Connections and Symbols

COGNITION Special Issues

The titles in this series are paperback, readily accessible editions of the Special Issues of *COGNITION: An International Journal of Cognitive Science,* edited by Jacques Mehler and produced by special agreement with Elsevier Science Publishers B.V.

VISUAL COGNITION, Steven Pinker, guest editor

THE ONSET OF LITERACY: Cognitive Processes in Reading Acquisition, Paul Bertelson, guest editor

SPOKEN WORD RECOGNITION, Uli H. Frauenfelder and Lorraine Komisarjevsky Tyler, guest editors

CONNECTIONS AND SYMBOLS, Steven Pinker and Jacques Mehler, guest editors

Connections and Symbols

edited by
Steven Pinker and
Jacques Mehler

A Bradford Book
The MIT Press
Cambridge, Massachusetts
London, England

Second printing, 1989

First MIT Press edition, 1988

Reprinted from *Cognition: International Journal of Cognitive Science,* Volume 28 (1988). The MIT Press has exclusive license to sell this English-language book edition throughout the world.

Printed and bound in the United States of America.

Library of Congress Cataloging-in-Publication Data

Connections and symbols.

(Cognition special issues)
"Reprinted from Cognition . . . volume 28 (1988)—
Verso t.p.
"A Bradford book."
Includes index.
1. Connectionism. 2. Human information processing.
3. Psycholinguistics. 4. Symbolism (Psychology)
I. Pinker, Steven, 1954– II. Mehler, Jacques.
III. Series.
BF311.C63 1988   153   88-6774
ISBN 0-262-66064-4 (pbk.)

Contents

Connections and Symbols

Introduction

During the past two years there has been more discussion of the foundations of cognitive science than in the 25 years preceding. The impetus for this reexamination has been a new approach to studying the mind, called "Connectionism", "Parallel Distributed Processing", or "Neural Networks". The assumptions behind this approach differ in substantial ways from the "central dogma" of cognitive science, that intelligence is the result of the manipulation of structured symbolic expressions. Instead, connectionists suggest that intelligence is to be understood as the result of the transmission of activation levels in large networks of densely interconnected simple units.

Connectionism has spawned an enormous amount of research activity in a short time. Much of the excitement surrounding the movement has been inspired by the rich possibilities inherent in ideas such as massive parallel processing, distributed representation, constraint satisfaction, neurally-realistic cognitive models, and subsymbolic or microfeatural analyses. Models incorporating various combinations of these notions have been proposed for behavioral abilities as diverse as Pavlovian conditioning, visual recognition, and language acquisition.

Perhaps it is not surprising that in a burgeoning new field there have been few systematic attempts to analyze the core assumptions of the new approach in comparison with those of the approach it is trying to replace, and to juxtapose both sets of assumptions with the most salient facts about human cognition. Analyses of new scientific models have their place, but they are premature before substantial accomplishments in the new field have been reported and digested. Now that many connectionist efforts are well known, it may be time for a careful teasing apart of what is truly new and what is just a relabeling of old notions; of the empirical generalizations that are sound and those that are likely to be false; of the proposals that naturally belong together and those that are logically independent.

This special issue of *Cognition* on Connectionism and Symbol Systems is intended to start such a discussion. Each of the papers in the issue attempts to analyze in careful detail the accomplishments and liabilities of connectionist models of cognition. The papers were independently and coincidentally submitted to the journal—a sign, perhaps, that the time is especially right for reflection on the status of connectionist theories. Though each makes different points, there are noteworthy common themes. All the papers are highly critical of certain aspects of connectionist models, particularly as applied to language of the parts of cognition employing language-like operations. All of them try to pinpoint what it is about human cognition that supports the traditional physical symbol system hypothesis. Yet none of the papers is an outright dismissal—in each case, the authors discuss aspects of cognition for which connectionist models may yield critical insights.

Perhaps the most salient common theme in these papers is that many current connectionist proposals are not motivated purely by considerations of parallel processing, distributed representation, constraint satisfaction, or other computational issues, but seem to be tied more closely to an agenda of reviving associationism as a central doctrine of learning and mental functioning. As a result, discussions of connectionism involve a reexamination of debates about the strengths and weaknesses of associationist mechanisms that were a prominent part of cognitive theory 30 years ago and 300 years ago.

These papers comprise the first critical examination of connectionism as a scientific theory. The issues they raise go to the heart of our understanding of how the mind works. We hope that they begin a fruitful debate among scientists from different frameworks as to the respective roles of connectionist networks and physical symbol systems in explaining intelligence.

STEVEN PINKER
JACQUES MEHLER

Connectionism and cognitive architecture: A critical analysis*

JERRY A. FODOR
CUNY Graduate Center

ZENON W. PYLYSHYN
University of Western Ontario

Abstract

This paper explores differences between Connectionist proposals for cognitive architecture and the sorts of models that have traditionally been assumed in cognitive science. We claim that the major distinction is that, while both Connectionist and Classical architectures postulate representational mental states, the latter but not the former are committed to a symbol-level of representation, or to a 'language of thought': i.e., to representational states that have combinatorial syntactic and semantic structure. Several arguments for combinatorial structure in mental representations are then reviewed. These include arguments based on the 'systematicity' of mental representation: i.e., on the fact that cognitive capacities always exhibit certain symmetries, so that the ability to entertain a given thought implies the ability to entertain thoughts with semantically related contents. We claim that such arguments make a powerful case that mind/brain architecture is not Connectionist at the cognitive level. We then consider the possibility that Connectionism may provide an account of the neural (or 'abstract neurological') structures in which Classical cognitive architecture is implemented. We survey a number of the standard arguments that have been offered in favor of Connectionism, and conclude that they are coherent only on this interpretation.

*This paper is based on a chapter from a forthcoming book. Authors' names are listed alphabetically. We wish to thank the Alfred P. Sloan Foundation for their generous support of this research. The preparation of this paper was also aided by a Killam Research Fellowship and a Senior Fellowship from the Canadian Institute for Advanced Research to ZWP. We also gratefully acknowledge comments and criticisms of earlier drafts by: Professors Noam Chomsky, William Demopoulos, Lila Gleitman, Russ Greiner, Norbert Hornstein, Keith Humphrey, Sandy Pentland, Steven Pinker, David Rosenthal, and Edward Stabler. Reprints may be obtained by writing to either author: Jerry Fodor, CUNY Graduate Center, 33 West 42 Street, New York, NY 10036, U.S.A.; Zenon Pylyshyn, Centre for Cognitive Science, University of Western Ontario, London, Ontario, Canada N6A 5C2.

1. Introduction

Connectionist or *PDP* models are catching on. There are conferences and new books nearly every day, and the popular science press hails this new wave of theorizing as a breakthrough in understanding the mind (a typical example is the article in the May issue of *Science 86*, called "How we think: A new theory"). There are also, inevitably, descriptions of the emergence of Connectionism as a Kuhnian "paradigm shift". (See Schneider, 1987, for an example of this and for further evidence of the tendency to view Connectionism as the "new wave" of Cognitive Science.)

The fan club includes the most unlikely collection of people. Connectionism gives solace both to philosophers who think that relying on the pseudo-scientific intentional or semantic notions of folk psychology (like goals and beliefs) mislead psychologists into taking the computational approach (e.g., P.M. Churchland, 1981; P.S. Churchland, 1986; Dennett, 1986); and to those with nearly the opposite perspective, who think that computational psychology is bankrupt because it doesn't address issues of intentionality or meaning (e.g., Dreyfus & Dreyfus, in press). On the computer science side, Connectionism appeals to theorists who think that serial machines are too weak and must be replaced by radically new parallel machines (Fahlman & Hinton, 1986), while on the biological side it appeals to those who believe that cognition can only be understood if we study it as neuroscience (e.g., Arbib, 1975; Sejnowski, 1981). It is also attractive to psychologists who think that much of the mind (including the part involved in using imagery) is not discrete (e.g., Kosslyn & Hatfield, 1984), or who think that cognitive science has not paid enough attention to stochastic mechanisms or to "holistic" mechanisms (e.g., Lakoff, 1986), and so on and on. It also appeals to many young cognitive scientists who view the approach as not only anti-establishment (and therefore desirable) but also rigorous and mathematical (see, however, footnote 2). Almost everyone who is discontent with contemporary cognitive psychology and current "information processing" models of the mind has rushed to embrace "the Connectionist alternative".

When taken as a way of modeling *cognitive architecture*, Connectionism really does represent an approach that is quite different from that of the Classical cognitive science that it seeks to replace. Classical models of the mind were derived from the structure of Turing and Von Neumann machines. They are not, of course, committed to the details of these machines as exemplified in Turing's original formulation or in typical commercial computers; only to the basic idea that the kind of computing that is relevant to understanding cognition involves operations on symbols (see Fodor 1976, 1987; Newell, 1980, 1982; Pylyshyn, 1980, 1984a, b). In contrast, Connectionists propose to design systems that can exhibit intelligent behavior without storing, retrieving, or otherwise operating on structured symbolic expressions. The style of processing carried out in such models is thus strikingly unlike what goes on when conventional machines are computing some function.

Connectionist systems are networks consisting of very large numbers of simple but highly interconnected "units". Certain assumptions are generally made both about the units and the connections: Each unit is assumed to receive real-valued activity (either excitatory or inhibitory or both) along its input lines. Typically the units do little more than sum this activity and change their state as a function (usually a threshold function) of this sum. Each connection is allowed to modulate the activity it transmits as a function of an intrinsic (but modifiable) property called its "weight". Hence the activity on an input line is typically some non-linear function of the state of activity of its sources. The behavior of the network as a whole is a function of the initial state of activation of the units and of the weights on its connections, which serve as its only form of memory.

Numerous elaborations of this basic Connectionist architecture are possible. For example, Connectionist models often have stochastic mechanisms for determining the level of activity or the state of a unit. Moreover, units may be connected to outside environments. In this case the units are sometimes assumed to respond to a narrow range of combinations of parameter values and are said to have a certain "receptive field" in parameter-space. These are called "value units" (Ballard, 1986). In some versions of Connectionist architecture, environmental properties are encoded by the pattern of states of entire populations of units. Such "coarse coding" techniques are among the ways of achieving what Connectionist call "distributed representation".[1] The term 'Connectionist model' (like 'Turing Machine' or 'Van Neumann machine') is thus applied to a family of mechanisms that differ in details but share a galaxy of architectural commitments. We shall return to the characterization of these commitments below.

Connectionist networks have been analysed extensively—in some cases

---

[1] The difference between Connectionist networks in which the state of a single unit encodes properties of the world (i.e., the so-called 'localist' networks) and ones in which the pattern of states of an entire population of units does the encoding (the so-called 'distributed' representation networks) is considered to be important by many people working on Connectionist models. Although Connectionists debate the relative merits of localist (or 'compact') versus distributed representations (e.g., Feldman, 1986), the distinction will usually be of little consequence for our purposes, for reasons that we give later. For simplicity, when we wish to refer indifferently to either single unit codes or aggregate distributed codes, we shall refer to the 'nodes' in a network. When the distinction is relevant to our discussion, however, we shall explicitly mark the difference by referring either to units or to aggregate of units.

using advanced mathematical techniques.[2] They have also been simulated on computers and shown to exhibit interesting aggregate properties. For example, they can be "wired" to recognize patterns, to exhibit rule-like behavioral regularities, and to realize virtually any mapping from patterns of (input) parameters to patterns of (output) parameters—though in most cases multi-parameter, multi-valued mappings require very large numbers of units. Of even greater interest is the fact that such networks can be made to learn; this is achieved by modifying the weights on the connections as a function of certain kinds of feedback (the exact way in which this is done constitutes a preoccupation of Connectionist research and has lead to the development of such important techniques as "back propagation").

In short, the study of Connectionist machines has led to a number of striking and unanticipated findings; it's surprising how much computing can be done with a uniform network of simple interconnected elements. Moreover, these models have an appearance of neural plausibility that Classical architectures are sometimes said to lack. Perhaps, then, a new Cognitive Science based on Connectionist networks should replace the old Cognitive Science based on Classical computers. Surely this is a proposal that ought to be taken seriously: if it is warranted, it implies a major redirection of research.

Unfortunately, however, discussions of the relative merits of the two architectures have thus far been marked by a variety of confusions and irrelevances. It's our view that when you clear away these misconceptions what's left is a real disagreement about the nature of mental processes and mental representations. But it seems to us that it is a matter that was substantially put to rest about thirty years ago; and the arguments that then appeared to militate decisively in favor of the Classical view appear to us to do so still.

In the present paper we will proceed as follows. First, we discuss some methodological questions about levels of explanation that have become enmeshed in the substantive controversy over Connectionism. Second, we try to say what it is that makes Connectionist and Classical theories of mental

---

[2] One of the attractions of Connectionism for many people is that it does employ some heavy mathematical machinery, as can be seen from a glance at many of the chapters of the two volume collection by Rumelhart, McClelland and the PDP Research Group (1986). But in contrast to many other mathematically sophisticated areas of cognitive science, such as automata theory or parts of Artificial Intelligence (particularly the study of search, or of reasoning and knowledge representation), the mathematics has not been used to map out the limits of what the proposed class of mechanisms can do. Like a great deal of Artificial Intelligence research, the Connectionist approach remains almost entirely experimental; mechanisms that look interesting are proposed and explored by implementing them on computers and subjecting them to empirical trials to see what they will do. As a consequence, although there is a great deal of mathematical work within the tradition, one has very little idea what various Connectionist networks and mechanisms are good for in general.

structure incompatible. Third, we review and extend some of the traditional arguments for the Classical architecture. Though these arguments have been somewhat recast, very little that we'll have to say here is entirely new. But we hope to make it clear how various aspects of the Classical doctrine cohere and why rejecting the Classical picture of reasoning leads Connectionists to say the very implausible things they do about logic and semantics. In part four, we return to the question what makes the Connectionist approach appear attractive to so many people. In doing so we'll consider some arguments that have been offered in favor of Connectionist networks as general models of cognitive processing.

Levels of explanation

There are two major traditions in modern theorizing about the mind, one that we'll call 'Representationalist' and one that we'll call 'Eliminativist'. Representationalists hold that postulating representational (or 'intentional' or 'semantic') states is essential to a theory of cognition; according to Representationalists, there are states of the mind which function to encode states of the world. Eliminativists, by contrast, think that psychological theories can dispense with such semantic notions as representation. According to Eliminativists the appropriate vocabulary for psychological theorizing is neurological or, perhaps behavioral, or perhaps syntactic; in any event, not a vocabulary that characterizes mental states in terms of what they represent. (For a neurological version of eliminativism, see P.S. Churchland, 1986; for a behavioral version, see Watson, 1930; for a syntactic version, see Stich, 1983.)

Connectionists are on the Representationalist side of this issue. As Rumelhart and McClelland (1986a, p. 121) say, PDPs "are explicitly concerned with the problem of internal representation". Correspondingly, the specification of what the states of a network *represent* is an essential part of a Connectionist model. Consider, for example, the well-known Connectionist account of the bistability of the Necker cube (Feldman & Ballard, 1982). "Simple units representing the visual features of the two alternatives are arranged in competing coalitions, with inhibitory ... links between rival features and positive links within each coalition .... The result is a network that has two dominant stable states" (see Figure 1). Notice that, in this as in all other such Connectionist models, the commitment to mental representation is explicit: the label of a node is taken to express the representational content of the state that the device is in when the node is excited, and there are nodes corresponding to monadic and to relational properties of the reversible cube when it is seen in one way or the other.

Figure 1. *A Connectionist network model illustrating the two stable representations of the Necker cube. (Reproduced from Feldman and Ballard, 1982, p. 221, with permission of the publisher, Ablex Publishing Corporation.)*

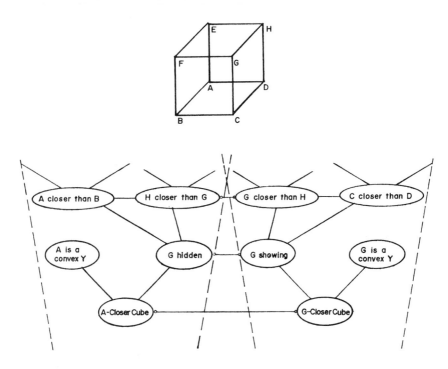

There are, to be sure, times when Connectionists appear to vacillate between Representationalism and the claim that the "cognitive level" is dispensable in favor of a more precise and biologically-motivated level of theory. In particular, there is a lot of talk in the Connectionist literature about processes that are "sub-symbolic"—and therefore presumably *not* representational. But this is misleading: Connectionist modeling is consistently Representationalist in practice, and Representationalism is generally endorsed by the very theorists who also like the idea of cognition 'emerging from the subsymbolic'. Thus, Rumelhart and McClelland (1986a, p. 121) insist that PDP models are "... strongly committed to the study of representation and process". Similarly, though Smolensky (1988, p. 2) takes Connectionism to articulate regularities at the "sub-symbolic level" of analysis, it turns out that sub-sym-

bolic states do have a semantics, though it's not the semantics of representations at the "conceptual level". According to Smolensky, the semantical distinction between symbolic and sub-symbolic theories is just that "entities that
are typically represented in the symbolic paradigm by [single] symbols are
typically represented in the sub-symbolic paradigm by a large number of
sub-symbols".[3] Both the conceptual and the sub-symbolic levels thus postulate representational states, but sub-symbolic theories slice them thinner.

We are stressing the Representationalist character of Connectionist
theorizing because much Connectionist methodological writing has been
preoccupied with the question 'What level of explanation is appropriate for
theories of cognitive architecture? (see, for example, the exchange between
Broadbent, 1985, and Rumelhart & McClelland, 1985). And, as we're about
to see, what one says about the levels question depends a lot on what stand
one takes about whether there are representational states.

It seems certain that the world has causal structure at very many different
levels of analysis, with the individuals recognized at the lowest levels being,
in general, very small and the individuals recognized at the highest levels
being, in general, very large. Thus there is a scientific story to be told about
quarks; and a scientific story to be told about atoms; and a scientific story to
be told about molecules ... ditto rocks and stones and rivers ... ditto galaxies.
And the story that scientists tell about the causal structure that the world has
at any one of these levels may be quite different from the story that they tell
about its causal structure at the next level up or down. The methodological
implication for psychology is this: If you want to have an argument about
cognitive architecture, you have to specify the level of analysis that's supposed
to be at issue.

If you're *not* a Representationalist, this is quite tricky since it is then not
obvious what makes a phenomenon cognitive. But specifying the level of
analysis relevant for theories of cognitive architecture is no problem for either
Classicists or Connectionists. Since Classicists and Connectionists are both
Representationalists, for them any level at which states of the system are
taken to encode properties of the world counts as a *cognitive* level; and no
other levels do. (Representations of "the world" include of course, representations of symbols; for example, the concept WORD is a construct at the
cognitive level because it represents something, namely words.) Correspond-

---

[3]Smolensky seems to think that the idea of postulating a level of representations with a semantics of
subconceptual features is unique to network theories. This is an extraordinary view considering the extent to
which *Classical* theorists have been concerned with feature analyses in every area of psychology from phonetics
to visual perception to lexicography. In fact, the question whether there are 'sub-conceptual' features is *neutral*
with respect to the question whether cognitive architecture is Classical or Connectionist.

ingly, it's the architecture of representational states and processes that discussions of *cognitive architecture* are about. Put differently, the architecture of the cognitive system consists of the set of basic operations, resources, functions, principles, etc. (generally the sorts of properties that would be described in a "user's manual" for that architecture if it were available on a computer), whose domain and range are the *representational states* of the organism.[4]

It follows, that, if you want to make good the Connectionist theory *as a theory of cognitive architecture*, you have to show that the processes which operate on *the representational states* of an organism are those which are specified by a Connectionist architecture. It is, for example, *no use at all*, from the cognitive psychologist's point of view, to show that the *non*representational (e.g., neurological, or molecular, or quantum mechanical) states of an organism constitute a Connectionist network, because that would *leave open* the question whether the mind is a such a network *at the psychological level*. It is, in particular, perfectly possible that nonrepresentational neurological states are interconnected in the ways described by Connectionist models *but that the representational states themselves are not*. This is because, just as it is possible to implement a *Connectionist* cognitive architecture in a network of causally interacting nonrepresentational elements, so too it is perfectly possible to implement a *Classical* cognitive architecture in such a network.[5] In fact, the question whether Connectionist networks should be treated as models at some level of implementation is moot, and will be discussed at some length in Section 4.

It is important to be clear about this matter of levels on pain of simply trivializing the issues about cognitive architecture. Consider, for example, the following remark of Rumelhart's: "It has seemed to me for some years now that there must be a unified account in which the so-called rule-governed and [the] exceptional cases were dealt with by a unified underlying process—a

---

[4]Sometimes, however, even Representationalists fail to appreciate that it is *representation* that distinguishes cognitive from noncognitive levels. Thus, for example, although Smolensky (1988) is clearly a Representationalist, his official answer to the question "What distinguishes those dynamical systems that are cognitive from those that are not?" makes the mistake of appealing to complexity rather than intentionality: "A river ... fails to be a cognitive dynamical system only because it cannot satisfy a *large* range of goals under a *large* range of conditions." But, of course, that depends on how you individuate goals and conditions; the river that wants to get to the sea wants first to get half way to the sea, and then to get half way more, ..., and so on; quite a lot of goals all told. The real point, of course, is that states that represent goals play a role in the etiology of the behaviors of people but not in the etiology of the 'behavior' of rivers.

[5]That Classical architectures can be implemented in networks is not disputed by Connectionists; see for example Rumelhart and McClelland (1986a, p. 118): "... one can make an arbitrary computational machine out of linear threshold units, including, for example, a machine that can carry out all the operations necessary for implementing a Turing machine; the one limitation is that real biological systems cannot be Turing machines because they have finite hardware.".

process which produces rule-like and rule-exception behavior through the application of a single process ... [In this process] ... both the rule-like and non-rule-like behavior is a product of the interaction of a very large number of 'sub-symbolic' processes." (Rumelhart, 1984, p. 60). It's clear from the context that Rumelhart takes this idea to be very tendentious; one of the Connectionist claims that Classical theories are required to deny.

But in fact it's not. For, *of course* there are 'sub-symbolic' interactions that implement both rule like and rule violating behavior; for example, quantum mechanical processes do. *That's* not what Classical theorists deny; indeed, it's not denied by anybody who is even vaguely a materialist. Nor does a Classical theorist deny that rule-following and rule-violating behaviors are both implemented by the very same neurological machinery. For a Classical theorist, neurons implement *all* cognitive processes in precisely the same way: viz., by supporting the basic operations that are required for symbol-processing.

What *would* be an interesting and tendentious claim is that there's no distinction between rule-following and rule-violating mentation *at the cognitive or representational or symbolic level*; specifically, that it is not the case that the etiology of rule-following behavior is mediated by the representation of explicit rules.[6] We will consider this idea in Section 4, where we will argue that it too is *not* what divides Classical from Connectionist architecture; Classical models *permit* a principled distinction between the etiologies of mental processes that are explicitly rule-governed and mental processes that aren't; but they don't *demand* one.

In short, the issue between Classical and Connectionist architecture is not about the explicitness of rules; as we'll presently see, Classical architecture is not, per se, committed to the idea that explicit rules mediate the etiology of behavior. And it is not about the reality of representational states; Classicists and Connectionists are all Representational Realists. And it is not about nonrepresentational architecture; a Connectionist neural network can perfectly well implement a Classical architecture at the cognitive level.

So, then, what *is* the disagreement between Classical and Connectionist architecture about?

---

[6]There is a different idea, frequently encountered in the Connectionist literature, that this one is easily confused with: viz., that the distinction between regularities and exceptions is merely stochastic (what makes 'went' an irregular past tense is just that the *more frequent* construction is the one exhibited by 'walked'). It seems obvious that if this claim is correct it can be readily assimilated to Classical architecture (see Section 4).

2. The nature of the dispute

Classicists and Connectionists all assign semantic content to *something*. Roughly, Connectionists assign semantic content to 'nodes' (that is, to units or aggregates of units; see footnote 1)—i.e., to the sorts of things that are typically labeled in Connectionist diagrams; whereas Classicists assign semantic content to *expressions*—i.e., to the sorts of things that get written on the tapes of Turing machines and stored at addresses in Von Neumann machines.[7] But Classical theories disagree with Connectionist theories about what primitive relations hold among these content-bearing entities. Connectionist theories acknowledge *only causal connectedness* as a primitive relation among nodes; when you know how activation and inhibition flow among them, you know everything there is to know about how the nodes in a network are related. By contrast, Classical theories acknowledge not only causal relations among the semantically evaluable objects that they posit, but also a range of structural relations, of which constituency is paradigmatic.

This difference has far reaching consequences for the ways that the two kinds of theories treat a variety of cognitive phenomena, some of which we will presently examine at length. But, underlying the disagreements about details are two architectural differences between the theories:

(1)   *Combinatorial syntax and semantics for mental representations.* Classical theories—but not Connectionist theories—postulate a 'language of thought' (see, for example, Fodor, 1975); they take mental representations to have *a combinatorial syntax and semantics*, in which (a) there is a distinction between structurally atomic and structurally molecular representations; (b) structurally molecular representations have syntactic constituents that are themselves either structurally molecular or structurally atomic; and (c) the semantic content of a (molecular) representation is a function of the semantic contents of its syntactic parts, together with its constituent structure. For purposes of convenience, we'll sometime abbreviate (a)–(c) by speaking of Classical theories as

---

[7]This way of putting it will do for present purposes. But a subtler reading of Connectionist theories might take it to be total machine *states* that have content, e.g., the state of *having such and such a node excited.* Postulating connections among labelled nodes would then be equivalent to postulating causal relations among the corresponding content bearing machine states: To say that the excitation of the node labelled 'dog' is caused by the excitation of nodes labelled [d], [o], [g] is to say that the machine's representing its input as consisting of the phonetic sequence [dog] causes it to represent its input as consisting of the word 'dog'. And so forth. Most of the time the distinction between these two ways of talking does not matter for our purposes, so we shall adopt one or the other as convenient.

committed to "complex" mental representations or to "symbol structures".[8]

(2) *Structure sensitivity of processes.* In Classical models, the principles by
which mental states are transformed, or by which an input selects the
corresponding output, are defined over structural properties of mental
representations. Because Classical mental *representations* have combinatorial structure, it is possible for Classical mental *operations* to apply
to them by reference to their form. The result is that a paradigmatic
Classical mental process operates upon any mental representation that
satisfies a given structural description, and transforms it into a mental
representation that satisfies another structural description. (So, for
example, in a model of inference one might recognize an operation that
applies to any representation of the form $P\&Q$ and transforms it into a
representation of the form P.) Notice that since formal properties can
be defined at a variety of levels of abstraction, such an operation can
apply equally to representations that differ widely in their structural
complexity. The operation that applies to representations of the form
$P\&Q$ to produce P is satisfied by, for example, an expression like
"(AvBvC) & (DvEvF)", from which it derives the expression
"(AvBvC)".

We take (1) and (2) as the claims that define Classical models, and we take
these claims quite literally; they constrain the physical realizations of symbol
structures. In particular, the symbol structures in a Classical model are assumed to correspond to real physical structures in the brain and the *combinatorial structure* of a representation is supposed to have a counterpart in
structural relations among physical properties of the brain. For example, the
relation 'part of', which holds between a relatively simple symbol and a more
complex one, is assumed to correspond to some physical relation among
brain states.[9] This is why Newell (1980) speaks of computational systems such
as brains and Classical computers as "*physical* symbols systems".

---

[8]Sometimes the difference between simply postulating representational states and postulating representations with a combinatorial syntax and semantics is marked by distinguishing theories that postulate *symbols*
from theories that postulate *symbol systems*. The latter theories, but not the former, are committed to a
"language of thought". For this usage, see Kosslyn and Hatfield (1984) who take the refusal to postulate
symbol systems to be the characteristic respect in which Connectionist architectures differ from Classical
architectures. We agree with this diagnosis.

[9]Perhaps the notion that relations among physical properties of the brain instantiate (or encode) the
combinatorial structure of an expression bears some elaboration. One way to understand what is involved is
to consider the conditions that must hold on a mapping (which we refer to as the 'physical instantiation
mapping') from expressions to brain states if the causal relations among brain states are to depend on the

This bears emphasis because the Classical theory is committed not only to there being a system of physically instantiated symbols, but also to the claim that the physical properties onto which the structure of the symbols is mapped *are the very properties that cause the system to behave as it does*. In other words the physical counterparts of the symbols, and their structural properties, *cause* the system's behavior. A system which has symbolic expressions, but whose operation does not depend upon the structure of these expressions, does not qualify as a Classical machine since it fails to satisfy condition (2). In this respect, a Classical model is very different from one in which behavior is caused by mechanisms, such as energy minimization, that are not responsive to the physical encoding of the structure of representations.

From now on, when we speak of 'Classical' models, we will have in mind *any* model that has complex mental representations, as characterized in (1) and structure-sensitive mental processes, as characterized in (2). Our account of Classical architecture is therefore neutral with respect to such issues as whether or not there is a separate executive. For example, Classical machines can have an "object-oriented" architecture, like that of the computer language *Smalltalk*, or a "message passing" architecture, like that of Hewett's

---

combinatorial structure of the encoded expressions. In defining this mapping it is not enough merely to specify a physical encoding for each symbol; in order for the *structures* of expressions to have causal roles, structural relations must be encoded by physical properties of brain states (or by sets of functionally equivalent physical properties of brain state).

Because, in general, Classical models assume that the expressions that get physically instantiated in brains have a generative syntax, the definition of an appropriate physical instantiation mapping has to be built up in terms of (a) the definition of a primitive mapping from atomic symbols to relatively elementary physical states, and (b) a specification of how the structure of complex expressions maps onto the structure of relatively complex or composite physical states. Such a structure-preserving mapping is typically given recursively, making use of the combinatorial syntax by which complex expressions are built up out of simpler ones. For example, the physical instantiation mapping **F** for complex expressions would be defined by recursion, given the definition of **F** for *atomic* symbols and given the *structure* of the complex expression, the latter being specified in terms of the 'structure building' rules which constitute the generative syntax for complex expressions. Take, for example, the expression '(A&B)&C'. A suitable definition for a mapping in this case might contain the statement that for any expressions P and Q, $F[P\&Q] = B(F[P],F[Q])$, where the function B specifies the physical relation that holds between physical states $F[P]$ and $F[Q]$. Here the property B serves to physically encode, (or 'instantiate') the relation that holds between the expressions P and Q, on the one hand, and the expressions $P\&Q$ on the other.

In using this rule for the example above P and Q would have the values 'A&B' and 'C' respectively, so that the mapping rule would have to be applied twice to pick the relevant physical structures. In defining the mapping recursively in this way we ensure that the relation between the expressions 'A' and 'B', and the composite expression 'A&B', is encoded in terms of a physical relation between constituent states that is identical (or functionally equivalent) to the physical relation used to encode the relation between expressions 'A&B' and 'C', and their composite expression '(A&B)&C'. This type of mapping is well known because of its use in Tarski's definition of an interpretation of a language in a model. The idea of a mapping from symbolic expressions to a structure of physical states is discussed in Pylyshyn (1984a, pp. 54–69), where it is referred to as an 'instantiation function' and in Stabler (1985), where it is called a 'realization mapping'.

(1977) *Actors*—so long as the objects or the messages have a combinatorial structure which is causally implicated in the processing. Classical architecture is also neutral on the question whether the operations on the symbols are constrained to occur one at a time or whether many operations can occur at the same time.

Here, then, is the plan for what follows. In the rest of this section, we will sketch the Connectionist proposal for a computational architecture that does away with complex mental representations and structure sensitive operations. (Although our purpose here is merely expository, it turns out that describing exactly what Connectionists are committed to requires substantial reconstruction of their remarks and practices. Since there is a great variety of points of view within the Connectionist community, we are prepared to find that some Connectionists in good standing may not fully endorse the program when it is laid out in what we take to be its bare essentials.) Following this general expository (or reconstructive) discussion, Section 3 provides a series of arguments favoring the Classical story. Then the remainder of the paper considers some of the reasons why Connectionism appears attractive to many people and offers further general comments on the relation between the Classical and the Connectionist enterprise.

2.1. Complex mental representations

To begin with, consider a case of the most trivial sort; two machines, one Classical in spirit and one Connectionist.[10] Here is how the Connectionist machine might reason. There is a network of labelled nodes as in Figure 2. Paths between the nodes indicate the routes along which activation can spread (that is, they indicate the consequences that exciting one of the nodes has for determining the level of excitation of others). Drawing an inference from A&B to A thus corresponds to an excitation of node 2 being caused by an excitation of node 1 (alternatively, if the system is in a state in which node 1 is excited, it eventually settles into a state in which node 2 is excited; see footnote 7).

Now consider a Classical machine. This machine has a tape on which it writes expressions. Among the expressions that can appear on this tape are:

[10]This illustration has not any particular Connectionist model in mind, though the caricature presented is, in fact, a simplified version of the Ballard (1987) Connectionist theorem proving system (which actually uses a more restricted proof procedure based on the *unification* of Horn clauses). To simplify the exposition, we assume a 'localist' approach, in which each semantically interpreted node corresponds to a single Connectionist unit; but nothing relevant to this discussion is changed if these nodes actually consist of patterns over a cluster of units.

Figure 2.   *A possible Connectionist network for drawing inferences from A&B to A or to B.*

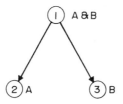

'A', 'B', 'A&B', 'C', 'D', 'C&D', 'A&C&D' ... etc. The machine's causal constitution is as follows: whenever a token of the form P&Q appears on the tape, the machine writes a token of the form P. An inference from A&B to A thus corresponds to a tokening of type 'A&B' on the tape causing a tokening of type 'A'.

So then, what does the architectural difference between the machines consist in? In the Classical machine, the objects to which the content A&B is ascribed (viz., tokens of the expression 'A&B') literally contain, as proper parts, objects to which the content A is ascribed (viz., tokens of the expression 'A'.) Moreover, the semantics (e.g., the satisfaction conditions) of the expression 'A&B' is determined in a uniform way by the semantics of its constituents.[11] By contrast, in the Connectionist machine none of this is true; the object to which the content A&B is ascribed (viz., node 1) is causally connected to the object to which the content A is ascribed (viz., node 2); but there is no structural (e.g., no part/whole) relation that holds between them. In short, it is characteristic of Classical systems, but not of Connectionist systems, to exploit arrays of symbols some of which are atomic (e.g., expressions like 'A') but indefinitely many of which have other symbols as syntactic and semantic parts (e.g., expressions like 'A&B').

It is easy to overlook this difference between Classical and Connectionist architectures when reading the Connectionist polemical literature or examining a Connectionist model. There are at least four ways in which one might be lead to do so: (1) by failing to understand the difference between what arrays of symbols do in Classical machines and what node labels do in Con-

---

[11]This makes the "compositionality" of data structures a defining property of Classical architecture. But, of course, it leaves open the question of the degree to which *natural* languages (like English) are also compositional.

nectionist machines; (2) by confusing the question whether the nodes in Connectionist networks have *constituent* structure with the question whether they are *neurologically distributed*; (3) by failing to distinguish between a representation having semantic and syntactic constituents and a concept being encoded in terms of microfeatures, and (4) by assuming that since representations of Connectionist networks have a graph structure, it follows that the nodes in the networks have a corresponding constituent structure. We shall now need rather a long digression to clear up these misunderstandings.

2.1.1. The role of labels in Connectionist theories

In the course of setting out a Connectionist model, intentional content will be assigned to machine states, and the expressions of some language or other will, of course, be used to express this assignment; for example, nodes may be labelled to indicate their representational content. Such labels often have a combinatorial syntax and semantics; in this respect, they can look a lot like Classical mental representations. The point to emphasize, however, is that it doesn't follow (and it isn't true) that the nodes to which these labels are assigned have a combinatorial syntax and semantics. 'A&B', for example, can be tokened on the tape of the Classical machine *and can also appear as a label in a Connectionist machine* as it does in diagram 2 above. And, of course, the expression 'A&B' is syntactically and semantically complex: it has a token of 'A' as one of its syntactic constituents, and the semantics of the expression 'A&B' is a function of the semantics of the expression 'A'. But it isn't part of the intended reading of the diagram that node 1 itself has constituents; the node—unlike its label—has no semantically interpreted parts.

It is, in short, important to understand the difference between Connectionist labels and the symbols over which Classical computations are defined. The difference is this: Strictly speaking, the labels play *no role at all* in determining the operation of a Connectionist machine; in particular, the operation of the machine is unaffected by the syntactic and semantic relations that hold among the expressions that are used as labels. To put this another way, the node labels in a Connectionist machine are not part of the causal structure of the machine. Thus, the machine depicted in Figure 2 will continue to make the same state transitions regardless of what labels we assign to the nodes. Whereas, by contrast, the state transitions of Classical machines are causally determined *by the structure—including the constituent structure—of the symbol arrays that the machines transform:* change the symbols and the system behaves quite differently. (In fact, since the behavior of a Classical machine is sensitive to the syntax of the representations it computes on, even interchanging *synonymous*—semantically equivalent—representations affects the course of computation). So, although the Connectionist's labels and the Classicist's data structures both constitute languages, only the latter language constitutes a medium of computation.[12]

2.1.2. Connectionist networks and graph structures

The *second* reason that the lack of syntactic and semantic structure in Connectionist representations has largely been ignored may be that Connectionist networks look like general graphs; and it is, of course, perfectly possible to use graphs to describe the internal structure of a complex symbol. That's precisely what linguists do when they use 'trees' to exhibit the constituent structure of sentences. Correspondingly, one could imagine a graph notation that expresses the internal structure of mental representations by using arcs and labelled nodes. So, for example, you might express the syntax of the mental representation that corresponds to the thought that John loves the girl like this:

John → loves → the girl

Under the intended interpretation, this would be the structural description of a mental representation whose content is that John loves the girl, and whose constituents are: a mental representation that refers to *John*, a mental representation that refers to *the girl*, and a mental representation that expresses the two-place relation represented by '→ loves →'.

But although graphs can sustain an interpretation as specifying the logical syntax of a complex mental representation, this interpretation is inappropriate for graphs of Connectionist networks. Connectionist graphs are not structural descriptions of mental representations; they're specifications of causal relations. All that a Connectionist can mean by a graph of the form X → Y is: *states of node X causally affect states of node Y.* In particular, the graph can't mean *X is a constituent of Y* or *X is grammatically related to Y* etc., since these sorts of relations are, in general, not defined for the kinds of mental representations that Connectionists recognize.

Another way to put this is that the links in Connectionist diagrams are not generalized pointers that can be made to take on different functional signifi-

---

[12]Labels aren't part of the *causal structure* of a Connectionist machine, but they may play an essential role in its *causal history* insofar as designers wire their machines to respect the semantic relations that the labels express. For example, in Ballard's (1987) Connectionist model of theorem proving, there is a mechanical procedure for wiring a network which will carry out proofs by unification. This procedure is a function from a set of node labels to a wired-up machine. There is thus an interesting and revealing respect in which node labels are relevant to the operations that get performed when the function is executed. But, of course, the machine on which the labels have the effect is not the machine whose states they are labels of; and the effect of the labels occurs at the time that the theorem-proving machine is constructed, not at the time its reasoning process is carried out. *This* sort of case of labels 'having effects' is thus quite different from the way that symbol tokens (e.g., tokened data structures) can affect the causal processes of a Classical machine.

cance *by an independent interpreter*, but are confined to meaning something like "sends activation to". The intended interpretation of the links as causal connections is intrinsic to the theory. If you ignore this point, you are likely to take Connectionism to offer a much richer notion of mental representation than it actually does.

2.1.3. Distributed representations

The *third* mistake that can lead to a failure to notice that the mental representations in Connectionist models lack combinatorial syntactic and semantic structure is the fact that many Connectionists view representations as being *neurologically distributed*; and, presumably, whatever is distributed must have parts. It doesn't follow, however, that whatever is distributed must have *constituents*; being neurologically distributed is very different from having semantic or syntactic constituent structure.

You have constituent structure when (and only when) the parts of semantically evaluable entities are themselves semantically evaluable. Constituency relations thus hold among objects all of which are at the representational level; they are, in that sense, *within* level relations.[13] By contrast, neural distributedness—the sort of relation that is assumed to hold between 'nodes' and the 'units' by which they are realized—is a *between* level relation: The nodes, but not the units, count as representations. To claim that a node is neurally distributed is presumably to claim that its states of activation correspond to patterns of neural activity—to aggregates of neural 'units'—rather than to activations of single neurons. The important point is that nodes that are distributed in this sense can perfectly well be syntactically and semantically atomic: Complex spatially-distributed implementation in no way implies constituent structure.

There is, however, a different sense in which the representational states in a network might be distributed, and this sort of distribution also raises questions relevant to the constituency issue.

2.1.4. Representations as 'distributed' over microfeatures

Many Connectionists hold that the mental representations that correspond to commonsense concepts (CHAIR, JOHN, CUP, etc.) are 'distributed' over galaxies of lower level units which themselves have representational content. To use common Connectionist terminology (see Smolensky, 1988), the higher or "conceptual level" units correspond to vectors in a "sub-conceptual" space

---

[13]Any relation specified as holding among representational states is, by definition, within the 'cognitive level'. It goes without saying that relations that are 'within-level' by this criterion can count as 'between-level' when we use criteria of finer grain. There is, for example, nothing to prevent hierarchies of levels of representational states.

of microfeatures. The model here is something like the relation between a defined expression and its defining feature analysis: thus, the concept BACHELOR might be thought to correspond to a vector in a space of features that includes ADULT, HUMAN, MALE, and MARRIED; i.e., as an assignment of the value + to the first two features and − to the last. Notice that distribution over microfeatures (unlike distribution over neural units) is a relation among representations, hence a relation at the cognitive level.

Since microfeatures are frequently assumed to be derived automatically (i.e., via learning procedures) from the statistical properties of samples of stimuli, we can think of them as expressing the sorts of properties that are revealed by multivariate analysis of sets of stimuli (e.g., by multidimensional scaling of similarity judgments). In particular, they need not correspond to English words; they can be finer-grained than, or otherwise atypical of, the terms for which a non-specialist needs to have a word. Other than that, however, they are perfectly ordinary semantic features, much like those that lexicographers have traditionally used to represent the meanings of words.

On the most frequent Connectionist accounts, theories articulated in terms of microfeature vectors are supposed to show how concepts are *actually* encoded, hence the feature vectors are intended to *replace* "less precise" specifications of macrolevel concepts. For example, where a Classical theorist might recognize a psychological state of entertaining the concept CUP, a Connectionist may acknowledge only a *roughly analogous* state of tokening the corresponding feature vector. (One reason that the analogy is only rough is that which feature vector 'corresponds' to a given concept may be viewed as heavily context dependent.) The generalizations that 'concept level' theories frame are thus taken to be only approximately true, the exact truth being stateable only in the vocabulary of the microfeatures. Smolensky, for example (p. 11), is explicit in endorsing this picture: "Precise, formal descriptions of the intuitive processor are generally tractable not at the conceptual level, but only at the subconceptual level."[14] This treatment of the relation between

---

[14]Smolensky (1988, p. 14) remarks that "unlike symbolic tokens, these vectors lie in a topological space, in which some are close together and others are far apart." However, this seems to radically conflate claims about the Connectionist model and claims about its implementation (a conflation that is not unusual in the Connectionist literature as we'll see in Section 4). If the space at issue is *physical*, then Smolensky is committed to extremely strong claims about adjacency relations in the brain; claims which there is, in fact, no reason at all to believe. But if, as seems more plausible, the space at issue is *semantical* then what Smolensky says isn't true. Practically any cognitive theory will imply distance measures between mental representations. In Classical theories, for example, the distance between two representations is plausibly related to the number of computational steps it takes to derive one representation from the other. In Connectionist theories, it is plausibly related to the number of intervening nodes (or to the degree of overlap between vectors, depending on the version of Connectionism one has in mind). The interesting claim is not that an architecture offers *a* distance measure but that it offers the *right* distance measure—one that is empirically certifiable.

commonsense concepts and microfeatures is exactly analogous to the standard Connectionist treatment of rules; in both cases, macrolevel theory is said to provide a vocabulary adequate for formulating generalizations that roughly approximate the facts about behavioral regularities. But the constructs of the macrotheory do *not* correspond to the causal mechanisms that generate these regularities. If you want a theory of these mechanisms, you need to replace talk about rules and concepts with talk about nodes, connections, microfeatures, vectors and the like.[15]

Now, it is among the major misfortunes of the Connectionist literature that the issue about whether commonsense concepts should be represented by sets of microfeatures has gotten thoroughly mixed up with the issue about combinatorial structure in mental representations. The crux of the mixup is the fact that sets of microfeatures can overlap, so that, for example, if a microfeature corresponding to '+ has-a-handle' is part of the array of nodes over which the commonsense concept CUP is distributed, then you might think of the theory as representing '+ has-a-handle' as a *constituent* of the concept CUP; from which you might conclude that Connectionists have a notion of constituency after all, contrary to the claim that Connectionism is not a language-of-thought architecture (see Smolensky, 1988).

A moment's consideration will make it clear, however, that even on the assumption that concepts are distributed over microfeatures, '+ has-a-handle' is not a constituent of CUP in anything like the sense that 'Mary' (the word) is a constituent of (the sentence) 'John loves Mary'. In the former case, "constituency" is being (mis)used to refer to a semantic relation between predicates; roughly, the idea is that macrolevel predicates like CUP are defined by sets of microfeatures like 'has-a-handle', so that it's some sort of semantic truth that CUP applies to a subset of what 'has-a-handle' applies to. Notice that while the extensions of these predicates are in a set/subset relation, the predicates themselves are not in any sort of part-to-whole relation. The expression 'has-a-handle' isn't *part of* the expression CUP any more

---

[15]The primary use that Connectionists make of microfeatures is in their accounts of generalization and abstraction (see, for example, Hinton, McClelland, & Rumelhart, 1986). Roughly, you get generalization by using overlap of microfeatures to define a similarity space, and you get abstraction by making the vectors that correspond to *types* be subvectors of the ones that correspond to their *tokens*. Similar proposals have quite a long history in traditional Empiricist analysis; and have been roundly criticized over the centuries. (For a discussion of abstractionism see Geach, 1957; that similarity is a primitive relation—hence not reducible to partial identity of feature sets—was, of course, a main tenet of Gestalt psychology, as well as more recent approaches based on "prototypes"). The treatment of microfeatures in the Connectionist literature would appear to be very close to early proposals by Katz and Fodor (1963) and Katz and Postal (1964), where both the idea of a feature analysis of concepts and the idea that relations of semantic containment among concepts should be identified with set-theoretic relations among feature arrays are explicitly endorsed.

than the English phrase 'is an unmarried man' is part of the English phrase 'is a bachelor'.

Real constituency does have to do with parts and wholes; the symbol 'Mary' is literally a part of the symbol 'John loves Mary'. It is because their symbols enter into real-constituency relations that natural languages have both atomic symbols and complex ones. By contrast, the definition relation can hold in a language where *all* the symbols are syntactically atomic; e.g., a language which contains both 'cup' and 'has-a-handle' as atomic predicates. This point is worth stressing. The question whether a representational system has real-constituency is independent of the question of microfeature analysis; it arises both for systems in which you have CUP as semantically primitive, and for systems in which the semantic primitives are things like '+ has-a-handle' and CUP and the like are defined in terms of these primitives. It really is very important not to confuse the semantic distinction between primitive expressions and defined expressions with the syntactic distinction between atomic symbols and complex symbols.

So far as we know, there are no worked out attempts in the Connectionist literature to deal with the syntactic and semantical issues raised by relations of real-constituency. There is, however, a proposal that comes up from time to time: viz., that what are traditionally treated as complex symbols should actually be viewed as just sets of units, with the role relations that traditionally get coded by constituent structure represented by units belonging to these sets. So, for example, the mental representation corresponding to the belief that John loves Mary might be the feature vector {+*John-subject;* +*loves;* +*Mary-object*}. Here 'John-subject' 'Mary-object' and the like are the labels of units; that is, they are atomic (i.e., micro-) features, whose status is analogous to 'has-a-handle'. In particular, they have no internal syntactic analysis, and there is no structural relation (except the orthographic one) between the feature 'Mary-object' that occurs in the set {John-subject; loves; Mary-object } and the feature 'Mary-subject' that occurs in the set {Mary-subject; loves; John-object}. (See, for example, the discussion in Hinton, 1987 of "role-specific descriptors that represent the conjunction of an identity and a role [by the use of which] we can implement part-whole hierarchies using set intersection as the composition rule." See also, McClelland, Rumelhart & Hinton, 1986, p. 82–85, where what appears to be the same treatment is proposed in somewhat different terms.)

Since, as we remarked, these sorts of ideas aren't elaborated in the Connectionist literature, detailed discussion is probably not warranted here. But it's worth a word to make clear what sort of trouble you would get into if you were to take them seriously.

As we understand it, the proposal really has two parts: On the one hand, it's suggested that although Connectionist representations cannot exhibit real-constituency, nevertheless the Classical distinction between complex symbols and their constituents can be replaced by the distinction between feature sets and their subsets; and, on the other hand, it's suggested that role relations can be captured by features. We'll consider these ideas in turn.

(1) Instead of having complex symbols like "John loves Mary" in the representational system, you have feature sets like {+*John-subject; +loves; +Mary-object*}. Since this set has {+*John-subject*}, {+*loves; +Mary-object*} and so forth as sub-sets, it may be supposed that the force of the constituency relation has been captured by employing the subset relation.

However, it's clear that this idea won't work since not all subsets of features correspond to genuine constituents. For example, among the subsets of {+*John-subject; +loves; +Mary-object*} are the sets {+*John-subject; +Mary-object*}) and the set {+*John-subject; + loves*} which do not, of course, correspond to constituents of the complex symbol "John loves Mary".

(2) Instead of defining roles in terms of relations among constituents, as one does in Classical architecture, introduce them as microfeatures.

Consider a system in which the mental representation that is entertained when one believes that John loves Mary is the feature set {+*John-subject; +loves; +Mary-object*}. What representation corresponds to the belief that John loves Mary and Bill hates Sally? Suppose, pursuant to the present proposal, that it's the set {+*John-subject; +loves; +Mary-object; +Bill-subject; +hates; +Sally-object*}. We now have the problem of distinguishing that belief from the belief that John loves Sally and Bill hates Mary; and from the belief that John hates Mary and Bill loves Sally; and from the belief that John hates Mary and Sally and Bill loves Mary; etc., since these other beliefs will all correspond to precisely the same set of features. The problem is, of course, that nothing in the representation of Mary as +*Mary-object* specifies whether it's the loving or the hating that she is the object of; similarly, mutatis mutandis, for the representation of John as +*John-subject*.

What has gone wrong isn't disastrous (yet). All that's required is to enrich the system of representations by recognizing features that correspond not to (for example) just being a subject, but rather to being the subject of a loving of Mary (the property that John has when John loves Mary) and being the subject of a hating of Sally (the property that Bill has when Bill hates Sally). So, the representation of John that's entertained when one believes that John loves Mary and Bill hates Sally might be something like +*John-subject-hates-Mary-object*.

The disadvantage of this proposal is that it requires rather a lot of micro-features.[16] How many? Well, a number of the order of magnitude of the *sentences* of a natural language (whereas one might have hoped to get by with a vocabulary of basic expressions that is not vastly larger than the *lexicon* of a natural language; after all, natural languages do). We leave it to the reader to estimate the number of microfeatures you would need, assuming that there is a distinct belief corresponding to every grammatical sentence of English of up to, say, fifteen words of length, and assuming that there is an average of, say, five roles associated with each belief. (Hint: George Miller once estimated that the number of well-formed 20-word sentences of English is of the order of magnitude of the number of seconds in the history of the universe.)

The alternative to this grotesque explosion of atomic symbols would be to have *a combinatorial syntax and semantics for the features*. But, of course, this is just to give up the game since the syntactic and semantic relations that hold among the parts of the complex feature +*((John subject) loves (Mary object))* are the very same ones that Classically hold among the constituents of the complex symbol "John loves Mary"; these include the role relations which Connectionists had proposed to reconstruct using just sets of atomic features. It is, of course, no accident that the Connectionist proposal for dealing with role relations runs into these sorts of problems. Subject, object and the rest are Classically defined *with respect to the geometry of constituent structure trees*. And Connectionist representations don't have constituents.

The idea that we should capture role relations by allowing features like *John-subject* thus turns out to be bankrupt; and there doesn't seem to be any other way to get the force of structured symbols in a Connectionist architecture. Or, if there is, nobody has given any indication of how to do it. This becomes clear once the crucial issue about structure in mental representations is disentangled from the relatively secondary (and orthogonal) issue about whether the representation of commonsense concepts is 'distributed' (i.e., from questions like whether it's CUP or 'has-a-handle' or both that is semantically primitive in the language of thought).

It's worth adding that these problems about expressing the role relations are actually just a symptom of a more pervasive difficulty: A consequence of restricting the vehicles of mental representation to sets of atomic symbols is a notation that fails quite generally to express the way that concepts group

[16]Another disadvantage is that, strictly speaking it doesn't work; although it allows us to distinguish the belief that John loves Mary and Bill hates Sally from the belief that John loves Sally and Bill hates Mary, we don't yet have a way to distinguish believing that (John loves Mary because Bill hates Sally) from believing that (Bill hates Sally because John loves Mary). Presumably nobody would want to have microfeatures corresponding to these.

into propositions. To see this, let's continue to suppose that we have a network in which the nodes represent concepts rather than propositions (so that what corresponds to the thought that John loves Mary is a distribution of activation over the set of nodes {JOHN; LOVES; MARY} rather than the activation of a single node labelled JOHN LOVES MARY). Notice that it cannot plausibly be assumed that all the nodes that happen to be active at a given time will correspond to concepts that are constituents of the *same* proposition; least of all if the architecture is "massively parallel" so that many things are allowed to go on—many concepts are allowed to be entertained—simultaneously in a given mind. Imagine, then, the following situation: at time t, a man is looking at the sky (so the nodes corresponding to SKY and BLUE are active) and thinking that John loves Fido (so the nodes corresponding to JOHN, LOVES, and FIDO are active), and the node FIDO is connected to the node DOG (which is in turn connected to the node ANIMAL) in such fashion that DOG and ANIMAL are active too. We can, if you like, throw it in that the man has got an itch, so ITCH is also on.

According to the current theory of mental representation, this man's mind at t is specified by the vector {+JOHN, +LOVES, +FIDO, +DOG, +SKY, +BLUE, +ITCH, +ANIMAL}. And the question is: *which subvectors of this vector correspond to thoughts that the man is thinking?* Specifically, what is it about the man's representational state that determines that the simultaneous activation of the nodes, {JOHN, LOVES, FIDO} constitutes his thinking that John loves Fido, but the simultaneous activation of FIDO, ANIMAL and BLUE does *not* constitute his thinking that Fido is a blue animal? It seems that we made it too easy for ourselves when we identified the thought that John loves Mary with the vector {+JOHN, +LOVES, +MARY}; at best that works only on the assumption that JOHN, LOVES and MARY are the only nodes active when someone has that thought. And that's an assumption to which no theory of mental representation is entitled.

It's important to see that this problem arises precisely because the theory is trying to use sets of atomic representations to do a job that you really need complex representations for. Thus, the question we're wanting to answer is: Given the total set of nodes active at a time, what distinguishes the subvectors that correspond to propositions from the subvectors that don't? This question has a straightforward answer if, contrary to the present proposal, complex representations are assumed: When representations express concepts that belong to the same proposition, they are not merely simultaneously active, but also *in construction with each other*. By contrast, representations that express concepts that don't belong to the same proposition may be simultaneously active; but, they are ipso facto *not* in construction with each other.

In short, you need two degrees of freedom to specify the thoughts that an intentional system is entertaining at a time: one parameter (active vs inactive) picks out the nodes that express concepts that the system has in mind; the other (in construction vs not) determines how the concepts that the system has in mind are distributed in the propositions that it entertains. For symbols to be "in construction" in this sense is just for them to be constituents of a complex symbol. Representations that are in construction form parts of a geometrical whole, *where the geometrical relations are themselves semantically significant*. Thus the representation that corresponds to the thought that John loves Fido is not a *set* of concepts but something like a *tree* of concepts, and it's the geometrical relations in this tree that mark (for example) the difference between the thought that John loves Fido and the thought that Fido loves John.

We've occasionally heard it suggested that you could solve the present problem consonant with the restriction against complex representations if you allow networks like this:

The intended interpretation is that the thought that Fido bites corresponds to the simultaneous activation of these nodes; that is, to the vector {+FIDO, + SUBJECT OF, + BITES}—with similar though longer vectors for more complex role relations.

But, on second thought, this proposal merely begs the question that it set out to solve. For, if there's a problem about what justifies assigning the proposition *John loves Fido* as the content of the set {JOHN, LOVES, FIDO}, there is surely the same problem about what justifies assigning the proposition *Fido is the subject of bites* to the set {FIDO, SUBJECT-OF, BITES}. If this is not immediately clear, consider the case where the simultaneously active nodes are {FIDO, SUBJECT-OF, BITES, JOHN}. Is the propositional content that Fido bites or that John does?[17]

---

[17]It's especially important at this point not to make the mistake of confusing diagrams of Connectionist networks with constituent structure diagrams (see section 2.1.2 above). Connecting SUBJECT-OF with FIDO and BITES does not mean that when all three are active FIDO is the subject of BITES. A network diagram is not a specification of the internal structure of a complex mental representation. Rather, it's a specification of a pattern of causal dependencies among the states of activation of nodes. Connectivity in a network determines which sets of simultaneously active nodes are possible; but it has no *semantical* significance.

The difference between the paths between nodes that network diagrams exhibit and the paths between nodes that constituent structure diagrams exhibit is precisely that the latter but not the former specify parameters of mental representations. (In particular, they specify part/whole relations among the constituents of complex symbols.) Whereas network theories define semantic interpretations over sets of (causally intercon- →

Strikingly enough, the point that we've been making in the past several paragraphs is very close to one that Kant made against the Associationists of his day. In "Transcendental Deduction (B)" of The First Critique, Kant remarks that:

> ... if I investigate ... the relation of the given modes of knowledge in any judgement, and distinguish it, as belonging to the understanding, from the relation according to laws of the reproductive imagination [e.g., according to the principles of association], which has only subjective validity, I find that a judgement is nothing but the manner in which given modes of knowledge are brought to the objective unity of apperception. This is what is intended by the copula "is". It is employed to distinguish the objective unity of given representations from the subjective .... Only in this way does there arise from the relation a *judgement*, that is a relation which is *objectively valid*, and so can be adequately distinguished from a relation of the same representations that would have only subjective validity—as when they are connected according to laws of association. In the latter case, all that I could say would be 'If I support a body, I feel an impression of weight'; I could not say, 'It, the body, is heavy'. Thus to say 'The body is heavy' is not merely to state that the two representations have always been conjoined in my perception, ... what we are asserting is that they are combined *in the object* ... (CPR, p. 159; emphasis Kant's)

A modern paraphrase might be: A theory of mental representation must distinguish the case when two concepts (e.g., THIS BODY, HEAVY) are merely *simultaneously entertained* from the case where, to put it roughly, the property that one of the concepts expresses is predicated of the thing that the other concept denotes (as in the thought: THIS BODY IS HEAVY). The relevant distinction is that while both concepts are "active" in both cases, in the latter case but *not* in the former the active concepts are in construction. Kant thinks that "this is what is intended by the copula 'is' ". But of course there are other notational devices that can serve to specify that concepts are in construction; notably the bracketing structure of constituency trees.

There are, to reiterate, two questions that you need to answer to specify the content of a mental state: "Which concepts are 'active' " and "Which of the active concepts are in construction with which others?" Identifying mental states with sets of active nodes provides resources to answer the first of these questions but not the second. That's why the version of network theory that acknowledges sets of atomic representations but no complex representations fails, in indefinitely many cases, to distinguish mental states that are in fact distinct.

---

nected) representations of concepts, theories that acknowledge complex symbols define semantic interpretations over sets of representations of concepts *together with specifications of the constituency relations that hold among these representations.*

But we are *not* claiming that you can't reconcile a Connectionist architecture with an adequate theory of mental representation (specifically with a combinatorial syntax and semantics for mental representations). On the contrary, of course you can: All that's required is that you use your network to implement a Turing machine, and specify a combinatorial structure for its computational language. What it appears that you can't do, however, is have both a combinatorial representational system and a Connectionist architecture *at the cognitive level*.

So much, then, for our long digression. We have now reviewed one of the major respects in which Connectionist and Classical theories differ; viz., their accounts of mental *representations*. We turn to the second major difference, which concerns their accounts of mental *processes*.

2.2. Structure sensitive operations

Classicists and Connectionists both offer accounts of mental processes, but their theories differ sharply. In particular, the Classical theory relies heavily on the notion of the logico/syntactic form of mental representations to define the ranges and domains of mental operations. This notion is, however, unavailable to orthodox Connectionists since it presupposes that there are nonatomic mental representations.

The Classical treatment of mental processes rests on two ideas, each of which corresponds to an aspect of the Classical theory of computation. Together they explain why the Classical view postulates at least three distinct levels of organization in computational systems: not just a physical level and a semantic (or "knowledge") level, but a syntactic level as well.

The first idea is that it is possible to construct languages in which certain features of the syntactic structures of formulas correspond systematically to certain of their semantic features. Intuitively, the idea is that in such languages the syntax of a formula encodes its meaning; most especially, those aspects of its meaning that determine its role in inference. All the artificial languages that are used for logic have this property and English has it more or less. Classicists believe that it is a crucial property of the Language of Thought.

A simple example of how a language can use syntactic structure to encode inferential roles and relations among meanings may help to illustrate this point. Thus, consider the relation between the following two sentences:

(1)   John went to the store and Mary went to the store.
(2)   Mary went to the store.

On the one hand, from the semantic point of view, (1) entails (2) (so, of course, inferences from (1) to (2) are truth preserving). On the other hand, from the syntactic point of view, (2) is a constituent of (1). These two facts can be brought into phase by exploiting the principle that sentences with the *syntactic* structure '(S1 and S2)$_S$' entail their sentential constituents. Notice that this principle connects the syntax of these sentences with their inferential roles. Notice too that the trick relies on facts about the grammar of English; it wouldn't work in a language where the formula that expresses the conjunctive content *John went to the store and Mary went to the store* is *syntactically* atomic.[18]

Here is another example. We can reconstruct such truth preserving inferences as *if Rover bites then something bites* on the assumption that (a) the sentence 'Rover bites' is of the syntactic type **F**a, (b) the sentence 'something bites' is of the syntactic type ∃x (**F**x) and (c) every formula of the first type entails a corresponding formula of the second type (where the notion 'corresponding formula' is cashed syntactically; roughly the two formulas must differ only in that the one has an existentially bound variable at the syntactic position that is occupied by a constant in the other.) Once again the point to notice is the blending of syntactical and semantical notions: The rule of existential generalization applies to formulas in virtue of their syntactic form. But the salient property that's preserved under applications of the rule is semantical: What's claimed for the transformation that the rule performs is that it is *truth* preserving.[19]

There are, as it turns out, examples that are quite a lot more complicated than these. The whole of the branch of logic known as proof theory is devoted to exploring them.[20] It would not be unreasonable to describe Classical Cog-

[18]And it doesn't work uniformly for English conjunction. Compare: *John and Mary are friends* → **John are friends*; or *The flag is red, white and blue* → *The flag is blue*. Such cases show either that English is not the language of thought, or that, if it is, the relation between syntax and semantics is a good deal subtler for the language of thought than it is for the standard logical languages.

[19]It needn't, however, be strict truth-preservation that makes the syntactic approach relevant to cognition. Other semantic properties might be preserved under syntactic transformation in the course of mental processing—e.g., warrant, plausibility, heuristic value, or simply *semantic non-arbitrariness*. The point of Classical modeling isn't to characterize human thought as supremely logical; rather, it's to show how a family of types of semantically coherent (or knowledge-dependent) reasoning are mechanically possible. Valid inference is the paradigm only in that it is the best understood member of this family; the one for which syntactical analogues for semantic relations have been most systematically elaborated.

[20]It is not uncommon for Connectionists to make disparaging remarks about the relevance of logic to psychology, even thought they accept the idea that inference is involved in reasoning. Sometimes the suggestion seems to be that it's all right if Connectionism can't reconstruct the theory of inference that formal deductive logic provides since it has something even better on offer. For example, in their report to the U.S. National Science Foundation, McClelland, Feldman, Adelson, Bower & McDermott (1986) state that "... connectionist models realize an evidential logic *in contrast to* the symbolic logic of conventional computing (p. 6; our emphasis)" and that "evidential logics are becoming increasingly important in cognitive science and

nitive Science as an extended attempt to apply the methods of proof theory to the modeling of thought (and similarly, of whatever other mental processes are plausibly viewed as involving inferences; preeminently learning and perception). Classical theory construction rests on the hope that syntactic analogues can be constructed for nondemonstrative inferences (or informal, commonsense reasoning) in something like the way that proof theory has provided syntactic analogues for validity.

The second main idea underlying the Classical treatment of mental processes is that it is possible to devise machines whose function is the transformation of symbols, and whose operations are sensitive to the syntactical structure of the symbols that they operate upon. This is the Classical conception of a computer: it's what the various architectures that derive from Turing and Von Neumann machines all have in common.

Perhaps it's obvious how the two 'main ideas' fit together. If, in principle, syntactic relations can be made to parallel semantic relations, and if, in principle, you can have a mechanism whose operations on formulas are sensitive to their syntax, then it may be possible to construct a *syntactically* driven machine whose state transitions satisfy *semantical* criteria of coherence. Such a machine would be just what's required for a mechanical model of the semantical coherence of thought; correspondingly, the idea that the brain *is* such a machine is the foundational hypothesis of Classical cognitive science.

So much for the Classical story about mental processes. The Connectionist story must, of course, be quite different: Since Connectionists eschew postulating mental representations with combinatorial syntactic/semantic structure, they are precluded from postulating mental processes that operate on mental representations in a way that is sensitive to their structure. The sorts of operations that Connectionist models do have are of two sorts, depending on whether the process under examination is learning or reasoning.

2.2.1. Learning

If a Connectionist model is intended to learn, there will be processes that determine the weights of the connections among its units as a function of the character of its training. Typically in a Connectionist machine (such as a 'Boltzman Machine') the weights among connections are adjusted until the system's behavior comes to model the statistical properties of its inputs. In

---

have a natural map to connectionist modeling." (p. 7). It is, however, hard to understand the implied contrast since, on the one hand, evidential logic must surely be a fairly conservative extension of "the symbolic logic of conventional computing" (i.e., most of the theorems of the latter have to come out true in the former) and, on the other, there is not the slightest reason to doubt that an evidential logic would 'run' on a Classical machine. Prima facie, the problem about evidential logic isn't that we've got one that we don't know how to implement; it's that we haven't got one.

the limit, the stochastic relations among machine states recapitulates the stochastic relations among the environmental events that they represent.

This should bring to mind the old Associationist principle that the strength of association between 'Ideas' is a function of the frequency with which they are paired 'in experience' and the Learning Theoretic principle that the strength of a stimulus-response connection is a function of the frequency with which the response is rewarded in the presence of the stimulus. But though Connectionists, like other Associationists, are committed to learning processes that model statistical properties of inputs and outputs, the simple mechanisms based on co-occurrence statistics that were the hallmarks of old-fashioned Associationism have been augmented in Connectionist models by a number of technical devices. (Hence the 'new' in 'New Connectionism'.) For example, some of the earlier limitations of associative mechanisms are overcome by allowing the network to contain 'hidden' units (or aggregates) that are not directly connected to the environment and whose purpose is, in effect, to detect statistical patterns in the activity of the 'visible' units including, perhaps, patterns that are more abstract or more 'global' than the ones that could be detected by old-fashioned perceptrons.[21]

In short, sophisticated versions of the associative principles for weight-setting are on offer in the Connectionist literature. The point of present concern, however, is what all versions of these principles have in common with one another and with older kinds of Associationism: viz., these processes are all *frequency*-sensitive. To return to the example discussed above: if a Connectionist learning machine converges on a state where it is prepared to infer A from A&B (i.e., to a state in which when the 'A&B' node is excited it tends to settle into a state in which the 'A' node is excited) the convergence will typically be caused by statistical properties of the machine's training experience: e.g., by correlation between firing of the 'A&B' node and firing of the 'A' node, or by correlations of the firing of both with some feedback signal. Like traditional Associationism, Connectionism treats learning as basically a sort of statistical modeling.

2.2.2. Reasoning

Association operates to alter the structure of a network *diachronically* as a function of its training. Connectionist models also contain a variety of types of 'relaxation' processes which determine the *synchronic* behavior of a network; specifically, they determine what output the device provides for a given pattern of inputs. In this respect, one can think of a Connectionist

---

[21]Compare the "little s's" and "little r's" of neo-Hullean "mediational" Associationists like Charles Osgood.

model as a species of analog machine constructed to realize a certain function. The inputs to the function are (i) a specification of the connectedness of the machine (of which nodes are connected to which); (ii) a specification of the weights along the connections; (iii) a specification of the values of a variety of idiosyncratic parameters of the nodes (e.g., intrinsic thresholds; time since last firing, etc.) (iv) a specification of a pattern of excitation over the input nodes. The output of the function is a specification of a pattern of excitation over the output nodes; intuitively, the machine chooses the output pattern that is most highly associated to its input.

Much of the mathematical sophistication of Connectionist theorizing has been devoted to devising analog solutions to this problem of finding a 'most highly associated' output corresponding to an arbitrary input; but, once again, the details needn't concern us. What is important, for our purposes, is another property that Connectionist theories share with other forms of Associationism. In traditional Associationism, the probability that one Idea will elicit another is sensitive to the strength of the association between them (including 'mediating' associations, if any). And the strength of this association is in turn sensitive to the extent to which the Ideas have previously been correlated. Associative strength was not, however, presumed to be sensitive to features of the content or the structure of representations per se. Similarly, in Connectionist models, the selection of an output corresponding to a given input is a function of properties of the paths that connect them (including the weights, the states of intermediate units, etc.). And the weights, in turn, are a function of the statistical properties of events in the environment (or of relations between patterns of events in the environment and implicit 'predictions' made by the network, etc.). But the syntactic/semantic structure of the representation of an input is *not* presumed to be a factor in determining the selection of a corresponding output since, as we have seen, syntactic/semantic structure is not defined for the sorts of representations that Connectionist models acknowledge.

To summarize: Classical and Connectionist theories disagree about the nature of mental representation; for the former, but not for the latter, mental representations characteristically exhibit a combinatorial constituent structure and a combinatorial semantics. Classical and Connectionist theories also disagree about the nature of mental processes; for the former, but not for the latter, mental processes are characteristically sensitive to the combinatorial structure of the representations on which they operate.

We take it that these two issues define the present dispute about the nature of cognitive architecture. We now propose to argue that the Connectionists are on the wrong side of both.

3. The need for symbol systems: Productivity, systematicity, compositionality and inferential coherence

Classical psychological theories appeal to the constituent structure of mental representations to explain three closely related features of cognition: its productivity, its compositionality and its inferential coherence. The traditional argument has been that these features of cognition are, on the one hand, pervasive and, on the other hand, explicable only on the assumption that mental representations have internal structure. This argument—familiar in more or less explicit versions for the last thirty years or so—is still intact, so far as we can tell. It appears to offer something close to a demonstration that an empirically adequate cognitive theory must recognize not just causal relations among representational states but also relations of syntactic and semantic constituency; hence that the mind cannot be, in its general structure, a Connectionist network.

3.1. Productivity of thought

There is a classical productivity argument for the existence of combinatorial structure in any rich representational system (including natural languages and the language of thought). The representational capacities of such a system are, by assumption, unbounded under appropriate idealization; in particular, there are indefinitely many propositions which the system can encode.[22] However, this unbounded expressive power must presumably be achieved by finite means. The way to do this is to treat the system of representations as consisting of expressions belonging to a generated set. More precisely, the correspondence between a representation and the proposition it expresses is, in arbitrarily many cases, built up recursively out of correspondences between parts of the expression and parts of the proposition. But, of course, this strategy can operate only when an unbounded number of the expressions are non-atomic. So linguistic (and mental) representations must constitute *symbol systems* (in the sense of footnote 8). So the mind cannot be a PDP.

Very often, when people reject this sort of reasoning, it is because they doubt that human cognitive capacities are correctly viewed as productive. In

---

[22]This way of putting the productivity argument is most closely identified with Chomsky (e.g., Chomsky, 1965; 1968). However, one does not have to rest the argument upon a basic assumption of infinite generative capacity. Infinite generative capacity can be viewed, instead, as a consequence or a corollary of theories formulated so as to capture the greatest number of generalizations with the fewest independent principles. This more neutral approach is, in fact, very much in the spirit of what we shall propose below. We are putting it in the present form for expository and historical reasons.

the long run there can be no a priori arguments for (or against) idealizing to productive capacities; whether you accept the idealization depends on whether you believe that the inference from finite performance to finite capacity is justified, or whether you think that finite performance is typically a result of the interaction of an unbounded competence with resource constraints. Classicists have traditionally offered a mixture of methodological and empirical considerations in favor of the latter view.

From a methodological perspective, the least that can be said for assuming productivity is that it precludes solutions that rest on inappropriate tricks (such as storing all the pairs that define a function); tricks that would be unreasonable in practical terms even for solving finite tasks that place sufficiently large demands on memory. The idealization to unbounded productive capacity forces the theorist to separate the finite specification of a method for solving a computational problem from such factors as the resources that the system (or person) brings to bear on the problem at any given moment.

The empirical arguments for productivity have been made most frequently in connection with linguistic competence. They are familiar from the work of Chomsky (1968) who has claimed (convincingly, in our view) that the knowledge underlying linguistic competence is generative—i.e., that it allows us *in principle* to generate (/understand) an unbounded number of sentences. It goes without saying that no one does, or could, *in fact* utter or understand tokens of more than a finite number of sentence types; this is a trivial consequence of the fact that nobody can utter or understand more than a finite number of sentence tokens. But there are a number of considerations which suggest that, despite de facto constraints on performance, ones knowledge of ones language supports an unbounded productive capacity in much the same way that ones knowledge of addition supports an unbounded number of sums. Among these considerations are, for example, the fact that a speaker/hearer's performance can often be improved by relaxing time constraints, increasing motivation, or supplying pencil and paper. It seems very natural to treat such manipulations as affecting the transient state of the speaker's memory and attention rather than what he knows about—or how he represents—his language. But this treatment is available only on the assumption that the character of the subject's performance is determined by interactions between the available knowledge base and the available computational resources.

Classical theories are able to accommodate these sorts of considerations because they assume architectures in which there is a functional distinction between memory and program. In a system such as a Turing machine, where the length of the tape is not fixed in advance, changes in the amount of available memory *can be affected without changing the computational structure of the machine*; viz., by making more tape available. By contrast, in a finite state automaton or a Connectionist machine, adding to the memory (e.g., by adding units to a network) alters the connectivity relations among nodes and thus does affect the machine's computational structure. Connectionist cognitive architectures cannot, by their very nature, support an expandable memory, so they cannot support productive cognitive capacities. The long and short is that if productivity arguments are sound, then they show that the architecture of the mind can't be Connectionist. Connectionists have, by and large, acknowledged this; so they are forced to reject productivity arguments.

The test of a good scientific idealization is simply and solely whether it produces successful science in the long term. It seems to us that the productivity idealization has more than earned its keep, especially in linguistics and in theories of reasoning. Connectionists, however, have not been persuaded. For example, Rumelhart and McClelland (1986a, p. 119) say that they "... do not agree that [productive] capabilities are of the essence of human computation. As anyone who has ever attempted to process sentences like 'The man the boy the girl hit kissed moved' can attest, our ability to process even moderate degrees of center-embedded structure is grossly impaired relative to an ATN [Augmented Transition Network] parser .... What is needed, then, is not a mechanism for flawless and effortless processing of embedded constructions ... The challenge is to explain how those processes that others have chosen to explain in terms of recursive mechanisms can be better explained by the kinds of processes natural for PDP networks."

These remarks suggest that Rumelhart and McClelland think that the fact that center-embedding sentences are hard is somehow an *embarrassment* for theories that view linguistic capacities as productive. But of course it's not since, according to such theories, performance is an effect of interactions between a productive competence and restricted resources. There are, in fact, quite plausible Classical accounts of why center-embeddings ought to impose especially heavy demands on resources, and there is a reasonable amount of experimental support for these models (see, for example, Wanner & Maratsos, 1978).

In any event, it should be obvious that the difficulty of parsing center-embeddings can't be a consequence of their recursiveness per se since there are many recursive structures that are strikingly easy to understand. Consider: 'this is the dog that chased the cat that ate the rat that lived in the house that Jack built.' The Classicist's case for productive capacities in parsing rests on the transparency of sentences like these.[23] In short, the fact that center-em-

---

[23]McClelland and Kawamoto (1986) discuss this sort of recursion briefly. Their suggestion seems to be that parsing such sentences doesn't really require recovering their recursive structure: "... the job of the parser

bedded sentences are hard perhaps shows that there are some recursive structures that we can't parse. But what Rumelhart and McClelland need if they are to deny the productivity of linguistic capacities is the much stronger claim that there are no recursive structures that we can parse; and this stronger claim would appear to be simply false.

Rumelhart and McClelland's discussion of recursion (pp. 119–120) nevertheless repays close attention. They are apparently prepared to concede that PDPs can model recursive capacities only indirectly—viz., by implementing Classical architectures like ATNs; so that *if* human cognition exhibited recursive capacities, that would suffice to show that minds have Classical rather than Connectionist architecture at the psychological level. "We have not dwelt on PDP implementations of Turing machines and recursive processing engines *because we do not agree with those who would argue that such capacities are of the essence of human computation*" (p. 119, our emphasis). Their argument that recursive capacities *aren't* "of the essence of human computation" is, however, just the unconvincing stuff about center-embedding quoted above.

So the Rumelhart and McClelland view is apparently that if you take it to be independently obvious that some cognitive capacities are productive, then you should take the existence of such capacities to argue for Classical cognitive architecture and hence for treating Connectionism as at best an implementation theory. We think that this is quite a plausible understanding of the bearing that the issues about productivity and recursion have on the issues about cognitive architecture; in Section 4 we will return to the suggestion that Connectionist models can plausibly be construed as models of the implementation of a Classical architecture.

In the meantime, however, we propose to view the status of productivity arguments for Classical architectures as moot; we're about to present a different sort of argument for the claim that mental representations need an articulated internal structure. It is closely related to the productivity argument, but it doesn't require the idealization to unbounded competence. Its assumptions

---

[with respect to right-recursive sentences] is to spit out phrases in a way that captures their *local* context. Such a representation may prove sufficient to allow us to reconstruct the correct bindings of noun phrases to verbs and prepositional phrases to *nearby* nouns and verbs" (p. 324; emphasis ours). It is, however, by no means the case that all of the semantically relevant grammatical relations in readily intelligible embedded sentences are local in surface structure. Consider: 'Where did the man who owns the cat that chased the rat that frightened the girl say that he was going to move to (X)?' or 'What did the girl that the children loved to listen to promise your friends that she would read (X) to them?' Notice that, in such examples, a binding element (italicized) can be arbitrarily displaced from the position whose interpretation it controls (marked 'X') without making the sentence particularly difficult to understand. Notice too that the 'semantics' doesn't determine the binding relations in either example.

should thus be acceptable even to theorists who—like Connectionists—hold that the finitistic character of cognitive capacities is intrinsic to their architecture.

3.2. Systematicity of cognitive representation

The form of the argument is this: Whether or not cognitive capacities are really *productive*, it seems indubitable that they are what we shall call 'systematic'. And we'll see that the systematicity of cognition provides as good a reason for postulating combinatorial structure in mental representation as the productivity of cognition does: You get, in effect, the same conclusion, but from a weaker premise.

The easiest way to understand what the systematicity of cognitive capacities amounts to is to focus on the systematicity of language comprehension and production. In fact, the systematicity argument for combinatorial structure in *thought* exactly recapitulates the traditional Structuralist argument for constituent structure in sentences. But we pause to remark upon a point that we'll re-emphasize later; linguistic capacity is a paradigm of systematic cognition, but it's wildly unlikely that it's the only example. On the contrary, there's every reason to believe that systematicity is a thoroughly pervasive feature of human and infrahuman mentation.

What we mean when we say that linguistic capacities are *systematic* is that the ability to produce/understand some sentences is *intrinsically* connected to the ability to produce/understand certain others. You can see the force of this if you compare learning languages the way we really do learn them with learning a language by memorizing an enormous phrase book. The point isn't that phrase books are finite and can therefore exhaustively specify only *non-productive* languages; that's true, but we've agreed not to rely on productivity arguments for our present purposes. Our point is rather that you can learn *any part of a phrase book without learning the rest.* Hence, on the phrase book model, it would be perfectly possible to learn that uttering the form of words 'Granny's cat is on Uncle Arthur's mat' is the way to say (in English) that Granny's cat is on Uncle Arthur's mat, and yet have no idea at all how to say that it's raining (or, for that matter, how to say that Uncle Arthur's cat is on Granny's mat). Perhaps it's self-evident that the phrase book story must be wrong about language acquisition because a speaker's knowledge of his native language is never like that. You don't, for example, find native speakers who know how to say in English that John loves the girl but don't know how to say in English that the girl loves John.

Notice, in passing, that systematicity is a property of the mastery of the syntax of a language, not of its lexicon. The phrase book model really does fit what it's like to learn the *vocabulary* of English since when you learn English vocabulary you acquire a lot of basically *independent* capacities. So you might perfectly well learn that using the expression 'cat' is the way to refer to cats and yet have no idea that using the expression 'deciduous conifer' is the way to refer to deciduous conifers. Systematicity, like productivity, is the sort of property of cognitive capacities that you're likely to miss if you concentrate on the psychology of learning and searching lists.

There is, as we remarked, a straightforward (and quite traditional) argument from the systematicity of language capacity to the conclusion that sentences must have syntactic and semantic structure: If you assume that sentences are constructed out of words and phrases, and that many different sequences of words can be phrases of the same type, the very fact that one formula is a sentence of the language will often imply that other formulas must be too: in effect, systematicity follows from the postulation of constituent structure.

Suppose, for example, that it's a fact about English that formulas with the constituent analysis 'NP Vt NP' are well formed; and suppose that 'John' and 'the girl' are NPs and 'loves' is a Vt. It follows from these assumptions that 'John loves the girl,' 'John loves John,' 'the girl loves the girl,' and 'the girl loves John' must all be sentences. It follows too that anybody who has mastered the grammar of English must have linguistic capacities that are systematic in respect of these sentences; he *can't but* assume that all of them are sentences if he assumes that any of them are. Compare the situation on the view that the sentences of English are all atomic. There is then no structural analogy between 'John loves the girl' and 'the girl loves John' and hence no reason why understanding one sentence should imply understanding the other; no more than understanding 'rabbit' implies understanding 'tree'.[24]

On the view that the sentences are atomic, the systematicity of linguistic capacities is a mystery; on the view that they have constituent structure, the systematicity of linguistic capacities is what you would predict. So we should prefer the latter view to the former.

Notice that you can make this argument for constituent structure in sentences without idealizing to astronomical computational capacities. There are productivity arguments for constituent structure, but they're concerned with our ability—in principle—to understand sentences that are arbitrarily long. Systematicity, by contrast, appeals to premises that are much nearer home;

---

[24]See Pinker (1984, Chapter 4) for evidence that children never go through a stage in which they distinguish between the internal structures of NPs depending on whether they are in subject or object position; i.e., the dialects that children speak are always systematic with respect to the syntactic structures that can appear in these positions.

such considerations as the ones mentioned above, that no speaker understands the form of words 'John loves the girl' except as he also understands
the form of words 'the girl loves John'. The assumption that linguistic
capacities are productive "in principle" is one that a Connectionist might
refuse to grant. But that they are systematic *in fact* no one can plausibly deny.

We can now, finally, come to the point: the argument from the systematicity of linguistic capacities to constituent structure in sentences is quite clear.
But thought is systematic too, so there is a precisely parallel argument from
the systematicity of thought to syntactic and semantic structure in mental
representations.

What does it mean to say that thought is systematic? Well, just as you
don't find people who can understand the sentence 'John loves the girl' but
not the sentence 'the girl loves John,' so too you don't find people who can
think the thought that John loves the girl but can't think the thought that the
girl loves John. Indeed, in the case of verbal organisms the systematicity of
thought *follows from* the systematicity of language if you assume—as most
psychologists do—that understanding a sentence involves entertaining the
thought that it expresses; on that assumption, nobody *could* understand both
the sentences about John and the girl unless he were able to think both the
thoughts about John and the girl.

But now if the ability to think that John loves the girl is intrinsically connected to the ability to think that the girl loves John, that fact will somehow
have to be explained. For a Representationalist (which, as we have seen,
Connectionists are), the explanation is obvious: Entertaining thoughts requires being in representational states (i.e., it requires tokening mental representations). And, just as the systematicity of language shows that there
must be structural relations between the sentence 'John loves the girl' and
the sentence 'the girl loves John,' so the systematicity of thought shows that
there must be structural relations between the mental representation that
corresponds to the thought that John loves the girl and the mental representation that corresponds to the thought that the girl loves John;[25] namely, the
two mental representations, like the two sentences, *must be made of the same
parts*. But if this explanation is right (and there don't seem to be any others
on offer), then mental representations have internal structure and there is a

---

[25]It may be worth emphasizing that the structural complexity of a mental representation is not the same
thing as, and does *not* follow from, the structural complexity of its propositional content (i.e., of what we're
calling "the thought that one has"). Thus, Connectionists and Classicists can agree to agree that *the thought
that P&Q* is complex (and has the thought that *P* among its parts) while agreeing to disagree about whether
mental representations have internal syntactic structure.

language of thought. So the architecture of the mind is not a Connectionist network.[26]

To summarize the discussion so far: Productivity arguments infer the internal structure of mental representations from the presumed fact that nobody has a *finite* intellectual competence. By contrast, systematicity arguments infer the internal structure of mental representations from the patent fact that nobody has a *punctate* intellectual competence. Just as you don't find linguistic capacities that consist of the ability to understand sixty-seven unrelated sentences, so too you don't find cognitive capacities that consist of the ability to think seventy-four unrelated thoughts. Our claim is that this isn't, in either case, an accident: A linguistic theory that allowed for the possibility of punctate languages would have gone not just wrong, but *very profoundly* wrong. And similarly for a cognitive theory that allowed for the possibility of punctate minds.

But perhaps not being punctate is a property only of the minds of language users; perhaps the representational capacities of infraverbal organisms do have just the kind of gaps that Connectionist models permit? A Connectionist might then claim that he can do everything "up to language" on the assumption that mental representations lack combinatorial syntactic and semantic structure. Everything up to language may not be everything, but it's a lot. (On the other hand, a lot may be a lot, but it isn't everything. Infraverbal cognitive architecture mustn't be so represented as to make the eventual acquisition of language in phylogeny and in ontogeny require a miracle.)

It is not, however, plausible that only the minds of verbal organisms are systematic. Think what it would mean for this to be the case. It would have to be quite usual to find, for example, animals capable of representing the state of affairs $a\mathbf{R}b$, but incapable of representing the state of affairs $b\mathbf{R}a$. Such animals would be, as it were, $a\mathbf{R}b$ sighted but $b\mathbf{R}a$ blind since, presumably, the representational capacities of its mind affect not just what an or-

---

[26]These considerations throw further light on a proposal we discussed in Section 2. Suppose that the mental representation corresponding to the thought that John loves the girl is the feature vector {+*John-subject; +loves; +the-girl-object*} where '*John-subject*' and '*the-girl-object*' are atomic features; as such, they bear no more structural relation to '*John-object*' and '*the-girl-subject*' than they do to one another or to, say, '*has-a-handle*'. Since this theory recognizes no structural relation between '*John-subject*' and '*John-object*', it offers no reason why a representational system that provides the means to express one of these concepts should also provide the means to express the other. This treatment of role relations thus makes a mystery of the (presumed) fact that anybody who can entertain the thought that John loves the girl can also entertain the thought that the girl loves John (and, mutatis mutandis, that any natural language that can express the proposition that John loves the girl can also express the proposition that the girl loves John). This consequence of the proposal that role relations be handled by "role specific descriptors that represent the conjunction of an identity and a role" (Hinton, 1987) offers a particularly clear example of how failure to postulate internal structure in representations leads to failure to capture the systematicity of representational systems.

ganism can think, but also what it can perceive. In consequence, such animals would be able to learn to respond selectively to *a*R*b* situations but quite *un*able to learn to respond selectively to *b*R*a* situations. (So that, though you could teach the creature to choose the picture with the square larger than the triangle, you couldn't for the life of you teach it to choose the picture with the triangle larger than the square.)

It is, to be sure, an empirical question whether the cognitive capacities of infraverbal organisms are often structured that way, but we're prepared to bet that they are not. Ethological cases are the exceptions that prove the rule. There *are* examples where salient environmental configurations act as 'gestalten'; and in such cases it's reasonable to doubt that the mental representation of the stimulus is complex. But the point is precisely that these cases are *exceptional*; they're exactly the ones where you expect that there will be some special story to tell about the ecological significance of the stimulus: that it's the shape of a predator, or the song of a conspecific ... etc. Conversely, when there is no such story to tell you expect structurally similar stimuli to elicit correspondingly similar cognitive capacities. That, surely, is the least that a respectable principle of stimulus generalization has got to require.

That infraverbal cognition is pretty generally systematic seems, in short, to be about as secure as any empirical premise in this area can be. And, as we've just seen, it's a premise from which the inadequacy of Connectionist models as cognitive theories follows quite straightforwardly; as straightforwardly, in any event, as it would from the assumption that such capacities are generally productive.

3.3. *Compositionality of representations*

Compositionality is closely related to systematicity; perhaps they're best viewed as aspects of a single phenomenon. We will therefore follow much the same course here as in the preceding discussion: first we introduce the concept by recalling the standard arguments for the compositionality of natural languages. We then suggest that parallel arguments secure the compositionality of mental representations. Since compositionality requires combinatorial syntactic and semantic structure, the compositionality of thought is evidence that the mind is not a Connectionist network.

We said that the systematicity of linguistic competence consists in the fact that "the ability to produce/understand some of the sentences is intrinsically connected to the ability to produce/understand certain of the others". We now add that which sentences are systematically related is not arbitrary from a semantic point of view. For example, being able to understand 'John loves the girl' goes along with being able to understand 'the girl loves John', and there are correspondingly close semantic relations between these sentences: in order for the first to be true, John must bear to the girl the very same relation that the truth of the second requires the girl to bear to John. By contrast, there is no intrinsic connection between understanding either of the John/girl sentences and understanding semantically unrelated formulas like 'quarks are made of gluons' or 'the cat is on the mat' or '$2 + 2 = 4$'; it looks as though semantical relatedness and systematicity keep quite close company.

You might suppose that this covariance is covered by the same explanation that accounts for systematicity per se; roughly, that sentences that are systematically related are composed from the same syntactic constituents. But, in fact, you need a further assumption, which we'll call the 'principle of compositionality': insofar as a language is systematic, a lexical item must make approximately the same semantic contribution to each expression in which it occurs. It is, for example, only insofar as 'the' 'girl', 'loves' and 'John' make the same semantic contribution to 'John loves the girl' that they make to 'the girl loves John' that understanding the one sentence implies understanding the other. Similarity of constituent structure accounts for the semantic relatedness between systematically related sentences only to the extent that the semantical properties of the shared constituents are context-independent.

Here it's idioms that prove the rule: being able to understand 'the', 'man', 'kicked' and 'bucket' isn't much help with understanding 'the man kicked the bucket', since 'kicked' and 'bucket' don't bear their standard meanings in this context. And, just as you'd expect, 'the man kicked the bucket' is *not* systematic even with respect to syntactically closely related sentences like 'the man kicked over the bucket' (for that matter, it's not systematic with respect to the 'the man kicked the bucket' read literally).

It's uncertain exactly how compositional natural languages actually are (just as it's uncertain exactly how systematic they are). We suspect that the amount of context induced variation of lexical meaning is often overestimated because other sorts of context sensitivity are misconstrued as violations of compositionality. For example, the difference between 'feed the chicken' and 'chicken to eat' must involve an *animal/food* ambiguity in 'chicken' rather than a violation of compositionality since if the context 'feed the ...' could *induce* (rather than select) the meaning *animal*, you would expect 'feed the veal', 'feed the pork' and the like.[27] Similarly, the difference between 'good book', 'good rest' and 'good fight' is probably not meaning shift but syncategorematicity. 'Good NP' means something like NP *that answers to the*

---

[27]We are indebted to Steve Pinker for this point.

relevant interest in NPs: a good book is one that answers to our interest in books (viz., it's good to read); a good rest is one that answers to our interest in rests (viz., it leaves one refreshed); a good fight is one that answers to our interest in fights (viz., it's fun to watch or to be in, or it clears the air); and so on. It's because the meaning of 'good' is syncategorematic and has a variable in it for relevant interests, that you can know that a good flurg is a flurg that answers to the relevant interest in flurgs without knowing what flurgs are or what the relevant interest in flurgs is (see Ziff, 1960).

In any event, the main argument stands: systematicity depends on compositionality, so to the extent that a natural language is systematic it must be compositional too. This illustrates another respect in which systematicity arguments can do the work for which productivity arguments have previously been employed. The traditional argument for compositionality is that it is required to explain how a finitely representable language can contain infinitely many nonsynonymous expressions.

Considerations about systematicity offer one argument for compositionality; considerations about entailment offer another. Consider predicates like '... is a brown cow'. This expression bears a straightforward semantical relation to the predicates '... is a cow' and '... is brown'; viz., that the first predicate is true of a thing if and only if both of the others are. That is, '... is a brown cow' severally entails '... is brown' and '... is a cow' and is entailed by their conjunction. Moreover—and this is important—this semantical pattern is not peculiar to the cases cited. On the contrary, it holds for a very large range of predicates (see '... is a red square,' '... is a funny old German soldier,' '... is a child prodigy;' and so forth).

How are we to account for these sorts of regularities? The answer seems clear enough; '... is a brown cow' entails '... is brown' because (a) the second expression is a constituent of the first; (b) the syntactical form '(adjective noun)$_N$' has (in many cases) the semantic force of a conjunction, and (c) 'brown' retains its semantical value under simplification of conjunction. Notice that you need (c) to rule out the possibility that 'brown' means *brown* when in it modifies a noun but (as it might be) *dead* when it's a predicate adjective; in which case '... is a brown cow' wouldn't entail '... is brown' after all. Notice too that (c) is just an application of the principle of composition.

So, here's the argument so far: you need to assume some degree of compositionality of English sentences to account for the fact that systematically related sentences are always semantically related; and to account for certain regular parallelisms between the syntactical structure of sentences and their entailments. So, beyond any serious doubt, the sentences of English must be compositional to some serious extent. But the principle of compositionality governs the semantic relations between words *and the expressions of which they are constituents.* So compositionality implies that (some) expressions *have* constituents. So compositionality argues for (specifically, presupposes) syntactic/semantic structure in sentences.

Now what about the compositionality of mental representations? There is, as you'd expect, a bridging argument based on the usual psycholinguistic premise that one uses language to express ones thoughts: Sentences are used to express thoughts; so if the ability to use some sentences is connected with the ability to use certain other, semantically related sentences, then the ability to think some thoughts must be correspondingly connected with the ability to think certain other, semantically related thoughts. But you can only think the thoughts that your mental representations can express. So, if the ability to think certain thoughts is interconnected, then the corresponding representational capacities must be interconnected too; specifically, the ability to be in some representational states must imply the ability to be in certain other, semantically related representational states.

But then the question arises: *how could* the mind be so arranged that the ability to be in one representational state is connected with the ability to be in others that are semantically nearby? What account of mental representation would have this consequence? The answer is just what you'd expect from the discussion of the linguistic material. Mental representations must have internal structure, just the way that sentences do. In particular, it must be that the mental representation that corresponds to the thought that John loves the girl contains, as its parts, the same constituents as the mental representation that corresponds to the thought that the girl loves John. That would explain why these thoughts are *systematically* related; *and, to the extent that the semantic value of these parts is context-independent, that would explain why these systematically related thoughts are also semantically related.* So, by this chain of argument, evidence for the compositionality of sentences is evidence for the compositionality of the representational states of speaker/hearers.

Finally, what about the compositionality of infraverbal thought? The argument isn't much different from the one that we've just run through. We assume that animal thought is largely systematic: the organism that can perceive (hence learn) that aRb can generally perceive (/learn) that bRa. But, systematically related thoughts (just like systematically related sentences) are generally semantically related too. It's no surprise that being able to learn that the triangle is above the square implies being able to learn that the square is above the triangle; whereas it would be *very* surprising if being able to learn the square/triangle facts implied being able to learn that quarks are made of gluons or that Washington was the first President of America.

So, then, what explains the correlation between systematic relations and semantic relations in infraverbal thought? Clearly, Connectionist models don't address this question; the fact that a network contains a node labelled X has, so far as the constraints imposed by Connectionist architecture are concerned, *no implications at all* for the labels of the other nodes in the network; in particular, it doesn't imply that there will be nodes that represent thoughts that are semantically close to X. This is just the semantical side of the fact that network architectures permit arbitrarily punctate mental lives.

But if, on the other hand, we make the usual Classicist assumptions (viz., that systematically related thoughts share constituents and that the semantic values of these shared constituents are context independent) the correlation between systematicity and semantic relatedness follows immediately. For a Classicist, this correlation is an 'architectural' property of minds; it couldn't but hold if mental representations have the general properties that Classical models suppose them to.

What have Connectionists to say about these matters? There is some textual evidence that they are tempted to deny the facts of compositionality wholesale. For example, Smolensky (1988) claims that: "Surely ... we would get quite a different representation of 'coffee' if we examined the difference between 'can with coffee' and 'can without coffee' or 'tree with coffee' and 'tree without coffee'; or 'man with coffee' and 'man without coffee' ... context insensitivity is not something we expect to be reflected in Connectionist representations ....".

It's certainly true that compositionality is not generally a feature of Connectionist representations. Connectionists can't acknowledge the facts of compositionality because they are committed to mental representations that don't have combinatorial structure. But to give up on compositionality is to take 'kick the bucket' as a model for the relation between syntax and semantics; and the consequence is, as we've seen, that you make the systematicity of language (and of thought) a mystery. On the other hand, to say that 'kick the bucket' is aberrant, and that the right model for the syntax/semantics relation is (e.g.) 'brown cow', is to start down a trail which leads, pretty inevitably, to acknowledging combinatorial structure in mental representation, hence to the rejection of Connectionist networks as cognitive models.

We don't think there's any way out of the need to acknowledge the compositionality of natural languages and of mental representations. However, it's been suggested (see Smolensky, op cit.) that while the principle of compositionality is false (because content isn't context invariant) there is nevertheless a "family resemblance" between the various meanings that a symbol has in the various contexts in which it occurs. Since such proposals generally aren't elaborated, it's unclear how they're supposed to handle the salient facts about systematicity and inference. But surely there are going to be serious problems. Consider, for example, such inferences as

(i)   Turtles are slower than rabbits.
(ii)   Rabbits are slower than Ferraris.
....
(iii) Turtles are slower than Ferraris.

The soundness of this inference appears to depend upon (a) the fact that the same relation (viz., *slower than*) holds between turtles and rabbits on the one hand, and rabbits and Ferraris on the other; and (b) the fact that that relation is transitive. If, however, it's assumed (contrary to the principle of compositionality) that 'slower than' means something different in premises (i) and (ii) (and presumably in (iii) as well)—so that, strictly speaking, the relation that holds between turtles and rabbits is *not* the same one that holds between rabbits and Ferraris—then it's hard to see why the inference should be valid.

Talk about the relations being 'similar' only papers over the difficulty since the problem is then to provide a notion of similarity that will guaranty that if (i) and (ii) are true, so too is (iii). And, so far at least, no such notion of similarity has been forthcoming. Notice that it won't do to require just that the relations all be similar in respect of their *transitivity*, i.e., that they all be transitive. On that account, the argument from 'turtles are slower than rabbits' and 'rabbits are furrier than Ferraris' to 'turtles are slower than Ferraris' would be valid since 'furrier than' is transitive too.

Until these sorts of issues are attended to, the proposal to replace the compositional principle of context invariance with a notion of "approximate equivalence ... across contexts" (Smolensky, 1988) doesn't seem to be much more than hand waving.

3.4. The systematicity of inference

In Section 2 we saw that, according to Classical theories, the syntax of mental representations mediates between their semantic properties and their causal role in mental processes. Take a simple case: It's a 'logical' principle that conjunctions entail their constituents (so the argument from $P\&Q$ to P and to Q is valid). Correspondingly, it's a psychological law that thoughts that $P\&Q$ tend to cause thoughts that P and thoughts that Q, all else being equal. Classical theory exploits the constituent structure of mental representations to account for both these facts, the first by assuming that the combinatorial semantics of mental representations is sensitive to their syntax and the second by assuming that mental processes apply to mental representations in virtue of their constituent structure.

A consequence of these assumptions is that Classical theories are committed to the following striking prediction: inferences that are of similar logical type ought, pretty generally,[28] to elicit correspondingly similar cognitive capacities. You shouldn't, for example, find a kind of mental life in which you get inferences from *P&Q&R* to *P* but you don't get inferences from *P&Q* to *P*. This is because, according to the Classical account, this logically homogeneous class of inferences is carried out by a correspondingly homogeneous class of psychological mechanisms: The premises of both inferences are expressed by mental representations that satisfy the same syntactic analysis (viz., $S_1\&S_2\&S_3\& \ldots S_n$); and the process of drawing the inference corresponds, in both cases, to the same formal operation of detaching the constituent that expresses the conclusion.

The idea that organisms should exhibit similar cognitive capacities in respect of logically similar inferences is so natural that it may seem unavoidable. But, on the contrary: there's nothing in principle to preclude a kind of cognitive model in which inferences that are quite similar from the logician's point of view are nevertheless computed by quite different mechanisms; or in which some inferences of a given logical type are computed and other inferences of the same logical type are not. Consider, in particular, the Connectionist account. A Connectionist can certainly model a mental life in which, if you can reason from *P&Q&R* to *P*, then you can also reason from *P&Q* to *P*. For example, the network in (Figure 3) would do:

Figure 3.   *A possible Connectionist network which draws inferences from P&Q&R to P and also draws inferences from P&Q to P.*

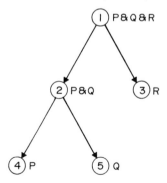

[28]The hedge is meant to exclude cases where inferences of the same logical type nevertheless differ in complexity in virtue of, for example, the length of their premises. The inference from $(A_\lor B_\lor C_\lor D_\lor E)$ and $(-B\&-C\&-D\&-E)$ to A is of the same logical type as the inference from $A_\lor B$ and $-B$ to A. But it wouldn't be very surprising, or very interesting, if there were minds that could handle the second inference but not the first.

But notice that *a Connectionist can equally model a mental life in which you get one of these inferences and not the other*. In the present case, since there is no structural relation between the *P&Q&R* node and the *P&Q* node (remember, all nodes are atomic; don't be misled by the node *labels*) there's no reason why a mind that contains the first should also contain the second, or vice versa. Analogously, there's no reason why you shouldn't get minds that simplify the premise *John loves Mary and Bill hates Mary* but no others; or minds that simplify premises with 1, 3, or 5 conjuncts, but don't simplify premises with 2, 4, or 6 conjuncts; or, for that matter, minds that simplify only premises that were acquired on Tuesdays ... etc.

In fact, the Connectionist architecture is *utterly indifferent* as among these possibilities. That's because it recognizes no notion of syntax according to which thoughts that are alike in inferential role (e.g., thoughts that are all subject to simplification of conjunction) are expressed by mental representations of correspondingly similar syntactic form (e.g., by mental representations that are all syntactically conjunctive). So, the Connectionist architecture tolerates gaps in cognitive capacities; it has no mechanism to enforce the requirement that logically homogeneous inferences should be executed by correspondingly homogeneous computational processes.

But, we claim, you don't find cognitive capacities that have these sorts of gaps. You don't, for example, get minds that are prepared to infer *John went to the store* from *John and Mary and Susan and Sally went to the store* and from *John and Mary went to the store* but not from *John and Mary and Susan went to the store*. Given a notion of logical syntax—the very notion that the Classical theory of mentation requires to get its account of mental processes off the ground—it is a *truism* that you don't get such minds. Lacking a notion of logical syntax, it is a *mystery* that you don't.

3.5. Summary

It is perhaps obvious by now that all the arguments that we've been reviewing—the argument from systematicity, the argument from compositionality, and the argument from influential coherence—are really much the same: If you hold the kind of theory that acknowledges structured representations, it must perforce acknowledge representations with *similar* or *identical* structures. In the linguistic cases, constituent analysis implies a taxonomy of sentences by their syntactic form, and in the inferential cases, it implies a taxonomy of arguments by their logical form. So, if your theory also acknowledges mental processes that are structure sensitive, then it will predict that similarly structured representations will generally play similar roles in thought. A theory that says that the sentence 'John loves the girl' is made out of the same parts as the sentence 'the girl loves John', and made by applications of the same rules of composition, will have to go out of its way to explain a linguistic competence which embraces one sentence but not the other. And similarly, if a theory says that the mental representation that corresponds to the thought that *P&Q&R* has the same (conjunctive) syntax as the mental representation that corresponds to the thought that *P&Q* and that mental processes of drawing inferences subsume mental representations in virtue of their syntax, it will have to go out of its way to explain inferential capacities which embrace the one thought but not the other. Such a competence would be, at best, an embarrassment for the theory, and at worst a refutation.

By contrast, since the Connectionist architecture recognizes no combinatorial structure in mental representations, gaps in cognitive competence should proliferate arbitrarily. It's not just that you'd expect to get them from time to time; it's that, on the 'no-structure' story, *gaps are the unmarked case*. It's the *systematic* competence that the theory is required to treat as an embarrassment. But, as a matter of fact, inferential competences are *blatantly* systematic. So there must be something deeply wrong with Connectionist architecture.

What's deeply wrong with Connectionist architecture is this: Because it acknowledges neither syntactic nor semantic structure in mental representations, it perforce treats them not as a generated set but as a list. But lists, qua lists, have no structure; any collection of items is a possible list. And, correspondingly, on Connectionist principles, any collection of (causally connected) representational states is a possible mind. So, as far as Connectionist architecture is concerned, there is nothing to prevent minds that are arbitrarily unsystematic. But that result is *preposterous*. Cognitive capacities come in structurally related clusters; their systematicity is pervasive. All the evidence suggests that *punctate minds can't happen*. This argument seemed conclusive against the Connectionism of Hebb, Osgood and Hull twenty or thirty years ago. So far as we can tell, nothing of any importance has happened to change the situation in the meantime.[29]

---

[29]Historical footnote: Connectionists are Associationists, but not every Associationist holds that mental representations must be unstructured. Hume didn't, for example. Hume thought that mental representations are rather like pictures, and pictures typically have a compositional semantics: the parts of a picture of a horse are generally pictures of horse parts.

On the other hand, allowing a compositional semantics for mental representations doesn't do an Associationist much good so long as he is true to this spirit of his Associationism. The virtue of having mental representations with structure is that it allows for structure sensitive operations to be defined over them; specifically, it allows for the sort of operations that eventuate in productivity and systematicity. Association is not, however, such an operation; all *it* can do is build an internal model of redundancies in experience by

A final comment to round off this part of the discussion. It's possible to imagine a Connectionist being prepared to admit that while systematicity doesn't *follow from*—and hence is not explained by—Connectionist architecture, it is nonetheless *compatible* with that architecture. It is, after all, perfectly possible to follow a policy of building networks that have *a*R*b* nodes only if they have *b*R*a* nodes ... etc. There is therefore nothing to stop a Connectionist from stipulating—as an independent postulate of his theory of mind—that all biologically instantiated networks are, de facto, systematic.

But this misses a crucial point: It's not enough just to stipulate systematicity; one is also required to specify a mechanism that is able to enforce the stipulation. To put it another way, it's not enough for a Connectionist to agree that all minds are systematic; he must also explain *how nature contrives to produce only systematic minds*. Presumably there would have to be some sort of mechanism, over and above the ones that Connectionism per se posits, the functioning of which insures the systematicity of biologically instantiated networks; a mechanism such that, in virtue of its operation, every network that has an *a*R*b* node also has a *b*R*a* node ... and so forth. There are, however, no proposals for such a mechanism. Or, rather, there is just one: The only mechanism that is known to be able to produce pervasive systematicity is Classical architecture. And, as we have seen, Classical architecture is not compatible with Connectionism since it requires internally structured representations.

4. The lure of Connectionism

The current popularity of the Connectionist approach among psychologists and philosophers is puzzling in view of the sorts of problems raised above; problems which were largely responsible for the development of a syntax-based (proof theoretic) notion of computation and a Turing-style, symbol-processing notion of cognitive architecture in the first place. There are, however, a number of apparently plausible arguments, repeatedly encountered

---

altering the probabilities of transitions among mental states. So far as the problems of productivity and systematicity are concerned, an Associationist who acknowledges structured representations is in the position of having the can but not the opener.

Hume, in fact, cheated: he allowed himself not just Association but also "Imagination", which he takes to be an 'active' faculty that can produce new concepts out of old parts by a process of analysis and recombination. (The idea of a unicorn is pieced together out of the idea of a horse and the idea of a horn, for example.) Qua associationist Hume had, of course, no right to active mental faculties. But allowing imagination in gave Hume precisely what modern Connectionists don't have: an answer to the question how mental processes can be productive. The moral is that if you've got structured representations, the temptation to postulate structure sensitive operations and an executive to apply them is practically irresistible.

in the literature, that stress certain limitations of conventional computers as models of brains. These may be seen as favoring the Connectionist alternative. We will sketch a number of these before discussing the general problems which they appear to raise.

- *Rapidity of cognitive processes in relation to neural speeds: the "hundred step" constraint.* It has been observed (e.g., Feldman & Ballard, 1982) that the time required to execute computer instructions is in the order of nanoseconds, whereas neurons take tens of milliseconds to fire. Consequently, in the time it takes people to carry out many of the tasks at which they are fluent (like recognizing a word or a picture, either of which may require considerably less than a second) a *serial* neurally-instantiated program would only be able to carry out about 100 instructions. Yet such tasks might typically require many thousands—or even millions—of instructions in present-day computers (if they can be done at all). Thus, it is argued, the brain must operate quite differently from computers. In fact, the argument goes, the brain must be organized in a highly parallel manner ("massively parallel" is the preferred term of art).
- *Difficulty of achieving large-capacity pattern recognition and content-based retrieval in conventional architectures.* Closely related to the issues about time constraints is the fact that humans can store and make use of an enormous amount of information—apparently without effort (Fahlman & Hinton, 1987). One particularly dramatic skill that people exhibit is the ability to recognize patterns from among tens or even hundreds of thousands of alternatives (e.g., word or face recognition). In fact, there is reason to believe that many expert skills may be based on large, fast recognition memories (see Simon & Chase, 1973). If one had to search through one's memory serially, the way conventional computers do, the complexity would overwhelm any machine. Thus, the knowledge that people have must be stored and retrieved differently from the way conventional computers do it.
- *Conventional computer models are committed to a different etiology for "rule-governed" behavior and "exceptional" behavior.* Classical psychological theories, which are based on conventional computer ideas, typically distinguish between mechanisms that cause regular and divergent behavior by postulating systems of explicit unconscious rules to explain the former, and then attributing departures from these rules to secondary (performance) factors. Since the divergent behaviors occur very frequently, a better strategy would be to try to account for both types of behavior in terms of the same mechanism.

● *Lack of progress in dealing with processes that are nonverbal or intuitive.*
Most of our fluent cognitive skills do not consist in accessing verbal
knowledge or carrying out deliberate conscious reasoning (Fahlman &
Hinton, 1987; Smolensky, 1988). We appear to know many things that
we would have great difficulty in describing verbally, including how to
ride a bicycle, what our close friends look like, and how to recall the
name of the President, etc. Such knowledge, it is argued, must not be
stored in linguistic form, but in some other "implicit" form. The fact
that conventional computers typically operate in a "linguistic mode",
inasmuch as they process information by operating on syntactically structured expressions, may explain why there has been relatively little success in modeling implicit knowledge.

● *Acute sensitivity of conventional architectures to damage and noise.* Unlike digital circuits, brain circuits must tolerate noise arising from spontaneous neural activity. Moreover, they must tolerate a moderate degree
of damage without failing completely. With a few notable exceptions, if
a part of the brain is damaged, the degradation in performance is usually
not catastrophic but varies more or less gradually with the extent of the
damage. This is especially true of memory. Damage to the temporal
cortex (usually thought to house memory traces) does not result in selective loss of particular facts and memories. This and similar facts about
brain damaged patients suggests that human memory representations,
and perhaps many other cognitive skills as well, are *distributed* spatially,
rather than being neurally localized. This appears to contrast with conventional computers, where hierarchical-style control keeps the crucial
decisions highly localized and where memory storage consists of an array
of location-addressable registers.

● *Storage in conventional architectures is passive.* Conventional computers
have a passive memory store which is accessed in what has been called
a "fetch and execute cycle". This appears to be quite unlike human
memory. For example, according to Kosslyn and Hatfield (1984, pp.
1022, 1029):

> In computers the memory is static: once an entry is put in a given location,
> it just sits there until it is operated upon by the CPU .... But consider a
> very simple experiment: Imagine a letter *A* over and over again ... then
> switch to the letter *B*. In a model employing a Von Neumann architecture
> the 'fatigue' that inhibited imaging the *A* would be due to some quirk in
> the way the CPU executes a given instruction .... Such fatigue should
> generalize to all objects imaged because the routine responsible for imag-
> ing was less effective. But experiments have demonstrated that this is not
> true: specific objects become more difficult to image, not all objects. This

finding is more easily explained by an analogy to the way invisible ink fades of its own accord ...: with invisible ink, the representation itself is doing something—there is no separate processor working over it ... .

● *Conventional rule-based systems depict cognition as "all-or-none".* But cognitive skills appear to be characterized by various kinds of continuities. For example:

● *Continuous variation in degree of applicability of different principles,* or in the degree of relevance of different constraints, "rules", or procedures. There are frequent cases (especially in perception and memory retrieval), in which it appears that a variety of different constraints are brought to bear on a problem simultaneously and the outcome is a combined effect of all the different factors (see, for example, the informal discussion by McClelland, Rumelhart & Hinton, 1986, pp. 3–9). That's why "constraint propagation" techniques are receiving a great deal of attention in artificial intelligence (see Mackworth, 1987).

● *Nondeterminism of human behavior:* Cognitive processes are never rigidly determined or precisely replicable. Rather, they appear to have a significant random or stochastic component. Perhaps that's because there is randomness at a microscopic level, caused by irrelevant biochemical or electrical activity or perhaps even by quantum mechanical events. To model this activity by rigid deterministic rules can only lead to poor predictions because it ignores the fundamentally stochastic nature of the underlying mechanisms. Moreover, deterministic, all-or-none models will be unable to account for the gradual aspect of learning and skill acquisition.

● *Failure to display graceful degradation.* When humans are unable to do a task perfectly, they nonetheless do something reasonable. If the particular task does not fit exactly into some known pattern, or if it is only partly understood, a person will not give up or produce nonsensical behavior. By contrast, if a Classical rule-based computer program fails to recognize the task, or fails to match a pattern to its stored representations or rules, it usually will be unable to do anything at all. This suggests that in order to display graceful degradation, we must be able to represent prototypes, match patterns, recognize problems, etc., in various *degrees*.

● *Conventional models are dictated by current technical features of computers and take little or no account of the facts of neuroscience.* Classical symbol processing systems provide no indication of how the kinds of processes that they postulate could be realized by a brain. The fact that this gap between high-level systems and brain architecture is so large might be an indication that these models are on the wrong track.

Whereas the architecture of the mind has evolved under the pressures of natural selection, some of the Classical assumptions about the mind may derive from features that computers have only because they are explicitly designed for the convenience of programmers. Perhaps this includes even the assumption that the description of mental processes at the cognitive level can be divorced from the description of their physical realization. At a minimum, by building our models to take account of what is known about neural structures we may reduce the risk of being misled by metaphors based on contemporary computer architectures.

Replies: Why the usual reasons given for preferring a Connectionist architecture are invalid

It seems to us that, as arguments against Classical cognitive architecture, all these points suffer from one or other of the following two defects.

(1) The objections depend on properties that are not in fact intrinsic to Classical architectures, since there can be perfectly natural Classical models that don't exhibit the objectionable features. (We believe this to be true, for example, of the arguments that Classical rules are explicit and Classical operations are 'all or none'.)

(2) The objections are true of Classical architectures insofar as they are implemented on current computers, but need not be true of such architectures when differently (e.g., neurally) implemented. They are, in other words, directed at the implementation level rather than the cognitive level, as these were distinguished in our earlier discussion. (We believe that this is true, for example, of the arguments about speed, resistance to damage and noise, and the passivity of memory.)

In the remainder of this section we will expand on these two points and relate them to some of the arguments presented above. Following this analysis, we will present what we believe may be the most tenable view of Connectionism; namely that it is a theory of how (Classical) cognitive systems might be implemented, either in real brains or in some 'abstract neurology'.

Parallel computation and the issue of speed

Consider the argument that cognitive processes must involve large scale parallel computation. In the form that it takes in typical Connectionist discussions, this issue is irrelevant to the adequacy of Classical *cognitive* architecture. The "hundred step constraint", for example, is clearly directed at the implementation level. All it rules out is the (absurd) hypothesis that cognitive architectures are implemented in the brain in the same way as they are implemented on electronic computers.

If you ever have doubts about whether a proposal pertains to the implementation level or the symbolic level, a useful heuristic is to ask yourself whether what is being claimed is true of a conventional computer—such as the DEC VAX—at *its* implementation level. Thus although most algorithms that run on the VAX are serial,[30] at the implementation level such computers are 'massively parallel'; they quite literally involve simultaneous electrical activity throughout almost the entire device. For example, every memory access cycle involves pulsing every bit in a significant fraction of the system's memory registers—since memory access is essentially a destructive read and rewrite process, the system clock regularly pulses and activates most of the central processing unit, and so on.

The moral is that the absolute speed of a process is a property *par excellence* of its implementation. (By contrast, the *relative* speed with which a system responds to different inputs is often diagnostic of distinct processes; but this has always been a prime empirical basis for deciding among alternative algorithms in information processing psychology). Thus, the fact that individual neurons require tens of miliseconds to fire can have no bearing on the predicted speed at which an algorithm will run *unless there is at least a partial, independently motivated, theory of how the operations of the functional architecture are implemented in neurons.* Since, in the case of the brain, it is not even certain that the firing[31] of neurons is invariably the relevant implementation property (at least for higher level cognitive processes like learning and memory) the 100 step "constraint" excludes nothing.

Finally, absolute constraints on the number of serial steps that a mental process can require, or on the time that can be required to execute them, provide weak arguments against Classical architecture because Classical architecture in no way excludes parallel execution of multiple symbolic processes. Indeed, it seems extremely likely that many Classical symbolic processes

---

[30]Even in the case of a conventional computer, whether it should be viewed as executing a serial or a parallel algorithm depends on what 'virtual machine' is being considered in the case in question. After all, a VAX *can* be used to simulate (i.e., to implement) a virtual machine with a parallel architecture. In that case the relevant algorithm would be a parallel one.

[31]There are, in fact, a number of different mechanisms of neural interaction (e.g., the "local interactions" described by Rakic, 1975). Moreover, a large number of chemical processes take place at the dendrites, covering a wide range of time scales, so even if dendritic transmission were the only relevant mechanism, we still wouldn't know what time scale to use as our estimate of neural action in general (see, for example, Black, 1986).

are going on in parallel in cognition, and that these processes interact with one another (e.g., they may be involved in some sort of symbolic constraint propagation). Operating on symbols can even involve "massively parallel" organizations; that might indeed imply new architectures, but they are all *Classical* in our sense, since they all share the Classical conception of computation as symbol-processing. (For examples of serious and interesting proposals on organizing Classical processors into large parallel networks, see Hewett's, 1977, *Actor* system, Hillis', 1985, "Connection Machine", as well as any of a number of recent commercial multi-processor machines.) The point here is that an argument for a network of parallel computers is not in and of itself either an argument against a Classical architecture or an argument for a Connectionist architecture.

Resistance to noise and physical damage (and the argument for distributed representation)

Some of the other advantages claimed for Connectionist architectures over Classical ones are just as clearly aimed at the implementation level. For example, the "resistance to physical damage" criterion is so obviously a matter of implementation that it should hardly arise in discussions of cognitive-level theories.

It is true that a certain kind of damage-resistance appears to be incompatible with localization, and it is also true that representations in PDP's are distributed over groups of units (at least when "coarse coding" is used). But distribution over units achieves damage-resistance only if it entails that representations are also *neurally* distributed.[32] However, neural distribution of representations is just as compatible with Classical architectures as it is with Connectionist networks. In the Classical case all you need are memory registers that distribute their contents over physical space. You can get that with fancy storage systems like optical ones, or chemical ones, or even with registers made of Connectionist nets. Come to think of it, we already had it in the old style "ferrite core" memories!

---

[32]Unless the 'units' in a Connectionist network really are assumed to have different spatially-focused loci in the brain, talk about distributed representation is likely to be extremely misleading. In particular, if units are merely *functionally* individuated, any amount of distribution or functional entities is compatible with any amount of spatial compactness of their neural representations. But it is not clear that units do, in fact, correspond to any anatomically identifiable locations in the brain. In the light of the way Connectionist mechanisms are designed, it may be appropriate to view units and links as functional/mathematical entities (what psychologists would call "hypothetical constructs") whose neurological interpretation remains entirely open. (This is, in fact, the view that some Connectionists take; see Smolensky, 1988.) The point is that distribution over mathematical constructs does not buy you damage resistance; only *neural* distribution does!

The physical requirements of a Classical symbol-processing system are easily misunderstood. (Confounding of physical and functional properties is widespread in psychological theorizing in general; for a discussion of this confusion in relation to metrical properties in models of mental imagery, see Pylyshyn 1981.) For example, conventional architecture requires that there be distinct symbolic expressions for each state of affairs that it can represent. Since such expressions often have a structure consisting of concatenated parts, the adjacency relation must be instantiated by *some* physical relation when the architecture is implemented (see the discussion in footnote 9). However, since the relation to be physically realized is *functional* adjacency, there is no necessity that physical instantiations of adjacent symbols be *spatially* adjacent. Similarly, although complex expressions are made out of atomic elements, and the distinction between atomic and complex symbols must somehow be physically instantiated, there is no necessity that a token of an atomic symbol be assigned a smaller region in space than a token of a complex symbol; even a token of a complex symbol of which it is a constituent. In Classical architectures, as in Connectionist networks, functional elements can be physically distributed or localized to any extent whatever. In a VAX (to use our heuristic again) pairs of symbols may certainly be functionally adjacent, but the symbol tokens are nonetheless spatially spread through many locations in physical memory.

In short, the fact that a property (like the position of a symbol within an expression) is functionally local has no implications one way or the other for damage-resistance or noise tolerance unless the functional-neighborhood metric corresponds to some appropriate *physical* dimension. When that is the case, we may be able to predict adverse consequences that varying the physical property has on objects localized in functional space (e.g., varying the voltage or line frequency might damage the left part of an expression). But, of course, the situation is exactly the same for Connectionist systems: even when they are resistant to spatially-local damage, they may not be resistant to damage that is local along some other physical dimensions. Since spatially-local damage is particularly frequent in real world traumas, this may have important practical consequences. But so long as our knowledge of how cognitive processes might be mapped onto brain tissue remains very nearly nonexistent, its message for cognitive science remains moot.

"Soft" constraints, continuous magnitudes, stochastic mechanisms, and active symbols

The notion that "soft" constraints which can vary continuously (as degree of activation does), are incompatible with Classical rule-based symbolic systems is another example of the failure to keep the psychological (or symbol-processing) and the implementation levels separate. One can have a Classical rule system in which the decision concerning which rule will fire resides in the functional architecture and depends on continuously varying magnitudes. Indeed, this is typically how it is done in practical "expert systems" which, for example, use a Bayesian mechanism in their production-system rule-interpreter. The soft or stochastic nature or rule-based processes arises from the interaction of deterministic rules with real-valued properties of the implementation, or with noisy inputs or noisy information transmission.

It should also be noted that rule applications need not issue in "all or none" behaviors since several rules may be activated at once and can have interactive effects on the outcome. Or, alternatively, each of the activated rules can generate independent parallel effects, which might get sorted out later—depending say, on which of the parallel streams reaches a goal first. An important, though sometimes neglected point about such aggregate properties of overt behavior as continuity, "fuzziness", randomness, etc., is that they need not arise from underlying mechanisms that are themselves fuzzy, continuous or random. It is not only possible in principle, but often quite reasonable in practice, to assume that apparently variable or nondeterministic behavior arises from the interaction of multiple deterministic sources.

A similar point can be made about the issue of "graceful degradation". Classical architecture does not require that when the conditions for applying the available rules aren't precisely met, the process should simply fail to do anything at all. As noted above, rules could be activated in some measure depending upon how close their conditions are to holding. Exactly what happens in these cases may depend on how the rule-system is implemented. On the other hand, it could be that the failure to display "graceful degradation" really is an intrinsic limit of the current class of models or even of current approaches to designing intelligent systems. It seems clear that the psychological models now available are inadequate over a broad spectrum of measures, so their problems with graceful degradation may be a special case of their general unintelligence: They may simply not be smart enough to know what to do when a limited stock of methods fails to apply. But this needn't be a principled limitation of Classical architectures: There is, to our knowledge, no reason to believe that something like Newell's (1969) "hierarchy of weak methods" or Laird, Rosenberg and Newell's (1986) "universal subgoaling", is in principle incapable of dealing with the problem of graceful degradation. (Nor, to our knowledge, has any argument yet been offered that Connectionist architectures are in principle capable of dealing with it. In fact current Connectionist models are every bit as graceless in their modes of failure as ones based on Classical architectures. For example, contrary to some claims, models such as that of McClelland and Kawamoto, 1986, fail quite unnaturally when given incomplete information.)

In short, the Classical theorist can view stochastic properties of behavior as emerging from interactions between the model and the intrinsic properties of the physical medium in which it is realized. It is essential to remember that, from the Classical point of view, overt behavior is par excellence an interaction effect, and symbol manipulations are supposed to be only one of the interacting causes.

These same considerations apply to Kosslyn and Hatfield's remarks (quoted earlier) about the commitment of Classical models to 'passive' versus 'active' representations. It is true, as Kosslyn and Hatfield say, that the representations that Von Neumann machines manipulate 'don't *do* anything' until a CPU operates upon them (they don't decay, for example). But, even on the absurd assumption that the mind has *exactly* the architecture of some contemporary (Von Neumann) computer, it is obvious that its behavior, and hence the behavior of an organism, is determined not just by the logical machine that the mind instantiates, but also by the protoplasmic machine in which the logic is realized. Instantiated representations *are* therefore bound to be active, even according to Classical models; the question is whether the kind of activity they exhibit should be accounted for by the cognitive model or by the theory of its implementation. This question is empirical and must not be begged on behalf of the Connectionist view. (As it is, for example, in such passages as "The brain itself does not manipulate symbols; the brain is the medium in which the symbols are floating and in which they trigger each other. There is no central manipulator, no central program. There is simply a vast collection of 'teams'—patterns of neural firings that, like teams of ants, trigger other patterns of neural firings ... . We feel those symbols churning within ourselves in somewhat the same way we feel our stomach churning." (Hofstadter, 1983, p. 279). This appears to be a serious case of *Formicidae in machina:* ants in the stomach of the ghost in the machine.)

Explicitness of rules

According to McClelland, Feldman, Adelson, Bower, and McDermott (1986, p. 6), "... Connectionist models are leading to a reconceptualization of key psychological issues, such as the nature of the representation of knowledge ... . One traditional approach to such issues treats knowledge as a body of rules that are consulted by processing mechanisms in the course of processing; in Connectionist models, such knowledge is represented, often in widely distributed form, in the connections among the processing units."

As we remarked in the Introduction, we think that the claim that most psychological processes are rule-implicit, and the corresponding claim that divergent and compliant behaviors result from the same cognitive mechanisms, are both interesting and tendentious. We regard these matters as entirely empirical and, in many cases, open. In any case, however, one should not confuse the rule-implicit/rule-explicit distinction with the distinction between Classical and Connectionist architecture.[33]

This confusion is just ubiquitous in the Connectionist literature: it is universally assumed by Connectionists that Classical models are committed to claiming that regular behaviors must arise from explicitly encoded rules. But this is simply untrue. Not only is there no reason why Classical models are required to be rule-explicit but—as a matter of fact—arguments over which, if any, rules are explicitly mentally represented have raged for decades *within* the Classicist camp. (See, for relatively recent examples, the discussion of the explicitness of grammatical rules in Stabler, 1985, and replies; for a philosophical discussion, see Cummins, 1983.) The one thing that Classical theorists do agree about is that it *can't* be that *all* behavioral regularities are determined by explicit rules; at least some of the causal determinants of compliant behavior *must* be *im*plicit. (The arguments for this parallel Lewis Carroll's observations in "What the Tortoise Said to Achilles"; see Carroll 1956.) All other questions of the explicitness of rules are viewed by Classicists as moot; and every shade of opinion on the issue can be found in the Classicist camp.

The basic point is this: not all the functions of a Classical computer can be encoded in the form of an explicit program; some of them must be wired in. In fact, the entire program can be hard-wired in cases where it does not need to modify or otherwise examine itself. In such cases, Classical machines can be *rule implicit* with respect to their programs, and the mechanism of their state transitions is entirely subcomputational (i.e., subsymbolic).

---

[33]An especially flagrant example of how issues about architecture get confused with issues about the explicitness of rules in the Connectionist literature occurs in PDP, Chapter 4, where Rumelhart and McClelland argue that PDP models provide "... a rather plausible account of how we can come to have innate 'knowledge'. To the extent that stored knowledge is assumed to be in the form of explicit, inaccessible rules ... it is hard to see how it could 'get into the head' of the newborn. It seems to us implausible that the newborn possesses elaborate symbol systems and the systems for interpreting them required to put these explicit, inaccessible rules to use in guiding behavior. On our account, we do not need to attribute such complex machinery. If the innate knowledge is simply the prewired connections, it is encoded from the start in just the right way to be of use by the processing mechanisms." (p. 42). A priorizing about what it does and doesn't seem likely that newborns possess strikes us as a bad way to do developmental cognitive psychology. But Rumelhart and McClelland's argument is doubly beside the point since a Classicist who shares their prejudices can perfectly well avail himself of the same solution that they endorse. Classical architecture does *not* require "complex machinery" for "interpreting" explicit rules since classical machines do not *require* explicit rules at all. Classical architecture is therefore *neutral* on the Empiricism/Nativism issue (and so is Connectionism, as Rumelhart and McClelland elsewhere correctly remark).

What *does* need to be explicit in a Classical machine is not its program but the symbols that it writes on its tapes (or stores in its registers). These, however, correspond not to the machine's rules of state transition but to its data structures. Data structures are *the objects that the machine transforms, not the rules of transformation.* In the case of programs that parse natural language, for example, Classical architecture requires the explicit representation of the structural descriptions of sentences, but is entirely neutral on the explicitness of grammars, contrary to what many Connectionists believe.

One of the important inventions in the history of computers—the stored-program computer—makes it *possible* for programs to take on the role of data structures. But nothing in the architecture *requires* that they always do so. Similarly, Turing demonstrated that there exists an abstract machine (the so-called Universal Turing Machine) which can simulate the behavior of any target (Turing) machine. A Universal machine is "rule-explicit" about the machine it is simulating (in the sense that it has an explicit representation of that machine which is sufficient to specify its behavior uniquely). Yet the target machine can perfectly well be "rule-implicit" with respect to the rules that govern *its* behavior.

So, then, you can't attack Classical theories of cognitive architecture by showing that a cognitive process is rule-implicit; Classical architecture *permits* rule-explicit processes but does *not* require them. However, you *can* attack Connectionist architectures by showing that a cognitive process is rule *explicit* since, by definition, Connectionist architecture precludes the sorts of logico-syntactic capacities that are required to encode rules and the sorts of executive mechanisms that are required to apply them.[34]

If, therefore, there should prove to be persuasive arguments for rule explicit cognitive processes, that would be very embarrassing for Connectionists. A natural place to look for such arguments would be in the theory of the acquisition of cognitive competences. For example, much traditional work in linguistics (see Prince & Pinker, 1988) and all recent work in mathematical learning theory (see Osherson, Stov, & Weinstein, 1984), assumes that the characteristic output of a cognitive acquisition device is a recursive rule system (a grammar, in the linguistic case). Suppose such theories prove to be well-founded; then that would be incompatible with the assumption that the cognitive architecture of the capacities acquired is Connectionist.

---

[34]Of course, it *is* possible to simulate a "rule explicit process" in a Connectionist network by first implementing a Classical architecture in the network. The slippage between networks as architectures and as implementations is ubiquitous in Connectionist writings, as we remarked above.

On "Brain style" modeling

The relation of Connectionist models to neuroscience is open to many interpretations. On the one hand, people like Ballard (1986), and Sejnowski
(1981), are explicitly attempting to build models based on properties of
neurons and neural organizations, even though the neuronal units in question
are idealized (some would say more than a little idealized: see, for example
the commentaries following the Ballard, 1986, paper). On the other hand,
Smolensky (1988) views Connectionist units as mathematical objects which
can be given an interpretation in either neural or psychological terms. Most
Connectionists find themselves somewhere in between, frequently referring
to their approach as "brain-style" theorizing.[35]

Understanding both psychological principles *and* the way that they are
neurophysiologically implemented is much better (and, indeed, more empirically secure) than only understanding one or the other. That is not at issue.
The question is whether there is anything to be gained by designing "brain
style" models that are uncommitted about how the models map onto brains.

Presumably the point of "brain style" modeling is that theories of cognitive
processing should be influenced by the facts of biology (especially neuroscience). The biological facts that influence Connectionist models appear to
include the following: neuronal connections are important to the patterns of
brain activity; the memory "engram" does not appear to be spatially local;
to a first approximation, neurons appear to be threshold elements which sum
the activity arriving at their dendrites; many of the neurons in the cortex have
multidimension "receptive fields" that are sensitive to a narrow range of
values of a number of parameters; the tendency for activity at a synapse to
cause a neuron to "fire" is modulated by the frequency and recency of past
firings.

Let us suppose that these and similar claims are both true and relevant to
the way the brain functions—an assumption that is by no means unproblematic. The question we might then ask is: What follows from such facts that is
relevant to inferring the nature of the cognitive architecture? The unavoidable answer appears to be, very little. That's not an a priori claim. The degree
of relationship between facts at different levels of organization of a system is
an empirical matter. However, there is reason to be skeptical about whether
the sorts of properties listed above are reflected in any more-or-less direct

---

[35]The PDP Research Group views its goal as being "to replace the 'computer metaphor' as a model of the
mind with the 'brain metaphor' ..." (Rumelhart & McClelland, 1986a, Ch. 6, p. 75). But the issue is not at
all which metaphor we should adopt; metaphors (whether 'computer' or 'brain') tend to be a license to take
one's claims as something less than serious hypotheses. As Pylyshyn (1984a) points out, the claim that the
mind has the architecture of a Classical computer is not a metaphor but a literal empirical hypothesis.

way in the structure of the system that carries out reasoning.

Consider, for example, one of the most salient properties of neural systems: they are networks which transmit activation culminating in state changes of some quasi-threshold elements. Surely it is not warranted to conclude that reasoning consists of the spread of excitation among representations, or even among semantic components of representations. After all, a VAX is also correctly characterized as consisting of a network over which excitation is transmitted culminating in state changes of quasi-threshold elements. Yet at the level at which it processes representations, a VAX is *literally* organized as a Von Neumann architecture.

The point is that the structure of "higher levels" of a system are rarely isomorphic, or even similar, to the structure of "lower levels" of a system. No one expects the theory of protons to look very much like the theory of rocks and rivers, even though, to be sure, it is protons and the like that rocks and rivers are 'implemented in'. Lucretius got into trouble precisely by assuming that there must be a simple correspondence between the structure of macrolevel and microlevel theories. He thought, for example, that hooks and eyes hold the atoms together. He was wrong, as it turns out.

There are, no doubt, cases where special empirical considerations suggest detailed structure/function correspondences or other analogies between different levels of a system's organization. For example, the input to the most peripheral stages of vision and motor control *must* be specified in terms of anatomically projected patterns (of light, in one case, and of muscular activity in the other); and independence of structure and function is perhaps less likely in a system whose input or output must be specified somatotopically. Thus, at these stages it is reasonable to expect an anatomically distributed structure to be reflected by a distributed functional architecture. When, however, the cognitive process under investigation is as abstract as reasoning, there is simply no reason to expect isomorphisms between structure and function; as, indeed, the computer case proves.

Perhaps this is all too obvious to be worth saying. Yet it seems that the commitment to "brain style" modeling leads to many of the characteristic Connectionist claims about psychology, and that it does so via the implicit—and unwarranted—assumption that there ought to be similarity of structure among the different levels of organization of a computational system. This is distressing since much of the psychology that this search for structural analogies has produced is strikingly recidivist. Thus the idea that the brain is a neural network motivates the revival of a largely discredited Associationist psychology. Similarly, the idea that brain activity is anatomically distributed leads to functionally distributed representations for concepts which in turn leads to the postulation of microfeatures; yet the inadequacies of feature-based theories of concepts are well-known and, to our knowledge, micro-feature theory has done nothing to address them (see Bolinger, 1965; J.D. Fodor, 1977). Or again, the idea that the strength of a connection between neurons is affected by the frequency of their co-activation gets projected onto the cognitive level. The consequence is a resurgence of statistical models of learning that had been widely acknowledged (both in Psychology and in AI) to be extremely limited in their applicability (e.g., Minsky & Papert, 1972, Chomsky, 1957).

So although, *in principle*, knowledge of how the brain works could direct cognitive modeling in a beneficial manner, *in fact* a research strategy has to be judged by its fruits. The main fruit of "brain style modeling" has been to revive psychological theories whose limitations had previously been pretty widely appreciated. It has done so largely because assumptions about the structure of the brain have been adopted in an all-too-direct manner as hypotheses about cognitive architecture; it's an instructive paradox that the current attempt to be thoroughly modern and 'take the brain seriously' should lead to a psychology not readily distinguishable from the worst of Hume and Berkeley. The moral seems to be that one should be deeply suspicious of the heroic sort of brain modeling that purports to address the problems of cognition. We sympathize with the craving for biologically respectable theories that many psychologists seem to feel. But, given a choice, truth is more important than respectability.

Concluding comments: Connectionism as a theory of implementation

A recurring theme in the previous discussion is that many of the arguments for Connectionism are best construed as claiming that cognitive architecture is *implemented* in a certain kind of network (of abstract "units"). Understood this way, these arguments are neutral on the question of what the cognitive architecture is.[36] In these concluding remarks we'll briefly consider Connectionism from this point of view.

Almost every student who enters a course on computational or information-processing models of cognition must be disabused of a very general mis-

---

[36]Rumelhart and McClelland maintain that PDP models are more than *just* theories of implementation because (1) they add to our understanding of the problem (p. 116), (2) studying PDPs can lead to the postulation of different macrolevel processes (p. 126). Both these points deal with the heuristic value of "brain style" theorizing. Hence, though correct in principle, they are irrelevant to the crucial question whether Connectionism is best understood as an attempt to model neural implementation, or whether it really does promise a "*new*" theory of the mind" incompatible with Classical information-processing approaches. It is an empirical question whether the heuristic value of this approach will turn out to be positive or negative. We have already commented on our view of the recent history of this attempt.

understanding concerning the role of the physical computer in such models. Students are almost always skeptical about "the computer as a model of cognition" on such grounds as that "computers don't forget or make mistakes", "computers function by exhaustive search," "computers are too logical and unmotivated," "computers can't learn by themselves; they can only do what they're told," or "computers are too fast (or too slow)," or "computers never get tired or bored," and so on. If we add to this list such relatively more sophisticated complaints as that "computers don't exhibit graceful degradation" or "computers are too sensitive to physical damage" this list will begin to look much like the arguments put forward by Connectionists.

The answer to all these complaints has always been that the *implementation*, and all properties associated with the particular realization of the algorithm that the theorist happens to use in a particular case, is irrelevant to the psychological theory; only the algorithm and the representations on which it operates are intended as a psychological hypothesis. Students are taught the notion of a "virtual machine" and shown that *some* virtual machines *can* learn, forget, get bored, make mistakes and whatever else one likes, providing one has a theory of the origins of each of the empirical phenomena in question.

Given this principled distinction between a model and its implementation, a theorist who is impressed by the virtues of Connectionism has the option of proposing PDP's as theories of implementation. But then, far from providing a revolutionary new basis for cognitive science, these models are in principle neutral about the nature of cognitive processes. In fact, they might be viewed as advancing the goals of Classical information processing psychology by attempting to explain how the brain (or perhaps some idealized brain-like network) might realize the types of processes that conventional cognitive science has hypothesized.

Connectionists do sometimes explicitly take their models to be theories of implementation. Ballard (1986) even refers to Connectionism as "the implementational approach". Touretzky (1986) clearly views his BoltzCONS model this way; he uses Connectionist techniques to implement conventional symbol processing mechanisms such as pushdown stacks and other LISP facilities.[37]

---

[37]Even in this case, where the model is specifically designed to implement Lisp-like features, some of the rhetoric fails to keep the implementation-algorithm levels distinct. This leads to talk about "emergent properties" and to the claim that even when they implement Lisp-like mechanisms, Connectionist systems "can compute things in ways in which Turing machines and von Neumann computers can't." (Touretzky, 1986). Such a claim suggests that Touretzky distinguishes different "ways of computing" not in terms of different algorithms, but in terms of different ways of implementing the same algorithm. While nobody has proprietary rights to terms like "ways of computing", this is a misleading way of putting it; it means that a DEC machine has a "different way of computing" from an IBM machine even when executing the identical program.

Rumelhart and McClelland (1986a, p. 117), who are convinced that Connectionism signals a radical departure from the conventional symbol processing approach, nonetheless refer to "PDP implementations" of various mechanisms such as attention. Later in the same essay, they make their position explicit: Unlike "reductionists," they believe "... that new and useful concepts emerge at different levels of organization". Although they then defend the claim that one should understand the higher levels "... through the study of the interactions among lower level units", the basic idea that there *are* autonomous levels seems implicit everywhere in the essay.

But once one admits that there really are cognitive-level principles distinct from the (putative) architectural principles that Connectionism articulates, there seems to be little left to argue about. Clearly it is pointless to ask whether one should or shouldn't do cognitive science by studying "the interaction of lower levels" as opposed to studying processes at the cognitive level since we surely have to do *both*. Some scientists study geological principles, others study "the interaction of lower level units" like molecules. But since the fact that there are genuine, autonomously-stateable principles of geology is never in dispute, people who build molecular level models do not claim to have invented a "new theory of geology" that will dispense with all that old fashioned "folk geological" talk about rocks, rivers and mountains!

We have, in short, no objection at all to networks as potential implementation models, nor do we suppose that any of the arguments we've given are incompatible with this proposal. The trouble is, however, that if Connectionists do want their models to be construed this way, then they will have to radically alter their practice. For, it seems utterly clear that most of the Connectionist models that have actually been proposed must be construed as theories of cognition, not as theories of implementation. This follows from the fact that it is intrinsic to these theories to ascribe representational content to the units (and/or aggregates) that they postulate. And, as we remarked at the beginning, a theory of the relations among representational states is ipso facto a theory at the level of cognition, not at the level of implementation. It has been the burden of our argument that when construed as a cognitive theory, rather than as an implementation theory, Connectionism appears to have fatal limitations. The problem with Connectionist models is that all the reasons for thinking that they might be true are reasons for thinking that they couldn't be *psychology*.

Conclusion

What, in light of all of this, are the options for the further development of Connectionist theories? As far as we can see, there are four routes that they could follow:

(1) Hold out for unstructured mental representations as against the Classical view that mental representations have a combinatorial syntax and semantics. Productivity and systematicity arguments make this option appear not attractive.

(2) Abandon network architecture to the extent of opting for structured mental *representations* but continue to insist upon an Associationistic account of the nature of mental *processes*. This is, in effect, a retreat to Hume's picture of the mind (see footnote 29), and it has a problem that we don't believe can be solved: Although mental representations are, on the present assumption, structured objects, *association is not a structure sensitive relation.* The problem is thus how to reconstruct the semantical coherence of thought without postulating psychological processes that are sensitive to the structure of mental representations. (Equivalently, in more modern terms, it's how to get the causal relations among mental representations to mirror their semantical relations without assuming a proof-theoretic treatment of inference and—more generally—a treatment of semantic coherence that is syntactically expressed, in the spirit of proof-theory.) This is the problem on which traditional Associationism foundered, and the prospects for solving it now strike us as not appreciably better than they were a couple of hundred years ago. To put it a little differently: if you need structure in mental representations anyway to account for the productivity and systematicity of minds, why not postulate mental processes that are structure sensitive to account for the coherence of mental processes? Why not be a Classicist, in short.

In any event, notice that the present option gives the Classical picture a lot of what it wants: viz., the identification of semantic states with relations to structured arrays of symbols and the identification of mental processes with transformations of such arrays. Notice too that, as things now stand, this proposal is Utopian since there are no serious proposals for incorporating syntactic structure in Connectionist architectures.

(3) Treat Connectionism as an implementation theory. We have no principled objection to this view (though there are, as Connectionists are discovering, technical reasons why networks are often an awkward way to implement Classical machines). This option would entail rewriting quite a lot of the polemical material in the Connectionist literature, as well as redescribing

what the networks are doing as operating on symbol structures, rather than spreading activation among semantically interpreted nodes.

Moreover, this revision of policy is sure to lose the movement a lot of fans. As we have pointed out, many people have been attracted to the Connectionist approach because of its promise to (a) do away with the symbol level of analysis, and (b) elevate neuroscience to the position of providing evidence that bears directly on issues of cognition. If Connectionism is considered simply as a theory of how cognition is neurally implemented, it may constrain cognitive models no more than theories in biophysics, biochemistry, or, for that matter, quantum mechanics do. All of these theories are also concerned with processes that *implement* cognition, and all of them are likely to postulate structures that are quite different from cognitive architecture. The point is that 'implements' is transitive, and it goes all the way down.

(4) Give up on the idea that networks offer (to quote Rumelhart & McClelland, 1986a, p. 110) "... a reasonable basis for modeling cognitive processes in general". It could still be held that networks sustain *some* cognitive processes. A good bet might be that they sustain such processes as can be analyzed as the drawing of statistical inferences; as far as we can tell, what network models really are is just analog machines for computing such inferences. Since we doubt that much of cognitive processing does consist of analyzing statistical relations, this would be quite a modest estimate of the prospects for network theory compared to what the Connectionists themselves have been offering.

This is, for example, one way of understanding what's going on in the argument between Rumelhart and McClelland (1986b) and Prince and Pinker (1988), though neither paper puts it in quite these terms. In effect, Rumelhart and McClelland postulate a mechanism which, given a corpus of pairings that a 'teacher' provides as data, computes the statistical correlation between the phonological form of the ending of a verb and the phonological form of its past tense inflection. (The magnitude of the correlations so computed is analogically represented by the weights that the network exhibits at asymptote.) Given the problem of inflecting a new verb stem ending in a specified phonological sequence, the machine chooses the form of the past tense that was most highly correlated with that sequence in the training set. By contrast, Prince and Pinker argue (in effect) that more must be going on in learning past tense morphology than merely estimating correlations since the statistical hypothesis provides neither a close fit to the ontogenetic data nor a plausible account of the adult competence on which the ontogenetic processes converge. It seems to us that Pinker and Prince have, by quite a lot, the best of this argument.

There is an alternative to the Empiricist idea that all learning consists of a kind of statistical inference, realized by adjusting parameters; it's the Rationalist idea that some learning is a kind of theory construction, effected by framing hypotheses and evaluating them against evidence. We seem to remember having been through this argument before. We find ourselves with a gnawing sense of deja vu.

References

Arbib, M. (1975). Artificial intelligence and brain theory: Unities and diversities. *Biomedical Engineering, 3*, 238–274.

Ballard, D.H. (1986). Cortical connections and parallel processing: Structure and function. *The Behavioral and Brain Sciences, 9*, 67–120.

Ballard, D.H. (1987). Parallel Logical Inference and Energy Minimization. Report TR142, Computer Science Department, University of Rochester.

Black, I.B. (1986). Molecular memory mechanisms. In Lynch, G. (Ed.), *Synapses, circuits, and the beginnings of memory*. Cambridge, MA: M.I.T. Press, A Bradford Book.

Bolinger, D. (1965). The atomization of meaning. *Language, 41*, 555–573.

Broadbent, D. (1985). A question of levels: Comments on McClelland and Rumelhart. *Journal of Experimental Psychology: General, 114*, 189–192.

Carroll, L. (1956). What the tortoise said to Achilles and other riddles. In Newman, J.R. (Ed.), *The world of mathematics: Volume Four*. New York: Simon and Schuster.

Chomsky, N. (1957). *Syntactic structures*. The Hague: Mouton.

Chomsky, N. (1965). *Aspects of the theory of syntax*. Cambridge: MA: M.I.T. Press.

Chomsky, N. (1968). *Language and mind*. New York: Harcourt, Brace and World.

Churchland, P.M. (1981). Eliminative materialism and the propositional attitudes. *Journal of Philosophy, 78*, 67–90.

Churchland, P.S. (1986). *Neurophilosophy*. Cambridge, MA: M.I.T. Press.

Cummins, R. (1983). *The nature of psychological explanation*. Cambridge, MA: M.I.T. Press.

Dennett, D. (1986). The logical geography of computational approaches: A view from the east pole. In Brand, M. & Harnish, M. (Eds.), *The representation of knowledge*. Tuscon, AZ: The University of Arizona Press.

Dreyfus, H., & Dreyfus, S. (in press). Making a mind vs modelling the brain: A.I. back at a branch point. *Daedalus*.

Fahlman, S.E., & Hinton, G.E. (1987). Connectionist architectures for artificial intelligence. *Computer, 20*, 100–109.

Feldman, J.A. (1986). Neural representation of conceptual knowledge. Report TR189. Department of Computer Science, University of Rochester.

Feldman, J.A., & Ballard, D.H. (1982). Connectionist models and their properties. *Cognitive Science, 6*, 205–254.

Fodor, J. (1976). *The language of thought*, Harvester Press, Sussex. (Harvard University Press paperback).

Fodor, J.D. (1977). *Semantics: Theories of meaning in generative grammar*. New York: Thomas Y. Crowell.

Fodor, J. (1987). *Psychosemantics*. Cambridge, MA: M.I.T. Press.

Frohn, H., Geiger, H., & Singer, W. (1987). A self-organizing neural network sharing features of the mammalian visual system. *Biological Cybernetics, 55*, 333–343.

Geach, P. (1957). *Mental acts.* London: Routledge and Kegan Paul.

Hewett, C. (1977). Viewing control structures as patterns of passing messages. *The Artificial Intelligence Journal, 8,* 232–364.

Hillis, D. (1985). *The connection machine.* Cambridge, MA: M.I.T. Press.

Hinton, G. (1987). Representing part-whole hierarchies in connectionist networks. Unpublished manuscript.

Hinton, G.E., McClelland, J.L., & Rumelhart, D.E. (1986). Distributed representations. In Rumelhart, D.E., McClelland, J.L. and the PDP Research Group, *Parallel distributed processing: Explorations in the microstructure of cognition. Volume 1:* Foundations. Cambridge, MA: M.I.T. Press/Bradford Books.

Hofstadter, D.R. (1983). Artificial intelligence: Sub-cognition as computation. In F. Machlup & U. Mansfield (Eds.), *The study of information: Interdisciplinary messages.* New York: John Wiley & Sons.

Kant, I. (1929). *The critique of pure reason.* New York: St. Martins Press.

Katz, J.J. (1972). *Semantic theory.* New York: Harper & Row.

Katz, J.J., & Fodor, J.A. (1963). The structure of a semantic theory, *Language, 39,* 170–210.

Katz, J., & Postal, P. (1964). *An integrated theory of linguistic descriptions.* Cambridge, MA: M.I.T. Press.

Kosslyn, S.M., & Hatfield, G. (1984). Representation without symbol systems. *Social Research, 51,* 1019–1054.

Laird, J., Rosenbloom, P., & Newell, A. (1986). *Universal subgoaling and chunking: The automatic generation and learning of goal hierarchies.* Boston, MA: Kluwer Academic Publishers.

Lakoff, G. (1986). Connectionism and cognitive linguistics. Seminar delivered at Princeton University, December 8, 1986.

Mackworth, A. (1987). Constraint propagation. In Shapiro, S.C. (Ed.). *The encyclopedia of artificial intelligence, Volume 1.* New York: John Wiley & Sons.

McClelland, J.L., Feldman, J., Adelson, B., Bower, G., & McDermott, D. (1986). *Connectionist models and cognitive science: Goals, directions and implications.* Report to the National Science Foundation, June, 1986.

McClelland, J.L., & Kawamoto, A.H. (1986). Mechanisms of sentence processing: Assigning roles to constituents. In McClelland, Rumelhart and the PDP Research Group (Eds.), *Parallel distributed processing: volume 2.* Cambridge, MA: M.I.T. Press, Bradford Books.

McClelland, J.L., Rumelhart, D.E., & Hinton, G.E. (1986). The appeal of parallel distributed processing. In Rumelhart, McClelland and the PDP Research Group, (Eds.), *Parallel distributed processing: volume 1.* Cambridge, MA: M.I.T. Press/Bradford Books.

Minsky, M., & Papert, F. (1972). *Artificial Intelligence Progress Report,* AI Memo 252, Massachusetts Institute of Technology.

Newell, A. (1969). Heuristic programming: Ill-structured problems. In Aronofsky, J. (Ed.), *Progress in operations research, III.* New York: John Wiley & Sons.

Newell, A. (1980). Physical symbol systems. *Cognitive Science, 4,* 135–183.

Newell, A. (1982). The knowledge level. *Artificial Intelligence, 18,* 87–127.

Osherson, D., Stov, M., & Weinstein, S. (1984). Learning theory and natural language, *Cognition, 17,* 1–28.

Pinker, S. (1984). *Language, learnability and language development.* Cambridge: Harvard University Press.

Prince, A., & Pinker, S. (1988). On language and connectionism: Analysis of a parallel distributed processing model of language acquisition. *Cognition, 28,* this issue.

Pylyshyn, Z.W. (1980). Cognition and computation: Issues in the foundations of cognitive science. *Behavioral and Brain Sciences, 3:1,* 154–169.

Pylyshyn, Z.W. (1981). The imagery debate: Analogue media versus tacit knowledge. *Psychological Review, 88,* 16–45.

Pylyshyn, Z.W. (1984a). *Computation and cognition: Toward a foundation for cognitive science.* Cambridge, MA: M.I.T. Press, A Bradford Book.

Pylyshyn, Z.W. (1984b). Why computation requires symbols. *Proceedings of the Sixth Annual Conference of the Cognitive Science Society, Bolder, Colorado, August, 1984.* Hillsdale, NJ: Erlbaum.

Rakic, P. (1975). Local circuit neurons. *Neurosciences Research Program Bulletin, 13*, 299–313.

Rumelhart, D.E. (1984). The emergence of cognitive phenomena from sub-symbolic processes. In *Proceedings of the Sixth Annual Conference of the Cognitive Science Society, Bolder, Colorado, August, 1984.* Hillsdale, NJ: Erlbaum.

Rumelhart, D.E., & McClelland, J.L. (1985). Level's indeed! A response to Broadbent. *Journal of Experimental Psychology: General, 114*, 193–197.

Rumelhart, D.E., & McClelland, J.L. (1986a). PDP Models and general issues in cognitive science: In Rumelhart, McClelland and the PDP Research Group (Eds.), *Parallel distributed processing, volume 1.* Cambridge, MA: M.I.T. Press, A Bradford Book.

Rumelhart, D.E., & McClelland, J.L. (1986b). On learning the past tenses of English verbs. In Rumelhart, McClelland and the PDP Research Group (Eds.), *Parallel distributed processing, volume 1.* Cambridge, MA: M.I.T. Press, A Bradford Book.

Schneider, W. (1987). Connectionism: Is it a paradigm shift for psychology? *Behavior Research Methods, Instruments, & Computers, 19*, 73–83.

Sejnowski, T.J. (1981). Skeleton filters in the brain. In Hinton, G.E., & Anderson, A.J. (Eds.), *Parallel models of associative memory.* Hillsdale, NJ: Erlbaum.

Simon, H.A., & Chase, W.G. (1973). Skill in chess. *American Scientist, 621*, 394–403.

Smolensky, P. (1988). On the proper treatment of connectionism. *The Behavioral and Brain Sciences, 11*, forthcoming.

Stabler, E. (1985). How are grammars represented? *Behavioral and Brain Sciences, 6*, 391–420.

Stich, S. (1983). *From folk psychology to cognitive science.* Cambridge, MA: M.I.T. Press.

Touretzky, D.S. (1986). BoltzCONS: Reconciling connectionism with the recursive nature of stacks and trees. *Proceedings of the Eighth Annual Conference of the Cognitive Science Society.* Amherst, MA, August, 1986. Hillsdale, NJ: Erlbaum.

Wanner, E., & Maratsos, M. (1978). An ATN approach to comprehension. In Halle, M., Bresnan, J., & Miller, G.A. (Eds.), *Linguistic theory and psychological reality.* Cambridge, MA: M.I.T. Press.

Watson, J. (1930). *Behaviorism,* Chicago: University of Chicago Press.

Woods, W.A. (1975). What's in a link? in Bobrow, D., & Collins, A. (Eds.), *Representation and understanding.* New York: Academic Press.

Ziff, P. (1960). *Semantic analysis.* Ithaca, NY: Cornell University Press.

On language and connectionism: Analysis of a parallel distributed processing model of language acquisition*

STEVEN PINKER

Massachusetts Institute of Technology

ALAN PRINCE

Brandeis University

Abstract

Does knowledge of language consist of mentally-represented rules? Rumelhart and McClelland have described a connectionist (parallel distributed processing) model of the acquisition of the past tense in English which successfully maps many stems onto their past tense forms, both regular (walk/walked) *and irregular* (go/went), *and which mimics some of the errors and sequences of development of children. Yet the model contains no explicit rules, only a set of neuron-style units which stand for trigrams of phonetic features of the stem, a set of units which stand for trigrams of phonetic features of the past form, and an array of connections between the two sets of units whose strengths are modified during learning. Rumelhart and McClelland conclude that linguistic rules may be merely convenient approximate fictions and that the real causal processes in language use and acquisition must be characterized as the transfer of activation levels among units and the modification of the weights of their connections. We analyze both the linguistic and the developmental assumptions of the model in detail and discover that (1) it cannot represent certain words, (2) it cannot learn many rules, (3) it can learn rules found in no human language, (4) it cannot explain morphological and phonological regularities, (5) it cannot ex-*

*The authors contributed equally to this paper and list their names in alphabetical order. We are grateful to Jane Grimshaw and Brian MacWhinney for providing transcripts of children's speech from the Brandeis Longitudinal Study and the Child Language Data Exchange System, respectively. We also thank Tom Bever, Jane Grimshaw, Stephen Kosslyn, Dan Slobin, an anonymous reviewer from *Cognition*, and the Boston Philosophy and Psychology Discussion Group for their comments on earlier drafts, and Richard Goldberg for his assistance. Preparation of this paper was supported by NSF grant IST-8420073 to Jane Grimshaw and Ray Jackendoff of Brandeis University, by NIH grant HD 18381–04 and NSF grant 85–18774 to Steven Pinker, and by a grant from the Alfred P. Sloan Foundation to the MIT Center for Cognitive Science. Requests for reprints may be sent to Steven Pinker at the Department of Brain and Cognitive Sciences, MIT, Cambridge, MA 02139, U.S.A. or Alan Prince at the Linguistics and Cognitive Science Program, Brown 125, Brandeis University, Waltham MA 02254, U.S.A.*

*plain the differences between irregular and regular forms, (6) it fails at its
assigned task of mastering the past tense of English, (7) it gives an incorrect
explanation for two developmental phenomena: stages of overregularization of
irregular forms such as* bringed, *and the appearance of doubly-marked forms
such as* ated *and (8) it gives accounts of two others (infrequent overregularization of verbs ending in* t/d, *and the order of acquisition of different irregular
subclasses) that are indistinguishable from those of rule-based theories. In
addition, we show how many failures of the model can be attributed to its
connectionist architecture. We conclude that connectionists' claims about the
dispensability of rules in explanations in the psychology of language must be
rejected, and that, on the contrary, the linguistic and developmental facts provide good evidence for such rules.*

> If design govern in a thing so small.
> *Robert Frost*

1. Introduction

The study of language is notoriously contentious, but until recently, researchers who could agree on little else have all agreed on one thing: that linguistic knowledge is couched in the form of rules and principles. This conception
is consistent with—indeed, is one of the prime motivations for—the "central
dogma" of modern cognitive science, namely that intelligence is the result of
processing symbolic expressions. To understand language and cognition, according to this view, one must break them up into two aspects: the rules or
symbol-manipulating processes capable of generating a domain of intelligent
human performance, to be discovered by examining systematicities in people's perception and behavior, and the elementary symbol-manipulating mechanisms made available by the information-processing capabilities of neural
tissue, out of which the rules or symbol-manipulating processes would be
composed (see, e.g., Chomsky, 1965; Fodor, 1968, 1975; Marr, 1982; Minsky,
1963; Newell & Simon, 1961; Putnam, 1960; Pylyshyn, 1984).

One of the reasons this strategy is inviting is that we know of a complex
intelligent system, the computer, that can only be understood using this al-
gorithm-implementation or software-hardware distinction. And one of the
reasons that the strategy has remained compelling is that it has given us
precise, revealing, and predictive models of cognitive domains that have required few assumptions about the underlying neural hardware other than that
it makes available some very general elementary processes of comparing and
transforming symbolic expressions.

Of course, no one believes that cognitive models explicating the systematicities in a domain of intelligence can fly in the face of constraints provided by the operations made available by neural hardware. Some early cognitive models have assumed an underlying architecture inspired by the historical and technological accidents of current computer design, such as rapid reliable serial processing, limited bandwidth communication channels, or rigid distinctions between registers and memory. These assumptions are not only inaccurate as descriptions of the brain, composed as it is of slow, noisy and massively interconnected units acting in parallel, but they are unsuited to tasks such as vision where massive amounts of information must be processed in parallel. Furthermore, some cognitive tasks seem to require mechanisms for rapidly satisfying large sets of probabilistic constraints, and some aspects of human performance seem to reveal graded patterns of generalization to large sets of stored exemplars, neither of which is easy to model with standard serial symbol-matching architectures. And progress has sometimes been stymied by the difficulty of deciding among competing models of cognition when one lacks any constraints on which symbol-manipulating processes the neural hardware supplies "for free" and which must be composed of more primitive processes.

1.1. Connectionism and symbol processing

In response to these concerns, a family of models of cognitive processes originally developed in the 1950s and early 1960s has received increased attention. In these models, collectively referred to as "Parallel Distributed Processing" ("PDP") or "Connectionist" models, the hardware mechanisms are networks consisting of large numbers of densely interconnected units, which correspond to concepts (Feldman & Ballard, 1982) or to features (Hinton, McClelland, & Rumelhart, 1981). These units have activation levels and they transmit signals (graded or 1–0) to one another along weighted connections. Units "compute" their output signals through a process of weighting each of their input signals by the strength of the connection along which the signal is coming in, summing the weighted input signals, and feeding the result into a nonlinear output function, usually a threshold. Learning consists of adjusting the strengths of connections and the threshold-values, usually in a direction that reduces the discrepancy between an actual output in response to some input and a "desired" output provided by an independent set of "teaching" inputs. In some respects, these models are thought to resemble neural networks in meaningful ways; in others, most notably the teaching and learning mechanisms, there is no known neurophysiological analogue, and some authors are completely agnostic about how the units and connections are neur-

ally instantiated. ("Brain-style modeling" is the noncommittal term used by
Rumelhart & McClelland, 1986a.) The computations underlying cognitive
processes occur when a set of input units in a network is turned on in a
pattern that corresponds in a fixed way to a stimulus or internal input. The
activation levels of the input units then propagate through connections to the
output units, possibly mediated by one or more levels of intermediate units.
The pattern of activation of the output units corresponds to the output of the
computation and can be fed into a subsequent network or into response
effectors. Many models of perceptual and cognitive processes within this
family have been explored recently (for a recent collection of reports, including extensive tutorials, reviews, and historical surveys, see Rumelhart,
McClelland, & The PDP Research Group, 1986; and McClelland,
Rumelhart, & The PDP Research Group, 1986; henceforth, "PDPI" and
"PDPII").

There is no doubt that these models have a different feel than standard
symbol-processing models. The units, the topology and weights of the connections among them, the functions by which activation levels are transformed
in units and connections, and the learning (i.e., weight-adjustment) function
are all that is "in" these models; one cannot easily point to rules, algorithms,
expressions, and the like inside them. By itself, of course, this means little,
because the same is true for a circuit diagram of a digital computer implementing a theorem-prover. How, then, are PDP models related to the more
traditional symbol-processing models that have until now dominated cognitive psychology and linguistics?

It is useful to distinguish three possibilities. In one, PDP models would
occupy an intermediate level between symbol processing and neural
hardware: they would characterize the elementary information processes provided by neural networks that serve as the building blocks of rules or algorithms. Individual PDP networks would compute the primitive symbol associations (such as matching an input against memory, or pairing the input
and output of a rule), but the way the overall output of one network feeds
into the input of another would be isomorphic to the structure of the symbol
manipulations captured in the statements of rules. Progress in PDP modeling
would undoubtedly force revisions in traditional models, because traditional
assumptions about primitive mechanisms may be neurally implausible, and
complex chains of symbol manipulations may be obviated by unanticipated
primitive computational powers of PDP networks. Nonetheless, in this
scenario a well-defined division between rule and hardware would remain,
each playing an indispensable role in the explanation of a cognitive process.
Many existing types of symbol-processing models would survive mostly intact,
and, to the extent they have empirical support and explanatory power, would

dictate many fundamental aspects of network organization. In some expositions of PDP models, this is the proposed scenario (see, e.g., Hinton, 1981;
Hinton, McClelland, & Rumelhart, 1986, p. 78; also Touretzky, 1986 and
Touretzky & Hinton, 1985, where PDP networks implement aspects of LISP
and production systems, respectively). We call this "implementational connectionism".

An alternative possibility is that once PDP network models are fully developed, they will *replace* symbol-processing models as explanations of cognitive processes. It would be impossible to find a principled mapping between
the components of a PDP model and the steps or memory structures implicated by a symbol-processing theory, to find states of the PDP model that
correspond to intermediate states of the execution of the program, to observe
stages of its growth corresponding to components of the program being put
into place, or states of breakdown corresponding to components wiped out
through trauma or loss—the structure of the symbolic model would vanish.
Even the input–output function computed by the network model could differ
in special cases from that computed by the symbolic model. Basically, the
entire operation of the model (to the extent that it is not a black box) would
have to be characterized not in terms of interactions among entities possessing
both semantic *and* physical properties (e.g., different subsets of neurons or
states of neurons each of which represent a distinct chunk of knowledge), but
in terms of entities that had *only* physical properties, (e.g., the "energy landscape" defined by the activation levels of a large aggregate of interconnected
neurons). Perhaps the symbolic model, as an approximate description of the
performance in question, would continue to be useful as a heuristic, capturing
some of the regularities in the domain in an intuitive or easily-communicated
way, or allowing one to make convenient approximate predictions. But the
symbolic model would not be a literal account at any level of analysis of what
is going on in the brain, only an analogy or a rough summary of regularities.
This scenario, which we will call "eliminative connectionism", sharply contrasts with the hardware–software distinction that has been assumed in cognitive science until now: no one would say that a program is an "approximate"
description of the behavior of a computer, with the "exact" description existing at the level of chips and circuits; rather they are both exact descriptions
at different levels of analysis.

Finally, there is a range of intermediate possibilities that we have already
hinted at. A cognitive process might be profitably understood as a sequence
or system of isolable entities that would be symbolic inasmuch as one could
characterize them as having semantic properties such as truth values, consistency relations, or entailment relations, and one might predict the input–output function and systematicities in performance, development, or loss strictly

in terms of formal properties of these entities. However, they might bear little resemblance to the symbolic structures that one would posit by studying a domain of intelligence independent of implementation considerations. The primitive information-processing operations made available by the connectionist architecture (summation of weighted activation levels and threshold functions, etc.) might force a theorist to posit a radically different set of symbols and operations, which in turn would make different predictions about the functions that could be computed and the patterns of breakdown observable during development, disease, or intermediate stages of processing. In this way, PDP theory could lead to fundamental new discoveries about the character of symbol-processing, rather than implying that there was no such thing. Let us call this intermediate position "revisionist-symbol-processing connectionism".

Language: A crucial test case. From its inception, the study of language within the framework of generative grammar has been a prototypical example of how fundamental properties of a cognitive domain can be explained within the symbolic paradigm. Linguistic theories have posited symbolic representations, operations, and architectures of rule-systems that are highly structured, detailed, and constrained, testing them against the plentiful and complex data of language (both the nature of adults' mastery of language, and data about how such knowledge is learned and put to use in comprehension and speech). Historically, it has been the demands of these theories that have driven our conception of what the computational resources underlying cognition must provide at a minimum (e.g., Chomsky, 1957, 1965). A priori notions of neurally possible elementary information processes have been plainly too weak, at worst, or unenlightening because of the few constraints they impose, at best. Language has been the domain most demanding of articulated symbol structures governed by rules and principles and it is also the domain where such structures have been explored in the greatest depth and sophistication, within a range of theoretical frameworks and architectures, attaining a wide variety of significant empirical results. Any alternative model that either eschews symbolic mechanisms altogether, or that is strongly shaped by the restrictive nature of available elementary information processes and unresponsive to the demands of the high-level functions being computed, starts off at a seeming disadvantage. Many observers thus feel that connectionism, as a radical restructuring of cognitive theory, will stand or fall depending on its ability to account for human language.

1.2. The Rumelhart–McClelland model and theory

One of the most influential efforts in the PDP school has been a model of the acquisition of the marking of the past tense in English developed by David Rumelhart and James McClelland (1986b, 1987). Using standard PDP mechanisms, this model learns to map representations of present tense forms of English verbs onto their past tense versions. It handles both regular (*walk/walked*) and irregular (*feel/felt*) verbs, productively yielding past forms for novel verbs not in its training set, and it distinguishes the variants of the past tense morpheme (*t* versus *d* versus *id*) conditioned by the final consonant of the verb (*walked* versus *jogged* versus *sweated*). Furthermore, in doing so it displays a number of behaviors reminiscent of children. It passes through stages of conservative acquisition of correct irregular and regular verbs (*walked, brought, hit*) followed by productive application of the regular rule and overregularization to irregular stems (e.g. *bringed, hitted*), followed by mastery of both regular and irregular verbs. It acquires subclasses of irregular verbs (e.g. *fly/flew, sing/sang, hit/hit*) in an order similar to children. It makes certain types of errors (*ated, wented*) at similar stages. Nonetheless, nothing in the model corresponds in any obvious way to the rules that have been assumed to be an essential part of the explanation of the past tense formation process. None of the individual units or connections in the model corresponds to a word, a position within a word, a morpheme, a regular rule, an exception, or a paradigm. The intelligence of the model is distributed in the pattern of weights linking the simple input and output units, so that any relation to a rule-based account is complex and indirect at best.

Rumelhart and McClelland take the results of this work as strong support for eliminative connectionism, the paradigm in which rule- or symbol-based accounts are simply eliminated from direct explanations of intelligence:

> We suggest instead that implicit knowledge of language may be stored in connections among simple processing units organized into networks. While the behavior of such networks may be describable (at least approximately) as conforming to some system of rules, we suggest that an account of the fine structure of the phenomena of language use and language acquisition can best be formulated in models that make reference to the characteristics of the underlying networks. (Rumelhart & McClelland, 1987, p. 196)

> We have, we believe, provided a distinct alternative to the view that children learn the rules of English past-tense formation in any explicit sense. We have shown that a reasonable account of the acquisition of past tense can be provided without recourse to the notion of a "rule" as anything more than a *description* of the language. We have shown that, for this case, there is no *induction problem*. The child need not figure out what the rules are, nor even that there are rules. (Rumelhart & McClelland, 1986b, p. 267, their emphasis)

We view this work on past-tense morphology as a step toward a revised understanding of language knowledge, language acquisition, and linguistic information
processing in general. (Rumelhart & McClelland, 1986b, p. 268)

The Rumelhart–McClelland (henceforth, "RM") model, because it in-
spires these remarkable claims, figures prominently in general expositions of
connectionism that stress its revolutionary nature, such as Smolensky (in
press) and McClelland, Rumelhart, and Hinton (1986). Despite the radical
nature of these conclusions, it is our impression that they have gained acceptance in many quarters; that many researchers have been persuaded that
theories of language couched in terms of rules and rule acquisition may be
obsolete (see, e.g., Sampson, 1987). Other researchers have attempted to
blunt the force of the Rumelhart and McClelland's attack on rules by suggesting that the model really does contain rules, or that past tense acquisition is
an unrepresentatively easy problem, or that there is some reason in principle
why PDP models are incapable of being extended to language as a whole, or
that Rumelhart and McClelland are modeling 'performance' and saying little
about 'competence' or are modeling implementations but saying little about
algorithms. We believe that these quick reactions—be they conversion experiences or outright dismissals—are unwarranted. Much can be gained by taking
the model at face value as a theory of the psychology of the child and by
examining the claims of the model in detail. That is the goal of this paper.

The RM model, like many PDP models, is a *tour de force*. It is explicit
and mechanistic: precise empirical predictions flow out of the model as it
operates autonomously, rather than being continuously molded or reshaped
to fit the facts by a theorist acting as *deus ex machina*. The authors have made
a commitment as to the underlying computational architecture of the model,
rather than leaving it as a degree of freedom. The model is tested not only
against the phenomenon that inspired it—the three-stage developmental sequence of generalizations of the regular past tense morpheme—but against
several unrelated phenomena as well. Furthermore, Rumelhart and McClelland bring these developmental data to bear on the model in an unusually
detailed way, examining not only gross effects but also many of its more
subtle details. Several non-obvious but interesting empirical predictions are
raised in these examinations. Finally, the model uses clever mechanisms that
operate in surprising ways. These features are virtually unheard of in developmental psycholinguistics (see Pinker, 1979; Wexler & Culicover, 1980). There
is no doubt that our understanding of language acquisition would advance
more rapidly if theories in developmental psycholinguistics were held to such
standards.

Nonetheless, our analysis of the model will come to conclusions very different from those of Rumelhart and McClelland. In their presentation, the

model is evaluated only by a global comparison of its overall output behavior with that of children. There is no unpacking of its underlying theoretical assumptions so as to contrast them with those of a symbolic rule-based alternative, or indeed any alternative. As a result, there is no apportioning of credit or blame for the model's performance to properties that are essential versus accidental, or unique to it versus shared by any equally explicit alternative. In particular, Rumelhart and McClelland do not consider what it is about the standard symbol-processing theories that makes them "standard", beyond their first-order ability to relate stem and past tense. To these ends, we analyze the assumptions and consequences of the RM model, as compared to those of symbolic theories, and point out the crucial tests that distinguish them. In particular, we seek to determine whether the RM model is viable as a theory of human language acquisition—there is no question that it is a valuable demonstration of some of the surprising things that PDP models are capable of, but our concern is whether it is an accurate model of children.

Our analysis will lead to the following conclusions:

- Rumelhart and McClelland's actual explanation of children's stages of regularization of the past tense morpheme is demonstrably incorrect.
- Their explanation for one striking type of childhood speech error is also incorrect.
- Their other apparent successes in accounting for developmental phenomena either have nothing to do with the model's parallel distributed processing architecture, and can easily be duplicated by symbolic models, or involve major confounds and hence do not provide clear support for the model.
- The model is incapable of representing certain kinds of words.
- It is incapable of explaining patterns of psychological similarity among words.
- It easily models many kinds of rules that are not found in any human language.
- It fails to capture central generalizations about English sound patterns.
- It makes false predictions about derivational morphology, compounding, and novel words.
- It cannot handle the elementary problem of homophony.
- It makes errors in computing the past tense forms of a large percentage of the words it is tested on.
- It fails to generate any past tense form at all for certain words.
- It makes incorrect predictions about the reality of the distinction between regular rules and exceptions in children and in languages.

We will conclude that the claim that parallel distributed processing networks can eliminate the need for rules and for rule induction mechanisms in the explanation of human language is unwarranted. In particular, we argue that the shortcomings are in many cases due to central features of connectionist ideology and irremediable; or if remediable, only by copying tenets of the maligned symbolic theory. The implications for the promise of connectionism in explicating language are, we think, profound.

The paper is organized as follows. First, we examine in broad outline the phenomena of English verbal inflection. Then we describe the operation of the RM model and how it contrasts with the rule-based alternative, evaluating the merits of each. This amounts to an evaluation of the model in terms of its ability to handle the empirical properties of language in its adult state. In the next major section, we evaluate the model in terms of its ability to handle the empirical properties of children's path of development toward the adult state, comparing it with a simple model of symbolic rule acquisition. Finally, we evaluate the status of the radical claims about connectionism that were motivated by the RM model, and we determine the extent to which the performance of the RM model is a direct consequence of properties of its PDP architecture and thus bears on the promise of parallel distributed processing models in accounting for language and language acquisition.

2. A brief overview of English verbal inflection

2.1. The basic facts of English inflection

Rumelhart and McClelland aim to describe part of the system of verbal inflection in English. As background to our examination of their model, we briefly review the structure of the English verb, and present the basic flavor of a rule-based account of it.[1] When we evaluate the RM model, many additional details about the facts of English inflection and about linguistic theories of its structure will be presented.

English inflectional morphology is not notably complicated. Where the verb of classical Greek has about 350 distinct forms and the verb of current Spanish or Italian about 50, the regular English verb has exactly four:

---

[1]Valuable linguistic studies of the English verbal system include Bloch (1947), Bybee and Slobin (1982), Curme (1935), Fries (1940), Hoard and Sloat (1973), Hockett (1942), Jespersen (1942), Mencken (1936), Palmer (1930), Sloat and Hoard (1971), Sweet (1892). Chomsky and Halle (1968) and Kiparsky (1982a, b) are important general works touching on aspects of the system.

(1) a.   walk
     b.   walks
     c.   walked
     d.   walking

As is typical in morphological systems, there is rampant syncretism—use of the same phonological form to express different, often unrelated morphological categories. On syntactic grounds we might distinguish 13 categories filled by the four forms.

(2) a.   -∅   Present-everything but 3rd person singular:
                    I, you, we, they *open*.
               Infinitive:
                    They may *open*, They tried to *open*.
               Imperative:
                    Open!
               Subjunctive:
                    They insisted that it *open*.

     b.   -s   Present- 3rd person singular:
                    He, she, it *opens*.

     c.   -ed Past:
                    It *opened*.
               Perfect Participle:
                    It has *opened*.
               Passive Participle:
                    It was being *opened*.
               Verbal adjective:
                    A recently-*opened* box.

     d.   -ing Progressive Participle:
                    He is *opening*.
               Present Participle:
                    He tried *opening* the door.
               Verbal noun (gerund):
                    His incessant *opening* of the boxes.
               Verbal adjective:
                    A quietly-*opening* door.

The system is rendered more interesting by the presence of about 180 'strong' or 'irregular' verbs, which form the past tense other than by simple suffixation. There are, however, far fewer than 180 ways of modifying a stem to produce a strong past tense; the study upon which Rumelhart and McClelland depend, Bybee and Slobin (1982), divides the strong group into nine coarse and somewhat heterogeneous subclasses, which we discuss later. (See the Appendix for a précis of the entire system.)

Many strong verbs also maintain a further formal distinction, lost in (2c), between the past tense itself and the Perfect/Passive Participle, which is frequently marked with *-en*: 'he *ate*' vs. 'he has, was *eaten*'. These verbs mark the outermost boundary of systematic complexity in English, giving the learner five forms to keep track of, two of which—past and perfect/passive participle—are not predictable from totally general rules.[2]

2.2. *Basic features of symbolic models of inflection*

Rumelhart and McClelland write that "We chose the study of acquisition of past tense in part because the phenomenon of regularization is an example often cited in support of the view that children do respond according to general rules of language." What they mean is that when Berko (1958) first documented children's ability to inflect novel verbs for past tense (e.g. *jicked*), and when Ervin (1964) documented overregularizations of irregular past tense forms in spontaneous speech (e.g. *breaked*), it was effective evidence against any notion that language acquisition consisted of rote imitation. But it is important to note the general point that the ability to generalize beyond rote forms is *not* the only motivation for using rules (as behaviorists were quick to point out in the 1960s when they offered their own accounts of generalization). In fact, even the existence of competing modes of generalizing, such as the different past tense forms of regular and irregular verbs or of regular verbs ending in different consonants, is not the most important motivation for positing distinct rules. Rather, rules are generally invoked in linguistic explanations in order to *factor* a complex phenomenon into simpler components that feed representations into one another. Different types of rules apply to these intermediate representations, forming a cascade of structures and rule components. Rules are individuated not only because they *compete* and mandate different transformations of the same input structure (such as *break—breaked/broke*), but because they apply to different *kinds* of structures, and thus impose a factoring of a phenomenon into distinct components, rather than generating the phenomena in a single step mapping inputs to outputs. Such factoring allows orthogonal generalizations to be extracted and stated separately, so that observed complexity can arise through interaction and feeding of independent rules and processes, which often have rather

---

[2]Somewhat beyond this bound lies the verb 'be' with eight distinct forms: *be, am, is, are, was, were, been, being,* of which only the last is regular.

different parameters and domains of relevance. This is immediately obvious in most of syntax, and indeed, in most domains of cognitive processing (which is why the acquisition and use of internal representations in "hidden units" is an important technical problem in connectionist modeling; see Hinton & Sejnowski, 1986; Rumelhart, Hinton, & Williams, 1986).

However, it is not as obvious at first glance how rules feed each other in the case of past tense inflection. Thus to examine in what sense the RM model "has no rules" and thus differs from symbolic accounts, it is crucial to spell out how the different rules in the symbolic accounts are individuated in terms of the components they are associated with.

There is one set of "rules" inherent in the generation of the past tense in English that is completely outside the mapping that the RM model computes: those governing the interaction between the use of the past tense form and the type of sentence the verb appears in, which depends on semantic factors such as the relationship between the times of the speech act, referent event, and a reference point, combined with various syntactic and lexical factors such as the choice of a matrix verb in a complex sentence (*I helped her leave/*left* versus *I know she left/*leave*) and the modality and mood of a sentence (*I went/*go yesterday* versus *I didn't go/*went yesterday; If my grandmother had/*has balls she'd be my grandfather*). In other words, a speaker doesn't choose to produce a past tense form of a verb when and only when he or she is referring to an event taking place before the act of speaking. The distinction between the mechanisms governing these phenomena, and those that associate individual stems and past tense forms, is implicitly accepted by Rumelhart and McClelland. That is, presumably the RM model would be embedded in a collection of networks that would pretty much reproduce the traditional picture of there being one set of syntactic and semantic mechanisms that selects occasions for use of the past tense, feeding information into a distinct morphological-phonological system that associates individual stems with their tensed forms. As such, one must be cautious at the outset in saying that the RM model is an alternative to a rule-based account of the past tense in general; at most, it is an alternative to whatever decomposition is traditionally assumed within the part of grammar that associates stems and past tense forms.[3]

In symbolic accounts, this morphological-phonological part is subject to

---

[3]Furthermore, the RM model seeks only to *generate* past forms from stems; it has no facility for retrieving a stem given the past tense form as input. (There is no guarantee that a network will run 'backwards' and in fact some of the more sophisticated learning algorithms presuppose a strictly feed-forward design.) Presumably the human learner can go both ways from the very beginning of the process; later we present examples of children's back-formations in support of this notion. Rule-based theories, as accounts of knowledge rather than use of knowledge, are neutral with respect to the production/recognition distinction.

further decomposition. In particular, rule-based accounts rely on several fundamental distinctions:

- *Lexical item vs. phoneme string.* The lexical item is a unique, idiosyncratic set of syntactic, semantic, morphological, and phonological properties. The phoneme string is just one of these properties. Distinct items may share the same phonological composition (homophony). Thus the notion of lexical representation distinguishes phonologically ambiguous words such as *wring* and *ring*.
- *Morphological category vs. morpheme.* There is a distinction between a morphological category, such as 'past tense' or 'perfect aspect' or 'plural' or 'nominative case', and the realization(s) of it in phonological substance. The relation can be many-one in both directions: the same phonological entity can mark several categories (syncretism); and one category may have several (or indeed many) realizations, such as through a variety of suffixes or through other means of marking. Thus in English, *-ed* syncretistically marks the past, the perfect participle, the passive participle, and a verbal adjective—distinct categories; while the past tense category itself is manifested differently in such items as *bought, blew, sat, bled, bent, cut, went, ate, killed.*
- *Morphology vs. phonology.* Morphological rules describe the syntax of words—how words are built from morphemes—and the realization of abstract morphological categories. Phonological rules deal with the predictable features of sound structure, including adjustments and accommodations occasioned by juxtaposition and superposition of phonological elements. Morphology trades in such notions as 'stem', 'prefix', 'suffix', 'past tense'; phonology in such as 'vowel', 'voicing', 'obstruence', 'syllable'. As we will see in our examination of English morphology, there can be a remarkable degree of segregation of the two vocabularies into distinct rule systems: there are morphological rules which are blind to phonology, and phonological rules blind to morphological category.
- *Phonology vs. phonetics.* Recent work (Liberman & Pierrehumbert, 1984; Pierrehumbert & Beckman, 1986) refines the distinction between phonology proper, which establishes and maps between one phonological representation and another, and phonetic implementation, which takes a representation and relates it to an entirely different system of parameters (for example, targets in acoustic or articulatory space).

In addition, a rule-system is organized by principles which determine the interactions between rules: whether they compete or feed, and if they compete, which wins. A major factor in regulating the feeding relation is organization into components: morphology, an entire set of formation rules, feeds phonology, which feeds phonetics.[4] Competition among morphological alternatives is under the control of a principle of paradigm structure (called the 'Unique Entry Principle' in Pinker, 1984) which guarantees that in general each word will have one and only one form for each relevant morphological category; this is closely related to the 'Elsewhere Condition' of formal linguistics (Kiparsky, 1982a, b). The effect is that when a general rule (like Past(x) = x + ed) formally overlaps a specific rule (like Past(go) = $went$), the specific rule not only applies but also blocks the general one from applying.

The picture that emerges looks like this:

(3)

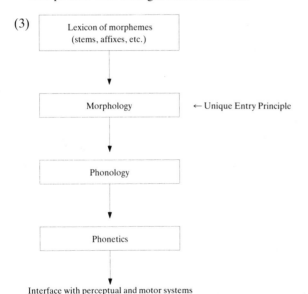

With this general structure in mind, we can now examine how the RM model differs in "not having rules".

3. The Rumelhart–McClelland model

Rumelhart and McClelland's goal is to model the acquisition of the past tense, specifically the *production* of the past tense, considered in isolation

---

[4]More intricate variations on this basic pattern are explored in recent work in "Lexical Phonology"; see Kiparsky (1982a, b).

from the rest of the English morphological system. They assume that the acquisition process establishes a direct mapping from the phonetic representation of the stem to the phonetic representation of the past tense form. The model therefore takes the following basic shape:

(4)   Uninflected stem → Pattern associator → Past form

This proposed organization of knowledge collapses the major distinctions embodied in the linguistic theory sketched in (3). In the following sections we ascertain and evaluate the consequences of this move.

The detailed structure of the RM model is portrayed in Figure 1.

In its trained state, the pattern associator is supposed to take any stem as input and emit the corresponding past tense form. The model's pattern associator is a simple network with two layers of nodes, one for representing input, the other for output. Each node represents a different property that an input item may have. Nodes in the RM model may only be 'on' or 'off'; thus the nodes represent binary features, 'off' and 'on' marking the simple absence or presence of a certain property. Each stem must be encoded as a unique subset of turned-on input nodes; each possible past tense form as a unique subset of output nodes turned on.

Here a nonobvious problem asserts itself. The natural assumption would be that words are strings on an alphabet, a concatenation of phonemes. But

Figure 1.   *The Rumelhart-McClelland model of past tense acquisition. (Reproduced from Rumelhart and McClelland, 1986b, p. 222, with permission of the publisher, Bradford Books/MIT Press.)*

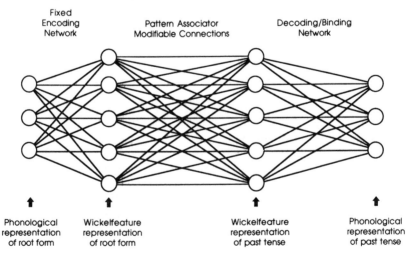

Fixed Encoding Network	Pattern Associator Modifiable Connections	Decoding/Binding Network

| Phonological representation of root form | Wickelfeature representation of root form | Wickelfeature representation of past tense | Phonological representation of past tense |

each datum fed to a network must decompose into an unordered set of properties (coded as turned-on units), and a string is a prime example of an
ordered entity. To overcome this, Rumelhart and McClelland turn to a
scheme proposed by Wickelgren (1969), according to which a string is represented as the set of the trigrams (3-character-sequences) that it contains.
(In order to locate word-edges, which are essential to phonology and morphology, it is necessary to assume that 'word-boundary' (#) is a character
in the underlying alphabet.) Rumelhart and McClelland call such trigrams
Wickelphones. Thus a word like *strip* translates, in their notation to $\{_{\#}s_t,$
$_st_r, _tr_i, _ri_p, _ip_\#\}$. Note that the word *strip* is uniquely reconstructible from the
cited trigram set. Although certain trigram sets are consistent in principle
with more than one string, Rumelhart and McClelland find that all words in
their sample are uniquely encoded. Crucially, each possible trigram must be
construed as an atomic property that a string may have or lack. Thus, writing
it out as we did above is misleading, because the order of the five Wickelphones is not represented anywhere in the RM system, and there is no selective access to the "central" phoneme t in a Wickelphone $_st_r$ or to the "context"
phonemes $_sX$ and X_r. It is more faithful to the actual mechanism to list the
Wickelphones in arbitrary (e.g., alphabetical) order and avoid any spurious
internal decomposition of Wickelphones, hence: {*ip#, rip, str, tri, #st*}.

For immediate expository purposes, we can think of each unit in the input
layer of the networks as standing for one of the possible Wickelphones;
likewise for each unit in the output layer. Any given word is encoded as a
pattern of node activations over the whole set of Wickelphone nodes—as a
set of Wickelphones. This gives a "distributed" representation: an individual
word does not register on its own node, but is analyzed as an ensemble of
properties, Wickelphones, which are the true primitives of the system. As
Figure 1 shows, Rumelhart and McClelland require an "encoder" of unspecified nature to convert an ordered phonetic string into a set of activated
Wickelphone units; we discuss some of its properties later.

The Wickelphone contains enough context to detect in gross the kind of
input–output relationships found in the stem-to-past tense mapping. Imagine
a pattern associator mapping from input Wickelphones to output Wickelphones. As is usual in such networks, every input node is connected to every
output node, giving each input Wickelphone node the chance to influence
every node in the output Wickelphone set. Suppose that a set of input nodes
is turned on, representing an input to the network. Whether a given output
node will turn on is determined jointly by the strength of its connections to
the active input nodes and by the output node's own overall susceptibility to
influence, its 'threshold'. The individual on/off decisions for the output units
are made probabilistically, on the basis of the discrepancy between total

input and threshold: the nearer the input is to the threshold, the more random the decision.

An untrained pattern associator starts out with no preset relations between input and output nodes—link weights at zero—or with random input–output relations; it's a tabula rasa that is either blank or meaninglessly noisy. (Rumelhart & McClelland's is blank.) Training involves presenting the network with an input form (in the present case, a representation of a stem) and comparing the output pattern actually obtained with the desired pattern for the past tense form, which is provided to the network by a "teacher" as a distinct kind of "teaching" input (not shown in Figure 1). The corresponding psychological assumption is that the child, through some unspecified process, has already figured out which past tense form is to be associated with which stem form. We call this the "juxtaposition process"; Rumelhart and McClelland adopt the not unreasonable idealization that it does not interact with the process of abstracting the nature of the mapping between stem and past forms.

The comparison between the actual output pattern computed by the connections between input and output nodes, and the desired pattern provided by the "teacher", is made on a node-by-node basis. Any output node that is in the wrong state becomes the target of adjustment. If the network ends up leaving a node off that ought to be on according to the teacher, changes are made to render that node more likely to fire in the presence of the particular input at hand. Specifically, the weights on the links connecting active input units to the recalcitrant output unit are increased slightly; this will increase the tendency for the currently active input units—those that represent the input form—to activate the target node. In addition, the target node's own threshold is lowered slightly, so that it will tend to turn on more easily across the board. If, on the other hand, the network incorrectly turns an output node *on*, the reverse procedure is employed: the weights of the connections from currently active input units are decremented (potentially driving the connection weight to a negative, inhibitory value) and the target node's threshold is raised; a hyperactive output node is thus made more likely to turn off given the same pattern of input node activation. Repeated cycling through input–output pairs, with concomitant adjustments, shapes the behavior of the pattern associator. This is the "perceptron convergence procedure" (Rosenblatt, 1962) and it is known to produce, in the limit, a set of weights that successfully maps the input activation vectors onto the desired output activation vectors, as long as such a set of weights exists.

In fact, the RM net, following about 200 training cycles of 420 stem-past pairs (a total of about 80,000 trials), is able to produce correct past forms for the stems when the stems are presented alone, that is, in the absence of "teaching" inputs. Somewhat surprisingly, a single set of connection weights in the network is able to map *look* to *looked, live* to *lived, melt* to *melted, hit* to *hit, make* to *made, sing* to *sang,* even *go* to *went.* The bits of stored information accomplishing these mappings are superimposed in the connection weights and node thresholds; no single parameter corresponds uniquely to a rule or to any single irregular stem-past pair.

Of course, it is necessary to show how such a network generalizes to stems it has not been trained on, not only how it reproduces a rote list of pairs. The circumstances under which generalization occurs in pattern associators with distributed representations is reasonably well understood. Any encoded (one is tempted to say 'en-noded') property of the input data that participates in a frequently attested pattern of input/output relations will play a major role in the development of the network. Because it is turned on during many training episodes, and because it stands in a recurrent relationship to a set of output nodes, its influence will be repeatedly enhanced by the learning procedure. A connectionist network does more than match input to output; it responds to regularities in the representation of the data and uses them to accomplish the mapping it is trained on and to generalize to new cases. In fact, the distinction between reproducing the memorized input–output pairs and generating novel outputs for novel inputs is absent from pattern associators: a single set of weights both reproduces trained pairs and produces novel outputs which are blends of the output patterns strongly associated with each of the properties defining the novel input.

The crucial step is therefore the first one: coding the data. If the patterns in the data relevant to generalizing to new forms are not encoded in the representation of the data, no network—in fact, no algorithmic system of any sort—will be able to find them. (This is after all the reason that so much research in the 'symbolic paradigm' has centered on the nature of linguistic representations.) Since phonological processes and relations (like those involved in past tense formation) do not treat phonemes as atomic, unanalyzable wholes but refer instead to their constituent phonetic properties like voicing, obstruency, tenseness of vowels, and so on, it is necessary that such fine-grained information be present in the network. The Wickelphone, like the phoneme, is too coarse to support generalization. To take an extreme example adapted from Morris Halle, any English speaker who labors to pronounce the celebrated composer's name as [bax] knows that if there were a verb *to Bach,* its past would be *baxt* and not *baxd* or *baxid,* even though no existing English word contains the velar fricative [x]. Any representation that does not characterize *Bach* as similar to *pass* and *walk* by virtue of ending in an unvoiced segment would fail to make this generalization. Wickelphones, of course, have this problem; they treat segments as opaque quarks and fail to display vital information about segmental similarity classes. A better representation would have units referring in some way to phonetic features rather than to phonemes, because of the well-known fact that the correct dimension of generalization from old to new forms must be in terms of such features.

Rumelhart and McClelland present a second reason for avoiding Wickelphone nodes. The number of possible Wickelphones for their representation of English is $35^3 + (2 \times 35^2) = 45{,}325$ (all triliterals + all biliterals beginning and ending with #). The number of distinct connections from the entire input Wickelvector to its output clone would be over two billion ($45{,}325^2$), too many to handle comfortably. Rumelhart and McClelland therefore assume a phonetic decomposition of segments into features which are in broad outline like those of modern phonology. On the basis of this phonetic analysis, a Wickelphone dissolves into a set of 'Wickelfeatures', a sequence of three features, one from each of the three elements of the Wickelphone. For example, the features "VowelUnvoicedInterrupted" and "HighStopStop" are two of the Wickelfeatures in the ensemble that would correspond to the Wickelphone "ipt". In the RM model, units represent Wickelfeatures, not Wickelphones; Wickelphones themselves play no role in the model and are only represented implicitly as sets of Wickelfeatures. Again, there is the potential for nondistinct representations, but it never occurred in practice for their verb set. Notice that the actual atomic properties recognized by the model are not phonetic features per se, but entities that can be thought of as 3-feature sequences. The Wickelphone/Wickelfeature is an excellent example of the kind of novel properties that revisionist-symbol-processing connectionism can come up with.

A further refinement is that not all definable Wickelfeatures have units dedicated to them: the Wickelfeature set was trimmed to exclude, roughly, feature-triplets whose first and third features were chosen from different phonetic dimensions.[5] The end result is a system of 460 nodes, each one representing a Wickelfeature. One may calculate that this gives rise to $460^2 = 211{,}600$ input–output connections.

The module that encodes words into input Wickelfeatures (the "Fixed Encoding Network" of Figure 1) and the one that decodes output Wickelfeatures into words (the "Decoding/Binding Network" of Figure 1) are perhaps not meant to be taken entirely seriously in the current implementation of the RM model, but several of their properties are crucially important in under-

---

[5]Although this move was inspired purely by considerations of computational economy, it or something like it has real empirical support; the reader familiar with current phonology will recognize its relation to the notion of a 'tier' of related features in autosegmental phonology.

standing and evaluating it. The input encoder is deliberately designed to activate some incorrect Wickelfeatures in addition to the precise set of Wickelfeatures in the stem: specifically, a randomly selected subset of those Wickelfeatures that encode the features of the central phoneme properly but encode incorrect feature values for one of the two context phonemes. This "blurred" Wickelfeature representation cannot be construed as random noise; the same set of incorrect Wickelfeatures is activated every time a word is presented, and no Wickelfeature encoding an incorrect choice of the *central* feature is ever activated. Rather, the blurred representation fosters generalization. Connectionist pattern associators are always in danger of capitalizing too much on idiosyncratic properties of words in the training set in developing their mapping from input to output and hence of not properly generalizing to new forms. Blurring the input representations makes the connection weights in the RM model less likely to be able to exploit the idiosyncrasies of the words in the training set and hence reduces the model's tendency toward conservatism.

The output decoder faces a formidable task. When an input stem is fed into the model, the result is a set of activated output Wickelfeature units. Which units are on in the output depends on the current weights of the connections from active input units and on the probabilistic process that converts the summed weighted inputs into a decision as to whether or not to turn on. Nothing in the model ensures that the set of activated output units will fit together to describe a legitimate word: the set of activated units do not have to have neighboring context features that "mesh" and hence implicitly "assemble" the Wickelfeatures into a coherent string; they do not have to be mutually consistent in the feature they mandate for a given position; and they do not have to define a set of features for a given position that collectively define an English phoneme (or any kind of phoneme). In fact, the output Wickelfeatures virtually *never* define a word exactly, and so there is no clear sense in which one knows which word the output Wickelfeatures are defining. In many cases, Rumelhart and McClelland are only interested in assessing how likely the model seems to be to output a given target word, such as the correct past tense form for a given stem; in that case they can peer into the model, count the number of desired Wickelfeatures that are successfully activated and vice versa, and calculate the goodness of the match. However, this does not reveal which phonemes, or which words, the model would actually output.

To assess how likely the model actually is to output a phoneme in a given context, that is, how likely a given *Wickelphone* is in the output, a *Wickelphone Binding Network* was constructed as part of the output decoder. This network has units corresponding to Wickelphones; these units "compete" with one another in an iterative process to "claim" the activated Wickelfeatures: the more Wickelfeatures that a Wickelphone unit uniquely accounts for, the greater its strength (Wickelfeatures accounted for by more than one Wickelphone are "split" in proportion to the number of other Wickelfeatures each Wickelphone accounts for uniquely) and, supposedly, the more likely that Wickelphone is to appear in the output. A similar mechanism, called the *Whole-String Binding Network*, is defined to estimate the model's relative tendencies to output any of a particular set of words when it is of interest to compare those words with one another as possible outputs. Rumelhart and McClelland choose a set of plausible output words for a given input stem, such as *break*, *broke*, *breaked* and *broked* for the past tense of *break*, and define a unit for each one. The units then compete for activated Wickelfeatures in the output vector, each one growing in strength as a function of the number of activated Wickelfeatures it uniquely accounts for (with credit for nonunique Wickelfeatures split between the words that can account for it), and diminishing as a function of the number of activated Wickelfeatures that are inconsistent with it. This amounts to a forced-choice procedure and still does not reveal what the model would output if left to its own devices—which is crucial in evaluating the model's ability to produce correct past tense forms for stems it has not been trained on. Rumelhart and McClelland envision an eventual "sequential readout process" that would convert Wickelfeatures into a single temporally ordered representation, but for now they make do with a more easily implemented substitute: an *Unconstrained Whole-String Binding Network*, which is a whole-string binding network with one unit for every possible string of phonemes less than 20 phonemes long—that is, a forced-choice procedure among all possible strings. Since this process would be intractable to compute on today's computers, and maybe even tomorrow's, they created whole-string units only for a sharply restricted subset of the possible strings, those whose Wickelphones exceed a threshold in the Wickelphone binding network competition. But the set was still fairly large and thus the model was in principle capable of selecting both correct past tense forms and various kinds of distortions of them. Even with the restricted set of whole strings available in the unconstrained whole-string binding network, the iterative competition process was quite time-consuming in the implementation, and thus Rumelhart and McClelland ran this network only in assessing the model's ability to produce past forms for untrained stems; in all other cases, they either counted features in the output Wickelfeature vector directly, or set up a restricted forced-choice test among a small set of likely alternatives in the whole-string binding network.

In sum, the RM model works as follows. The phonological string is cashed in for a set of Wickelfeatures by an unspecified process that activates all the correct and some of the incorrect Wickelfeature units. The pattern associator excites the Wickelfeature units in the output; during the training phase its parameters (weights and thresholds) are adjusted to reduce the discrepancy between the excited Wickelfeature units and the desired ones provided by the teacher. The activated Wickelfeature units may then be decoded into a string of Wickelphones by the Wickelphone binding network, or into one of a small set of words by the whole-string binding network, or into a free choice of an output word by the unconstrained whole-string binding network.

4. An analysis of the assumptions of the Rumelhart–McClelland model in comparison with symbolic accounts

It is possible to practice psycholinguistics with minimal commitment to explicating the internal representation of language achieved by the learner. Rumelhart and McClelland's work is emphatically not of this sort. Their model is offered precisely as a model of internal representation; the learning process is understood in terms of changes in a representational system as it converges on the mature state. It embodies claims of the greatest psycholinguistic interest: it has a theory of phonological representation, a theory of morphology, a theory (or rather anti-theory) of the role of the notion 'lexical item', and a theory of the relation between regular and irregular forms. In no case are these presupposed theories simply transcribed from familiar views; they constitute a bold new perspective on the central issues in the study of word-forms, rooted in the exigencies and strengths of connectionism.

The model largely exemplifies what we have called revisionist-symbol-processing connectionism, rather than implementational or eliminative connectionism. Standard symbolic rules are not embodied in it; nor does it posit an utterly opaque device whose operation cannot be understood in terms of symbol-processing of any sort. It is possible to isolate an abstract but unorthodox linguistic theory implicit in the model (though Rumelhart and McClelland do not themselves consider it in this light), and that theory can be analyzed and evaluated in the same way that more familiar theories are. These are the fundamental linguistic assumptions of the RM model:

- That the Wickelphone/Wickelfeature provides an adequate basis for phonological generalization, circumventing the need to deal with strings.
- That the past tense is formed by direct modification of the phonetics of the root, so that there is no need to recognize a more abstract level of morphological structure.
- That the formation of strong (irregular) pasts is determined by purely

phonetic considerations, so that there is no need to recognize the notion 'lexical item' to serve as a locus of idiosyncrasy.

● That the regular system is qualitatively the same as the irregular, differing only in the number and uniformity of their populations of exemplars, so that it is appropriate to handle the whole stem/past relation in a single, indissoluble facility.

These rather specific assumptions combine to support the broader claim that connectionism supplies a viable alternative to highly structured symbol-processing theories such as that sketched above. "We have shown," they write (PDPII, p. 267), "that a reasonable account of the acquisition of the past tense can be provided without recourse to the notion of a 'rule' as anything more than a description of the language." By this they mean that rules, as mere summaries of the data, are not intrinsically or causally involved in internal representations. Rumelhart and McClelland's argument for the broader claim is based entirely on the behavior of their model.

We will show that each of the listed assumptions grossly mischaracterizes the domain it is relevant to, in a way that seriously undermines the model's claim to accuracy and even 'reasonableness'. More positively, we will show how past tense formation takes its place within a larger, more inclusive system of phonological and morphological interactions. The properties of the larger system will provide us with a clear benchmark for measuring the value of linguistic and psycholinguistic models.

4.1. Wickelphonology

The Wickelphone/Wickelfeature has some useful properties. Rumelhart and McClelland hold that the finite Wickelphone set can encode strings of arbitrary length (PDPII, p. 269) and though false this is close enough to being true to give them a way to distinguish all the words in their data. In addition, a Wickelphone contains a chunk of context within which phonological dependencies can be found. These properties allow the RM model to get off the ground. If, however, the Wickelphone/Wickelfeature is to be taken seriously as even an approximate model of phonological representation, it must satisfy certain basic, uncontroversial criteria.[6]

Preserving distinctions. First of all, a phonological representation system for a language must preserve all the distinctions that are actually present in

---

[6]For other critiques of the Wickelphone hypothesis, antedating the RM model, see Halwes and Jenkins (1971) and Savin and Bever (1970).

the language. English orthography is a familiar representational system that fails to preserve distinctness: for example, the word spelled 'read' may be read as either [rid] or [rɛd];[7] whatever its other virtues, spelling is not an appropriate medium for phonological computation. The Wickelphone system fails more seriously, because there are distinctions that it is in principle incapable of handling. Certain patterns of repetitions will map distinct string-regions onto the same Wickelphone set, resulting in irrecoverable loss of information. This is not just a mathematical curiosity. For example, the Australian language Oykangand (Sommer, 1980) distinguishes between *algal* 'straight' and *algalgal* 'ramrod straight', different strings which share the Wickelphone set {alg, al#, gal, lga, #al}, as can be seen from the analysis in (5):

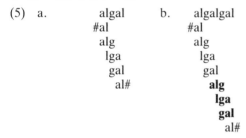

(5) a.   algal   b.   algalgal
                 #al   #al
                 alg   alg
                 lga   lga
                 gal   gal
                 al#   **alg**
                                   lga
                                   gal
                                   al#

Wickelphone sets containing subsets closed under cyclic permutation on the character string—{alg, gal, lga} in the example at hand—are infinitely ambiguous as to the strings they encode. This shows that Wickelphones cannot represent even relatively short strings, much less strings of arbitrary length, without loss of concatenation structure (loss is guaranteed for strings

---

[7]We will use the following phonetic notation and terminology (sparingly). Enclosure in square brackets [ ] indicates phonetic spelling.

The *tense* vowels are: [i] as in *beat*   [u] as in *shoe*
                        [e] as in *bait*   [o] as in *go*

The *lax* vowels are: [I] as in *bit*   [U] as in *put*
                        [ε] as in *bet*   [ɔ] as in *lost*

The low front vowel [æ] appears in *cat*. The low central vowel [ʌ] appears in *shut*. The low back vowel [ɔ] appears in *caught*. The diphthong [ay] appears in *might* and *bite*; the diphthong [aw] in *house*. The high lax central vowel [ɨ] is the second vowel in *melted, rose's*.

The symbol [č] stands for the voiceless palato-alveolar affricate that appears twice in *church*; the symbol [j] for its voiced counterpart, which appears twice in *judge*. [š] is the voiceless palato-alveolar fricative of *shoe* and [ž] is its voiced counterpart, the final consonant of *rouge*. The velar nasal ŋ is the final consonant in *sing*.

The term *sonorant consonant* refers to the liquids *l,r* and the nasals *m,n,*ŋ. The term *obstruent* refers to the complement set of oral stops, fricatives and affricates, such as *p,t,k,f,s,š,č,b,d,g,v,z,ž,j*. The term *coronal* refers to sounds made at the dental, alveolar, and palato-alveolar places of articulation. The term *sibilant* refers to the conspicuously noisy fricatives and affricates [s,z,š,ž,č,j].

over a certain length). On elementary grounds, then, the Wickelphone is demonstrably inadequate.

Supporting generalizations. A second, more sophisticated requirement is that a representation supply the basis for proper generalization. It is here that the phonetic vagaries of the most commonly encountered representation of English—its spelling—receive a modicum of justification. The letter *i*, for example, is implicated in the spelling of both [ay] and [I], allowing word-relatedness to be overtly expressed as identity of spelling in many pairs like those in (6):

(6) a. wr*i*te-wr*i*tten
     b. b*i*te-b*i*t
     c. ign*i*te-ign*i*tion
     d. sen*i*le-sen*i*lity
     e. der*i*ve-der*i*vative

The Wickelphone/Wickelfeature provides surprisingly little help in finding phonological generalizations. There are two domains in which significant similarities are operative: (1) among items in the input set, and (2) between an input item and its output form. Taking the trigram as the primitive unit of description impedes the discovery of inter-item similarity relations.

Consider the fact, noted by Rumelhart and McClelland, that the word *silt* and the word *slit* have no Wickelphones in common: the first goes to {#si, sil, ilt, lt#}, the second to {#sl, sli, lit, it#}. The implicit claim is that such pairs have no phonological properties in common. Although this result meets the need to distinguish the distinct, it shows that Wickelphone composition is a very unsatisfactory measure of psychological phonetic similarity. Indeed, historical changes of the type *slit* → *silt* and *silt* → *slit*, based on phonetic similarity, are fairly common in natural language. In the history of English, for example, we find *hross* → *horse, thrid* → *third, brid* → *bird* (Jespersen, 1942, p. 58). On pure Wickelphones such changes are equivalent to complete replacements; they are therefore no more likely, and no easier to master, than any other complete replacement, like *horse* going to *slit* or *bird* to *clam*. The situation is improved somewhat by the transition to Wickelfeatures, but remains unsatisfactory. Since phonemes *l* and *i* share features like voicing, Wickelphones like *sil* and *sli* will share Wickelfeatures like Voiceless-Voiced-Voiced. The problem is that the *l/i* overlap is the same as the overlap of *l* with any vowel and the same as the overlap of *r* with vowels. In Wickelfeatures it is just as costly—counting by number of replacements—to turn *brid* to phonetically distant *bald* or *blud* as it is to turn it to nearby *bird*.

Even in the home territory of the past tense, Wickelphonology is more an encumbrance than a guide. The dominant regularity of the language entails that a verb like *kill* will simply add one phone [d] in the past; in Wickelphones the map is as in (7):

(7) a. {#ki, kil, il#} → {#ki, kil, ild, ld#}
     b. il# → ild, ld#

The change, shown in (7b), is exactly the full replacement of one Wickelphone by two others. The Wickelphone is in principle incapable of representing an observation like 'add [d] to the end of a word when it ends in a voiced consonant', because there is no way to single out the one word-ending consonant and no way to add a phoneme without disrupting the stem; you must refer to the entire sequence AB#, whether A is relevant or not, and you must replace it entirely, regardless of whether the change preserves input string structure. Given time and space, the facts can be registered on a Wickelfeature-by-Wickelfeature basis, but the unifying pattern is undiscoverable. Since the relevant phonological process involves only a *pair* of representationally adjacent elements, the triune Wickelphone/Wickelfeature is quite generally incompetent to locate the relevant factors and to capitalize on them in learning, with consequences we will see when we examine the model's success in generalizing to new forms.

The "blurring" of the Wickelfeature representation, by which certain input units XBC and ABZ are turned on in addition to authentic ABC, is a tactical response to the problem of finding similarities among the input set. The reason that AYB is not also turned on—as one would expect, if "blurring" corresponded to neural noise of some sort—is in part that XBC and ABZ are units preserving the empirically significant adjacency pairing of segments: in many strings of the form ABC, we expect interactions within AB and BC, but not between A and C. Blurring both A and C helps to model processes in which only the presence of B is significant, and as Lachter and Bever (1988) show, partially recreates the notion of the single phoneme as a phonological unit. Such selective "blurring" is not motivated within Rumelhart and McClelland's theory or by general principles of PDP architecture; it is an external imposition that pushes it along more or less in the right direction. Taken literally, it is scarcely credible: the idea would be that the pervasive adjacency requirement in phonological processes is due to quasi-random confusion, rather than structural features of the representational apparatus and the physical system it serves.

Excluding the impossible. The third and most challenging requirement we can place on a representational system is that it should exclude the impossible. Many kinds of formally simple relations are absent from natural language, presumably because they cannot be mentally represented. Here the Wickelphone/Wickelfeature fails spectacularly. A quintessential unlinguistic map is relating a string to its mirror image reversal (this would relate *pit* to *tip*, *brag* to *garb*, *dumb* to *mud*, and so on); although neither physiology nor physics forbids it, no language uses such a pattern. But it is as easy to represent and learn in the RM pattern associator as the identity map. The rule is simply to replace each Wickelfeature ABC by the Wickelfeature CBA. In network terms, assuming link-weights from 0 to 1, weight the lines from ABC → CBA at 1 and all the (459) others emanating from ABC at 0. Since all weights start at 0 for Rumelhart and McClelland, this is exactly as easy to achieve as weighting the lines ABC → ABC at 1, with the others from ABC staying at 0; and it requires considerably less modification of weights than most other input–output transforms. Unlike other, more random replacements, the S → S^R map is guaranteed to preserve the stringhood of the input Wickelphone set. It is easy to define other processes over the Wickelphone that are equally unlikely to make their appearance in natural language: for example, no process turns on the identity of the entire first Wickelphone (#AB) or last Wickelphone (AB#)—compare in this regard the notions 'first (last) segment', 'first (last) syllable', frequently involved in actual morphological and phonological processes, but which appear as arbitrary disjunctions, if reconstructible at all, in the Wickelphone representation. The Wickelphone tells us as little about unnatural avenues of generalization as it does about the natural ones.

The root cause, we suggest, is that the Wickelphone is being asked to carry two contradictory burdens. Division into Wickelphones is primarily a way of multiplying out possible rule-contexts in advance. Since many phonological interactions are segmentally local, a Wickelphone-like decomposition into short substrings will pick out domains in which interaction is likely.[8] But any such decomposition must also retain enough information to allow the string to be reconstituted with a fair degree of certainty. Therefore, the minimum usable unit to reconstruct order is three segments long, even though many contexts for actual phonological processes span a window of only two seg-

---

[8] Of course, not all interactions are segmentally local. In vowel harmony, for example, a vowel typically reacts to a nearby vowel over an intervening string of consonants; if there are two intervening consonants, the interacting vowels will never be in the same Wickelphone and generalization will be impossible. Stress rules commonly skip over a string of one or two *syllables*, which may contain many segments: crucial notions such as 'second syllable' will have absolutely no characterization in Wickelphonology (see Sietsema, 1987, for further discussion). Phenomena like these show the need for more sophisticated representational resources, so that the relevant notion of domain of interaction may be adequately defined (see van der Hulst & Smith, 1982, for an overview of recent work). It is highly doubtful that Wickelphonology can be strengthened to deal with such cases, but we will not explore these broader problems, because our goal is to examine the Wickelphone as an alternative to the segmental concatenative structure which every theory of phonology includes.

ments. Similarly, if the blurring process were done thoroughly, so that ABC would set off all XBZ in the input set, there would be a full representation of the presence of B, but the identity of the input string would disappear. The RM model thus establishes a mutually subversive relation between representing the aspects of the string that figure in generalizations and representing its concatenation structure. In the end, neither is done satisfactorily.

Rumelhart and McClelland display some ambivalence about the Wickelfeature. At one point they dismiss the computational difficulty of recovering a string from a Wickelfeature set as one that is easily overcome by parallel processing "in biological hardware" (p. 262). At another point they show how the Wickelfeature-to-Wickelphone re-conversion can be done in a binding network that utilizes a certain genus of connectionist mechanisms, implying again that this process is to be taken seriously as part of the model. Yet they write (PDPII, p. 239):

> All we claim for the present coding scheme is its sufficiency for the task of representing the past tenses of the 500 most frequent verbs in English and the importance of the basic principles of distributed, coarse (what we are calling blurred), conjunctive coding that it embodies.

This disclaimer is at odds with the centrality of the Wickelfeature in the model's design. The Wickelfeature structure is not some kind of approximation that can easily be sharpened and refined; it is categorically the wrong kind of thing for the jobs assigned to it.[9] At the same time, the Wickelphone or something similar is demanded by the most radically distributed forms of distributed representations, which resolve order relations (like concatenation) into unordered sets of features. Without the Wickelphone, Rumelhart and McClelland have no account about how phonological strings are to be analyzed for significant patterning.

4.2. Phonology and morphology

The RM model maps from input to output in a single step, on the assumption that the past tense derives by a direct phonetic modification of the stem. The regular endings -t, -d, -id, make their appearance in the same way as the

---

[9]Compare in this regard certain other aspects of the model which are clearly inaccurate, but represent harmless oversimplifications. The actual set of phonetic features used to describe individual phones (p. 235) doesn't make enough distinctions for English, much less language at large, nor is it intended to; but the underlying strategy of featural analysis is solidly supported at the scientific literature. Similarly, the frequency classifications of the verbs in the study derive from the Kucera–Francis count over a written corpus, which shows obvious divergences from the input encountered by a learner (for examples, see footnote 24). Such aberrations, which have little impact on the model's behavior, could be corrected easily, with no structural re-design.

vowel changes $i \rightarrow a$ *(sing – sang)* or $u \rightarrow o$ *(choose – chose)*. Rumelhart and McClelland claim as an advantage of the model that "[a] uniform procedure is applied for producing the past-tense form in every case." (PDPII, p. 267) This sense of uniformity can be sustained, however, only if past tense formation is viewed in complete isolation from the rest of English phonology and morphology. We will show that Rumelhart and McClelland's very local uniformity must be paid for with extreme nonuniformity in the treatment of the broader patterns of the language.

The distribution of *t-d-id* follows a simple pattern: *id* goes after those stems ending in *t* or *d*; elsewhere, *t* (voiceless itself) goes after a voiceless segment and *d* (itself voiced) goes after a voiced segment. The real interest of this rule is that *none of it is specifically bound to the past tense*. The perfect/passive participle and the verbal adjective use the very same *t-d-id* scheme: *was kicked – was slugged – was patted; a kicked dog – a flogged horse – a patted cat*. These categories cannot be simply identified as copies of the past tense, because they have their own distinctive irregular formations. For example, past *drank* contrasts with the participle *drunk* and the verbal adjective *drunken*. Outside the verbal system entirely there is yet another process that uses the *t-d-id* suffix, with the variants distributed in exactly the same way as in the verb forms, to make adjectives from nouns, with the meaning 'having X' (Jespersen, 1942, p. 426 ff.):

(8)   -t   -d   -id

hooked   long-nosed   one-handed
saber-toothed   horned   talented
pimple-faced   winged   kind-hearted
foul-mouthed   moneyed   warm-blooded
thick-necked   bad-tempered   bareheaded

The full generality of the component processes inherent in the *t-d-id* alternation only becomes apparent when we examine the widespread *s-z-iz* alternation found in the diverse morphological categories collected below:

(9)   Category   -s   -z   -iz

a.	Plural	hawks	dogs	hoses
b.	3psg	hits	sheds	chooses
c.	Possessive	Pat's	Fred's	George's
d.	has	Pat's	Fred's	George's
e.	is	Pat's	Fred's	George's
f.	does	what's	where's	–
g.	Affective	Pats(y)	Wills, bonkers	–
h.	adverbial	thereabouts	towards, nowadays	–
i.	Linking -s	huntsman	landsman	–

These 9 categories show syncretism in a big way—they use the same phonetic resources to express very different distinctions.

The regular noun plural exactly parallels the 3rd person singular marking of the verb, despite the fact that the two categories (noun/verb, singular/plural) have no notional overlap. The rule for choosing among *s-z-iz* is this: *iz* goes after stems ending in sibilants ($s,z,š,ž,č,ǰ$); elsewhere, *s* (itself voiceless) goes after voiceless segments, *z* (voiced itself) goes after voiced segments. The distribution of *s/z* is exactly the same as that of *t/d*. The rule for *iz* differs from that for *id* only inasmuch as *z* differs from *d*. In both cases the rule functions to separate elements that are phonetically similar: as the sibilant *z* is to the sibilants, so the alveolar stop *d* is to the alveolar stops *t* and *d*.

The possessive marker and the fully reduced forms of the auxiliary *has* and the auxiliary/main verb *is* repeat the pattern. These three share the further interesting property that they attach not to nouns but to noun phrases, with the consequence that in ordinary colloquial speech they can end up on any kind of word at all, as shown in (10) below:

(10) a.   [my mother-in-law]'s hat (cf. plural: *mothers-in-law*)
     b.   [the man you met]'s dog
     c.   [the man you spoke to]'s here. (Main verb *be*)
     d.   [the student who did well]'s being escorted home. (Auxiliary *be*)
     e.   [the patient who turned yellow]'s been getting better. (Auxiliary *has*)

The remaining formal categories (10f–h) share the *s/z* part of the pattern. The auxiliary *does*, when unstressed, can reduce colloquially to its final sibilant:[10]

---

[10]A post-sibilant environment in which *iz* would be necessary seems somewhat less available in natural speech:

    (i)   ? What church's he go to?
    (ii)   ?? Whose lunch's he eat from?
    (iii)   ?? Which's he like better?
    (iv)   ?? Whose's he actually prefer?

We suspect that the problem here lies in getting *does* to reduce at all in such structural environments, regardless of phonology. If this is right, then (i) and (ii) should be as good (or bad) as structurally identical (v) and (vi), where the sibilant-sibilant problem doesn't arise:

    (v)   ? What synagogue's he go to?
    (vi)   ? Whose dinner's he eat from?

Sentence forms (iii) and (iv) use the wh-determines *which* and *whose* without following head nouns, which may introduce sufficient additional structural complexity to inhibit reduction. At any rate, this detail, though interesting in itself, is orthogonal to the question of what happens to *does* when it does reduce.

(11) a.   'Z he like beans?
    b.   What's he eat for lunch?
    c.   Where's he go for dinner?

The affective marker *s/z* forms nicknames in some dialects and argots, as in *Wills* from *William*, *Pats* from *Patrick*, and also shows up in various emotionally-colored neologisms like *bonkers*, *bats*, paralleling *-y* or *-o* (*batty*, *wacko*), with which it sometimes combines (*Patsy*, *fatso*). A number of adverbial forms are marked by *s/z*—*unawares*, *nowadays*, *besides*, *backwards*, *here/there/whereabouts*, *amidships*. A final, quite sporadic (but phonologically regular) use links together elements of compounds, as in *huntsman*, *statesman*, *kinsman*, *bondsman*.

The reason that the voiced/voiceless choice is made identically throughout English morphology is not hard to find: it reflects the prevailing and inescapable phonetics of consonant cluster voicing in the language at large. Even in unanalyzable words, final obstruent clusters have a single value for the voicing feature; we find only words like these:

(12) a.   ax, fix, box   [ks]
    b.   act, fact, product   [kt]
    c.   traipse, lapse, corpse [ps]
    d.   apt, opt, abrupt   [pt]
    e.   blitz, kibitz, Potts   [ts]
    f.   post, ghost, list   [st]

Entirely absent are words ending in a cluster with mixed voicing: [zt], [gs], [kz], etc.[11] Notice that after vowels, liquids, and nasals (non-obstruents) a voicing contrast is permitted:

(13) a.   lens – fence   [nz] – [ns]
    b.   furze – force   [rz] – [rs]
    c.   wild – wilt   [ld] – [lt]
    d.   bulb – help   [lb] – [lp]
    e.   goad – goat   [od] – [ot]
    f.   niece – sneeze [is] – [iz]

If we are to achieve uniformity in the treatment of consonant-cluster voicing, we must not spread it out over 10 or so distinct morphological form generators (i.e., 10 different networks), and then repeat it once again in the phonetic component that applies to unanalyzable words. Otherwise, we

---

[11]In noncomplex words obstruent clusters are overwhelmingly voiceless: the word *adze* [dz] pretty much stands alone.

would have no explanation for why English contains, and why generation after generation of children easily learn, the exact same pattern eleven or so different times. Eleven unrelated sets of cluster patternings would be just as likely. Rather, the voicing pattern must be factored out of the morphology and allowed to stand on its own.

Let's see how the cross-categorial generalizations that govern the surface shape of English morphemes can be given their due in a rule system. Suppose the phonetic content of the past tense marker is just /d/ and that of the diverse morphemes in (9) is /z/. There is a set of morphological rules that say how morphemes are assembled into words: for example, Verb-past = stem + /d/; Noun-pl = stem + /z/; Verb-3psg = stem + /z/. Given this, we can invoke a single rule to derive the occurrences of [t] and [s]:

(14) *Voicing Assimilation.* Spread the value of voicing from one obstruent to the next in word final position.[12]

Rule (14) is motivated by the facts of simplex words shown above: it holds of *ax* and *adze* and is restricted so as to allow *goat* and *horse* to escape unaffected—they end in single obstruents, not clusters. When a final cluster comes about via morphology, the rule works like this:

(15) a.   pig + /z/   Vacuous
     b.   pit + /z/   →   [pIts]
     c.   pea + /z/   No Change
     d.   rub + /d/   Vacuous
     e.   rip + /d/   →   [rIpt]
     f.   tow + /d/   No Change

The crucial effect of the rule is to devoice /d/ and /z/ after voiceless obstruents; after voiced obstruents its effect is vacuous and after nonobstruents—vowels, liquids, nasals—it doesn't apply at all, allowing the basic values to emerge unaltered.[13]

The environment of the variant with the reduced vowel *i* is similarly constant across all morphological categories, entailing the same sort of uniform treatment. Here again the simplex forms in the English vocabulary provide the key to understanding: in no case are the phonetic sequences [tt], [dd], [sibilant-sibilant] tolerated at the end of unanalyzable words, or even inside

---

[12]More likely, syllable-final position.

[13]Notice that if /t/ and /s/ were taken as basic, we would require a special rule of voicing, restricted to suffixes, to handle the case of words ending in vowels, liquids, and nasals. For example, *pea* + /s/ would have to go to *pea* + [z], even though this pattern of voicing is not generally required in the language: cf. the morphologically simplex word *peace*. Positing /d/ and /z/ as basic, on the other hand, allows the rule (14), which is already part of English, to derive the suffixal voicing pattern without further ado.

them.[14] English has very strong general restrictions against the clustering of identical or highly similar consonants. These are not mere conventions deriving from vocabulary statistics, but real limitations on what native speakers of English have learned to pronounce. (Such sequences are allowed in other languages.) Consequently, forms like [skIdd] from *skid* + /d/ or [jʌȷ̌z] from *judge* + /z/ are quite impossible. To salvage them, a vowel comes in to separate the ending from a too-similar stem final consonant. We can informally state the rule as (16):

(16) *Vowel Insertion.* Word-finally, separate with the vowel *i* adjacent consonants that are too similar in place and manner of articulation, as defined by the canons of English word phonology.

The two phonological rules have a competitive interaction. Words like *passes* [pæsɨz] and *pitted* [pItid] show that Vowel Insertion will always prevent Voicing Assimilation: from *pass* + /z/ and *pit* + /d/ we never get [pæsis] or [pItit], with assimilation to the voiceless final consonant. Various lines of explanation might be pursued; we tentatively suggest that the outcome of the competition follows from the rather different character of the two rules. Voicing Assimilation is highly phonetic in character, and might well be part of the system that implements phonological representations rather than part of the phonology proper, where representations are defined, constructed, and changed. If Vowel Insertion, as seems likely, actually changes the representation prior to implementation, then it is truly phonological in character. Assuming the componential organization of the whole system portrayed above, with a flow between components in the direction Morphology → Phonology → Phonetics, the pieces of the system fall naturally into place. Morphology provides the basic structure of stem + suffix. Phonology makes various representational adjustments, including Vowel Insertion, and Phonetics then implements the representations. In this scheme, Voicing Assimilation, sitting in the phonetic component, never sees the suffix as adjacent to a too-similar stem-final consonant.

Whatever the ultimate fate of the details of the competition, it is abundantly clear that the English system turns on a fundamental distinction between phonology and morphology. Essential phonological and phonetic processes are entirely insensitive to the specifics of morphological composition and sweep across categories with no regard for their semantic or syntactic content. Such processes define equivalences at one level over items that are distinct at the level of phonetics: for English suffixes, $t = d = id$ and $s = z$

---

[14]This is of course a phonological restriction, not an orthographic one. The words *petty* and *pity*, for example, have identical consonantal phonology.

= *iz*. As a consequence, the learner infers that there is one suffix for the regular past, not three; and one suffix, not three, for each of plural, 3rd person singular, possessive, and so on. The phonetic differences emerge automatically; as would be expected in such cases, uninstructed native speakers typically have no awareness of them.

Rumelhart and McClelland's pattern associator is hobbled by a doctrine we might dub "morphological localism": the assumption that there is for each morphological category an encapsulated system that handles every detail of its phonetics. This they mischaracterize as a theoretically desirable "uniformity". In fact, morphological localism destroys uniformity by preventing generalization across categories and by excluding inference based on larger-scale regularities. Thus it is inconsistent with the fact that the languages that people learn are shaped by these generalizations and inferences.

The shape of the system. It is instructive to note that although the various English morphemes discussed earlier all participate in the general phonological patterns of the language, like the past tense they can also display their own particularities and subpatterns. The 3rd person singular is extremely regular, with a few lexical irregularities (*is, has, does, says*) and a lexical class (modal auxiliaries) that can't be inflected (*can, will*, etc.). The plural has a minuscule number of non-/z/ forms (*oxen, children, geese, mice, ...*), a Ø suffixing class (*sheep, deer*), and a fricative-voicing subclass (*leaf-leaves, wreath-wreathes*). The possessive admits no lexical peculiarities (outside of the pronouns), presumably because it adds to phrases rather than lexical items, but it is lost after plural /z/ (*men's* vs. *dogs'*) and sporadically after other *z*'s. The fully reduced forms of *is* and *has* admit no lexical or morphologically-based peculiarities whatever, presumably because they are syntactic rather than lexical.

From these observations, we can put together a general picture of how the morphological system works. There are some embracing regularities:

1. All inflectional morphology is suffixing.
2. All nonsyllabic regular suffixes are formed from the phonetic substance /d/ or /z/; that is, they must be the same up to the one feature distinguishing *d* from *z*: sibilance.
3. All morphemes are liable to re-shaping by phonology and phonetics.
4. Categories, inasmuch as they are lexical, can support specific lexical peculiarities and subpatterns; inasmuch as they are nonlexical, they must be entirely regular.

Properties (1) and (2) are clearly English-bound generalizations, to be learned by the native speaker. Properties (3) and (4) are replicated from language to language and should therefore be referred to the general capacities of the learner rather than to the accidents of English. Notice that we have lived up to our promise to show that the rules governing the regular past tense are not idiosyncratic to it: beyond even the phonology discussed above, its intrinsic phonetic content is shared up to one feature with the other regular nonsyllabic suffixes; and the rule of inflectional suffixation itself is shared generally across categories. We have found a highly modular system, in which the mapping from uninflected stem to the phonetic representation of the past tense form breaks down into a cascade of independent rule systems, and each rule system treats its inputs identically regardless of how they were originally created.

It is a nontrivial problem to design a device that arrives at this characterization on its own. An unanalyzed single module like the RM pattern associator that maps from features to features cannot do so.

4.3. Lexical items

The notion of a 'word' or 'morpheme' is so basic to our intuitive understanding of language that it is easy to forget the role it plays in systematic linguistic explanation. As a result, use of the representational structure known as a 'lexical item' might be seen as mere tradition, and one of the revolutionary aspects of the RM model—that it contains nothing corresponding to a lexical item other than its phonetic composition—might be dismissed as a harmless iconoclasm. Here we show that, on the contrary, lexical items as explicit representations play a crucial role in many linguistic phenomena.

4.3.1. Preservation of stem and affix

The pattern associator suffers from a fundamental design problem which prevents it from truly grasping even the simplest morphological generalization. Because the relation between stem and past tense is portrayed as a transduction from one low-level featural representation to another, literally replacing every feature in the input, it becomes an inexplicable accident that the regular formation rule preserves the stem unaltered. The identity map has no cachet in the pattern associator; it is one among very many (including the reverse map) that happen to produce strings in the output. Yet a tendency toward preservation of stem identity, a typical linguistic phenomenon, is an immediate consequence of the existence of morphology as a level of description: if the rule is Word = Stem + Affix, then ceteris paribus the stem comes through. What makes ceteris not exactly paribus is the potential existence of phonological and phonetic accommodations, but even these will be relatively minute in a properly formulated theory.

The other side of the morphological coin is the preservation of *affix* identity. The suffixal variants *t* and *d* are matched with *id*, not with *iz* or *oz* or *og* or any other conceivable but phonetically distant form. Similarly, morphemes which show the *s/z* variants take *iz* in the appropriate circumstances, not *id* or *od* or *gu*. This follows directly from our hypothesis that the morphemes in question have just one basic phonetic content—/d/ or /z/—which is subject to minor contextual adjustments. The RM model, however, cannot grasp this generalization. To see this, consider the Wickelphone map involved in the *id* case, using the verb *melt* as an example:

(17) a.   {#me, mel, elt, lt#} → {#me, mel, elt, lti, tid, id#}
     b.   lt# → lti, tid, id#

The replacement Wickelphone (or more properly—Wickelfeature set) *id#* has no relation to the stem-final consonant and could just as well be *iz#* or *ig#*. Thus the RM model cannot explain the prevalence across languages of inflectional alternations that preserve stem and affix identities.

4.3.2. Operations on lexical items

The generalizations that the RM model extracts consist of specific correlations between particular phone sequences in the stem and particular phone sequences in the past form. Since the model contains no symbol corresponding to a stem per se, independent of the particular phone sequences that happen to have exemplified the majority of stems in the model's history, it cannot make any generalization that refers to stems per se, cutting across their individual phonetic contents. Thus a morphological process like reduplication, which in many languages copies an entire stem (e.g. yielding forms roughly analogous to *dum-dum* and *boom-boom*), cannot be acquired in its fully general form by the network. In many cases it can "memorize" *particular* patterns of reduplication, consisting of mappings between particular feature sequences and their reduplicated counterparts (though even here problems can arise because of the poverty of the Wickelfeature representation, as we pointed out in discussing Wickelphonology), but the concept "Copy the stem" itself is unlearnable; there is no unitary representation of a thing to be copied and no operation consisting of copying a variable regardless of its specific content. Thus when a new stem comes in that does not share many features with the ones encountered previously, it will not match any stored patterns and reduplication will not apply to it.[15]

[15]It is worth noting that reduplication, which always calls on a variable (if not 'stem', then 'syllable' or 'foot') is one of the most commonly used strategies of word-formation. In one form or another, it's found in hundreds, probably thousands, of the world's languages. For detailed analysis, see McCarthy and Prince (forthcoming).

The point strikes closer to home as well. The English regular past tense rule adds an affix to a stem. The rule doesn't care about the contents of the stem; it mentions a variable, "stem", that is cashed in independently for information stored in particular lexical entries. Thus the rule, once learned, can apply across the board independent of the set of stems encountered in the learner's history. The RM model, on the other hand, learns the past tense alternation by linking phonetic features of inflected forms directly to the particular affix features of the stem (for example, in *pat – patted* the *id#* Wickelfeatures are linked directly to the entire set of features for *pat*: *#pæ*, *pæt*, etc.). Though much of the activation for the affix features eventually is contributed by some stem features that cut across many individual stems, such as those at the end of a word, not all of it is; some contribution from the word-specific stem features that are well-represented in the input sample can play a role as well. Thus the RM model could fail to generate any past tense form for a new stem if the stem did not share enough features with those stems that were encountered in the past and that thus grew their own strong links with past tense features. When we examine the performance of the RM model, we will see how some of its failures can probably be attributed to the fact that what it learns is associated with particular phone sequences as opposed to variables standing for stems in general.

4.3.3. Lexical items as the locus of idiosyncrasy

For the RM model, membership in the strong classes is determined entirely by phonological criteria; there is no notion of a "lexical item", as distinct from the phone-sequences that make up the item, to which an 'irregular' tag can be affixed. In assessing their model, Rumelhart and McClelland write:

> The child need not decide whether a verb is regular or irregular. There is no question as to whether the inflected form should be stored directly in the lexicon or derived from more general principles. (PDPII, p. 267)

If Rumelhart and McClelland are right, there can be no homophony between regular and irregular verbs or between items in distinct irregular classes, because words are nothing but phone-sequences, and irregular forms are tied directly to these sequences. This basic empirical claim is transparently false. Within the strong class itself, there is a contrast between *ring* (past: *rang*) and *wring* (past: *wrung*) which are only orthographically distinct. Looking at the broader population, we find the string *lay* shared by the items *lie* (past: *lied*) 'prevaricate' and *lie* (past: *lay*) 'assume a recumbent position'. In many dialects, regular *hang* refers to a form of execution, strong *hang* means merely 'suspend'. One verb *fit* is regular, meaning 'adjust'; the other, which refers to the shape-or-size appropriateness of its subject, can be strong:

(18) a.   That shirt never fit/?fitted me.
    b.   The tailor fitted/*fit me with a shirt.

The sequence [kʌm] belongs to the strong system when it spells the morpheme *come*, not otherwise: contrast *become, overcome* with *succumb, encumber.*

An excellent source of counterexamples to the claim that past tense formation collapses the distinctions between words and their featural decomposition is supplied by verbs derived from other categories (like nouns or adjectives). The significance of these examples, which were first noticed in Mencken (1936), has been explored in Kiparsky (1982a, b)[16]

(19) a.   He braked the car suddenly. ≠ broke
    b.   He flied out to center field. ≠ flew
    c.   He ringed the city with artillery. *rang
    d.   Martina 2-setted Chris. *2-set
    e.   He subletted/sublet the apartment.
    f.   He sleighed down the hill. *slew
    g.   He de-flea'd his dog. *de-fled
    h.   He spitted the pig. *spat
    i.   He righted the boat. *rote
    j.   He high-sticked the goalie. *high-stuck
    k.   He grandstanded to the crowd. *grandstood.

This phenomenon becomes intelligible if we assume that irregularity is a property of verb *roots*. Nouns and adjectives by their very nature do not classify as irregular (or regular) with respect to the past tense, a purely verbal notion. Making a noun into a verb, which is done quite freely in English, cannot produce a new verb root, just a new verb. Such verbs can receive no special treatment and are inflected in accord with the regular system, regardless of any phonetic resemblance to strong roots.

In some cases, there is a circuitous path of derivation: V → N → V. But the end product, having passed through nounhood, must be regular no matter what the status of the original source verb. (By "derivation" we refer to relations intuitively grasped by the native speaker, not to historical etymology.) The baseball verb *to fly out*, meaning 'make an out by hitting a fly ball that gets caught', is derived from the baseball noun *fly (ball)*, meaning 'ball hit on a conspicuously parabolic trajectory', which is in turn related to the simple strong verb *fly* 'proceed through the air'. Everyone says "he flied out"; no mere mortal has yet been observed to have "flown out" to left field.

---

[16]Examples (19b) and (h) are from Kiparsky.

Similarly, the noun *stand* in the lexical compound *grandstand* is surely felt by speakers to be related to the homophonous strong verb, but once made a noun its verbal irregularity cannot be resurrected: **he grandstood*. A derived noun cannot retain any verbal properties of its base, like irregular tense formation, because nouns in general can't have properties such as tense. Thus it is not simply derivation that erases idiosyncrasy, but departure from the verb class: *stand* retains its verbal integrity in the verbs *withstand, understand*, as *throw* does in the verbs *overthrow, underthrow*.[17] Kiparsky (1982a, b) has pointed out that regularization-by-derivation is quite general and shows up wherever irregularity is to be found. In nouns, for example, we have the *Toronto Maple Leafs*, not **Leaves*, because use in a name strips a morpheme of its original content. Similar patterns of regularization are observed very widely in the world's languages.

One might be tempted to try to explain these phenomena in terms of the meanings of regular and irregular versions of a verb. For example, Lakoff (1987) appeals to the distinction between the 'central' and 'extended' senses of polysemous words, and claims that irregularity attaches only to the 'central sense' of an item. It is a remarkable fact—indeed, an insult to any naive idea that linguistic form is driven by meaning—that polysemy is irrelevant to the regularization phenomenon. Lakoff's proposed generalization is not sound. Consider these examples:

(20) a.   He wetted his pants.   *wet* regular in central sense.
      b.   He wet his pants.   *wet* irregular in extended sense.

(21) a.   They heaved the bottle   *heave* regular in central sense.
           overboard.
      b.   They hove to.   *heave* irregular in extended
                                            sense.

It appears that a low-frequency irregular can occasionally become locked into a highly specific use, regardless of whether the sense involved is 'central' or 'extended'. Thus the purely semantic or metaphorical aspect of sense extension has no predictive power whatsoever. Verbs like *come, go, do, have, set, get, put, stand* ... are magnificently polysemous (and become more so in combination with particles like *in, out, up, off*), yet they march in lockstep

---

[17]When the verb is the 'head' of the word it belongs to, it passes on its categorial features to the whole word, including both verb-ness and more specialized morphological properties like irregularity (Williams, 1981). Deverbal nouns [$_N$V] and denominal verbs [$_V$N] must therefore be headless, whereas prefixed verbs are headed [$_V$PREF-V]. Notice that there can be uncertainty and dialect differences in the interpretation of individual cases. The verb *sublet* can be thought of as denominal, [$_V$[$_N$sublet]] giving *subletted*, or as a prefixed form headed by the verb *to let*, giving past tense *sublet*.

through the same nonregular paradigms in central and extended senses—regardless of how strained or opaque the metaphor.[18] Similarly, they retain their nonregular forms when combined with bound affixes that recur in word-formation patterns in the language, even if the meaning of the whole is not composed of the meaning of its parts: *forget/forgot, forgive/forgave, understand/understood, undertake/undertook, overcome/overcame* (see Aronoff, 1976, for other examples of this kind of phenomenon). But when a verb is transparently derived from a noun or adjective, the irregular system is *predictably* by-passed. The critical factors are lexical category in the formal sense— noun, verb, adjective—and the structural analysis of the word into entities such as root, stem, head, prefix, which are purely and autonomously morphological.

To master the actual system, then, the learner must have access to lexical information about each item, ranging from its derivational status (is the item a primitive root? is it derived from a noun or another verb?) to its specific lexical identity (is the item at hand *ring* or *wring*, $hang_1$ or $hang_2$, lie_1 or lie_2, etc.?). The RM model does without the notion 'lexical item' at the cost of major lapses in accuracy and coverage.

Our basic finding is independent of how the notion 'lexical item' is implemented. If a lexical item is a distributed pattern of activation—that is to say, just a set of semantic, syntactic, morphological, and phonological features—it remains true that past tense formation must be sensitive to various aspects of the pattern. It is hardly acceptable, however, to allow past tense formation (or morphology in general) to access every scrap of lexical information. Categorial information like root vs. derived status figures in the morphology of language after language, and with comparable effects, whereas the specific semantic distinctions between, say, *ring* and *wring* are hardly the basis for any real generalization. (Such verbs could have their class assignments reversed with no consequences for the rest of the language. We return to this point in Sections 8.3.1 and 8.3.4.) What's important is that *ring* ≠ *wring*, $hang_1$ ≠ $hang_2$; that they are not the same items. From such cases, it is clear that classification is not driven by any particular feature of the lexical item; rather, arbitrary assignment to a strong class is *itself* a lexical feature. Because morphology is sensitive to gross distinctness (α is not the same as β)

<hr>

[18]Compare in this regard Ross's (1975) study of productive affixation, which uncovers an actual constraint involving the central/extended distinction. Ross finds that prefixes like *re-, un-, mis-*, which affect meaning, are sensitive in various ways to the meaning of the base they attach to. He amply documents the fact that such prefixes reject metaphorically extended bases. Thus: "Horace Silver (*re-)cut Liberace" (*cut* = 'played better than'), "Larry (*mis-)fed Dennis" (*fed* = 'passed the basketball to'). Examination of Ross's numerous examples shows *not one* where metaphorical extension affects irregularity. The contrast could not be starker. Notions like 'past tense form' have no systematic sensitivity to the lexical semantics of the base.

rather than to every possible semantic, syntactic, and pragmatic fillip, we can conclude that lexical items do indeed possess an accessible local identity as well as a distributed featural decomposition.

4.4. The strong system and the regular system

The RM model embodies the claim that the distinction between regular and irregular modes of formation is spurious. At this point, we have established the incorrectness of two assumptions that were supposed to support the broader claim of uniformity.

> Assumption #1. "All past tenses are formed by direct phonetic modification of the stem." We have shown that the regular forms are derived through affixation followed by phonological and phonetic adjustment.

> Assumption #2. "The inflectional class of any verb (regular, subregular, irregular) can be determined from its phonological representation alone." We have seen that membership in the strong classes depends on lexical and morphological information.

These results still leave open the question of disparity between the regular and strong systems. To resolve it, we need a firmer understanding of how the strong system works. We will find that the strong system has a number of distinctive peculiarities which are related to its being a partly structured list of exceptions. We will examine five:

1. Phonetic similarity criteria on class membership.
2. Prototypicality structure of classes.
3. Lexical distinctness of stem and past tense forms.
4. Failure of predictability in verb categorization.
5. Lack of phonological motivation for the strong-class changes.

4.4.1. Hypersimilarity

The strong classes are often held together, if not exactly defined, by phonetic similarity. The most pervasive constraint is monosyllabism: 90% of the strong verbs are monosyllabic, and the rest are composed of a monosyllable combined with an unstressed and essentially meaningless prefix.[19]

---

[19]The polysyllabic strong verbs are:
arise, awake
become, befall, beget, begin, behold, beset, beshit, bespeak
forbear, forbid, forget, forgive, forgo, forsake, forswear, foretell
mistake
partake

(continued) →

Within the various classes, there are often significant additional resemblances holding between the members. Consider the following sample of typical classes, arranged by pattern of change in past and past participle ("*x–y–z*" will mean that the verb has the vowel *x* in its stem, *y* in its past tense form, and *z* in its past participle). Our judgments about the cited forms are indicated as follows: *?Verb* means that usage of the irregular past form of *Verb* is somewhat less natural than usual; *??Verb* means that *Verb* is archaic or recherché-sounding in the past tense.

(22) Some strong verb types
　　a.　　x - [u] - x(o)+n
　　　　　　　blow, grow, know, throw
　　　　　　　draw, withdraw
　　　　　　　fly
　　　　　　　??slay
　　b.　　[e] - [U] - [e]+en
　　　　　　　take, mistake, forsake, shake
　　c.　　[ay] - [aw] - [aw]
　　　　　　　bind, find, grind, wind
　　d.　　[d] - [t] - [t]
　　　　　　　bend, send, spend, ?lend, ??rend
　　　　　　　build
　　e.　　[ɛ] - [ɔ] - [ɔ]+n
　　　　　　　swear, tear, wear, ?bear, ??forswear, ??forbear
　　　　　　　get, forget, ??beget
　　　　　　　?tread

The members of these classes share much more than just a pattern of changes. In the *blow*-group (22a), for example, the stem-vowel becomes [u] in the past; this change could in principle apply to all sorts of stems, but in fact the participating stems are all vowel-final, and all but *know* begin with a CC cluster. In the *find*-group (22c) the vowel change [ay] → [aw] could apply to any stem in [ay], but it only applies to a few ending in [nd]. The change of [d] to [t] in (22d) occurs only after sonorants [n, l] and mostly when the stem rhymes in *-end*. Rhyming is also important in (22b), where every-

---

understand, undergo
upset
withdraw, withstand
The prefixes *a-, be-, for-, under-, with-* do not carry any particular meaning, nor in fact do most of the stems. (There is nothing about 'for' and 'get', for example, that helps us interpret *forget*.) Their independent existence in other forms is sufficient to support a sense of compositeness; see Aronoff (1976). As mentioned, this shows that morphology is in some sense a separate, abstract component of language.

thing ends in -*ake* (and the base also begins with a coronal consonant), and in (22e), where -*ear* has a run.

Most of the multi-verb classes in the system are in fact organized around clusters of words that rhyme and share other structural similarities, which we will call *hypersimilarities*. (The interested reader is referred to the Appendix for a complete listing.) The regular system shows no signs of such organization. As we have seen, the regular morpheme can add onto any phonetic form—even those most heavily tied to the strong system, as long as the lexical item involved is not a primary verb root.

4.4.2. *Prototypicality*

The strong classes often have a kind of prototypicality structure. Along the phonetic dimension, Bybee and Slobin (1982) point out that class cohesion can involve somewhat disjunctive 'family resemblances' rather than satisfaction of a strict set of criteria. In the *blow*-class (22a), for example, the central exemplars are *blow, grow, throw*, all of the form [CRo], where R is a sonorant. The verb *know* [no] lacks the initial C in the modern language, but otherwise behaves like the exemplars. The stems *draw* [drɔ] and *slay* [sle] fit a slightly generalized pattern [CRV] and take the generalized pattern x–u–x in place of o–u–o. The verb *fly* [flay] has the diphthong [ay] for the vowel slot in [CRV], which is unsurprising in the context of English phonology, but unlike *draw* and *slay* it takes the concrete pattern of changes in the exemplars: x–u–o rather than x–u–x. Finally, all take -*n* in the past participle.

Another kind of prototypicality has to do with the degree to which strong forms allow regular variants. (This need not correlate with phonetic centrality—notice that all the words in the *blow*-class are quite secure in their irregular status.) Consider the class of verbs which add -t and lax the stem-vowel:

(23) V: - V - V(+t)
      keep, sleep, sweep, weep (?weeped/wept), creep (?creeped/crept),
      leap (leaped/leapt)
      feel, deal (?dealed/dealt), kneel (kneeled/?knelt)
      mean
      dream (dreamed/?dreamt)
      leave
      lose

Notice the hypersimilarities uniting the class: the almost exclusive prevalence of the vowel [i]; the importance of the terminations [-ip] and [-il].

The parenthetical material contains coexisting variants of the past forms that, according to our judgments, are acceptable to varying degrees. The range of prototypicality runs from 'can only be strong' (*keep*) through 'may be either' (*leap*) to 'may possibly be strong' (*dream*). The source of such variability is probably the low but nonzero frequency of the irregular form, often due to the existence of conflicting but equally high-status dialects (see Bybee, 1985).

The regular system, on the other hand, does not have prototypical exemplars and does not have a gradient of variation of category membership defined by dimensions of similarity. For example, there appears to be no sense in which *walked* is a better or worse example of the past tense form of *walk* than *genuflected* is of *genuflect*. In the case at hand, there is no reason to assume that regular verbs such as *peep, reap* function as a particularly powerful attracting cluster, pulling *weep, creep, leap* away from irregularity. Historically, we can clearly see attraction in the opposite direction: according to the *OED, knelt* appears first in the 19th century; such regular verbs as *heal, peel, peal, reel, seal, squeal* failed to protect it; as regular forms they could not do so, on our account, because their phonetic similarity is not perceived as relevant to their choice of inflection, so they do not form an attracting cluster.

4.4.3. Lexicality

The behavior of low-frequency forms suggests that the stem and its strong past are actually regarded as distinct lexical items, while a regular stem and its inflected forms, no matter how rare, are regarded as expressions of a single item.

Consider the verb *forgo*: though uncommon, it retains a certain liveliness, particularly in the sarcastic phrase "forgo the pleasure of ...". The past tense must surely be *forwent* rather than **forgoed*, but it seems entirely unusable. Contrast the following example, due to Jane Grimshaw:

(24) a. *Last night I forwent the pleasure of grading student papers.
     b. You will excuse me if I forgo the pleasure of reading your paper until it's published.

Similarly but more subtly, we find a difference in naturalness between stem and past tense when the verbs *bear* and *stand* mean 'tolerate':

(25) a. I don't know how she bears it.
     b. (?) I don't know how she bore it.
     c. I don't know how she stands him.
     d. (?) I don't know how she stood him.

The verb *rend* enjoys a marginal subsistence in the phrase *rend the fabric of society*, yet the past seems slightly odd: *The Vietnam War rent the fabric of American society*. The implication is that familiarity can accrue differentially to stem and past tense forms; the use of one in a given context does not always entail the naturalness of the other.

This phenomenon appears to be absent from the regular system. There are regular verbs that are trapped in a narrow range of idioms, like *eke* in "eke out", *crook* in "crook one's finger", *stint* in "stint no effort", yet all inflected forms seem equivalent. Furthermore, rare or self-conscious verbs like *anastomose, fleech, fleer, incommode, prescind* show no further increment of oddness or uncertainty in the past tense. Suppose that it is only the items actually listed in the lexicon that gain familiarity, rather than each individual inflected form. If regular forms are rule-generated from a single listed item, then all forms should freely inherit statistics from each other. Irregular forms, on the other hand, listed because unpredictable, should be able to part company even if they belong to a single paradigm.

4.4.4. Failures of predictability

Even when a verb matches the characteristic patterns of any of the classes in the strong system, no matter how closely, there can be no guarantee that the verb will be strong. If the verb is strong, its similarity to the characteristic patterns of the subclasses cannot always predict which of these subclasses it will fall into. Verbs like *flow, glow, crow* are as similar to the words in the set *blow, grow, throw, know* as the members of the set are to each other; yet they remain regular. (Indeed, *crow* has turned regular in the last few hundred years.) As for subcategorization into one of the strong subclasses, consider the clear subregularity associated with the [I - æ - ʌ] and [I - ʌ - ʌ] vowel-change classes:

(26) a.   I - æ - ʌ
            ring, sing, spring
            drink, shrink, sink, stink
            swim
            begin, spin, win
            ⟨run⟩
     b.   I - ʌ - ʌ
            cling, sling, sting, string, swing, wring, fling (?flinged/flung),
            slink (slinked/?slunk)
            stick
            dig
            ⟨hang⟩

The core members of these related classes end in *-ing* and *-ink*. (Bybee and Slobin note the family resemblance structure here, whereby the hallmark 'velar nasal' accommodates mere nasals on the one side (*swim*, etc.) and mere velars on the other (*stick, dig*); the stems *run* and *hang* differ from the norm in a vowel feature or two, as well.) Interestingly, no primitive English monosyllabic verb root that ends in -*ing* is regular. Forms like *ding, ping, zing*, which show no attraction to class (26), are tainted by onomatopoetic origins; forms like *ring* (surround), *king* (as in checkers), and *wing* are obviously derived from nouns. Thus the -*ing* class of verbs is the closest we have in English to a class that can be uniformly and, possibly, productively, inflected with anything other than the regular ending. Nevertheless, even for this subclass it is impossible to predict the actual forms from the fact of irregularity: *ring–rang* contrasts with *wring–wrung*; *spring–sprang* with *string–strung*; and *bring* belongs to an entirely unrelated class. This observation indicates that learners can pick up the general distinction regular/irregular at some remove from the particular patterns.

The regular system, in contrast, offers complete predictability.

4.4.5. Lack of phonological motivation for morphological rules

The rules that determine the shape of the regular morphemes of English are examples of true phonological (or even phonetic) rules: they examine a narrow window of the string and make a small-scale change. Such rules have necessary and sufficient conditions, which must be satisfied by elements present in the window under examination in order for the rule to apply. The conditioning factors are intrinsically connected with the change performed. Voicelessness in the English suffixes directly reflects the voicelessness of the stem-final consonant. Insertion of the vowel *i* resolves the inadmissible adjacency of (what English speakers regard as) excessively similar consonants.

The relations between stem and past tense in the various strong verb classes are defined on phonological substance, but the factors affecting the relationship are not like those found in true phonological rules. In particular, the changes are for the most part entirely unmotivated by phonological conditions in the string. There is nothing in the environment *b_nd* that encourages [ay] to become [aw]; nothing about [CRo], the basic scheme of the *blow*- class, that causes a change to [CRu] or makes such a change more likely than in some other environment. These are arbitrary though easily definable changes tied arbitrarily to certain canonical forms, in order to mark an abstract morphological category: past tense. The patterns of similarity binding the classes together actually play no causal role in determining the changes that occur. A powerful association may exist, but it is merely conventional and could quite easily be otherwise (and indeed in the different dialects of the language spoken now or in the past, there are many different systems). Similarity relations serve essentially to qualify entry into a strong class rather than to provide an environment that causes a rule to happen.

There is one region of the strong system where discernibly phonological factors do play a role: the treatment of stems ending in [-t] and [-d]. No strong verb takes the suffix *id* (*bled/*bledded, got/*gotted*); the illicit cluster that would be created by suffixing /d/ is resolved instead by eliminating the suffix. This is a strategy that closely resembles the phonological process of degemination (simplification of identical adjacent consonants to a single consonant), which is active elsewhere in English. Nevertheless, if we examine the class of affected items, we see the same arbitrariness, prototypicality, and incomplete predictiveness we have found above. Consider the "no-change" class, which uses a single form for stem, past tense, and past participle—by far the largest single class of strong verbs, with about 25 members. In these examples, a word preceded by '?' has no natural-sounding past tense form in our dialect; words followed by two alternatives in parentheses have two possible forms, often with one of them (indicated by '?') worse-sounding than the other:

(27) No-change verbs

> hit, slit, split, quit, spit (spit/spat), knit (knitted/?knit), ?shit, ??beshit
> bid, rid
> shed, spread, wed
> let, set, upset, ?beset, wet (wetted/wet)
> cut, shut
> put
> burst, cast, cost
> thrust (thrusted/thrust), hurt

Although ending in [-t, d] is a necessary condition for no-change status, it is by no means sufficient. First of all, the general constraint of monosyllabism applies, even though it is irrelevant to degemination. Second, there is a strong favoritism for the vowels [I] and [ε], followed by a single consonant; again, this is of no conceivable relevance to a truly phonological process simplifying [td] and [dd] to [t] and [d]. Absent from the class, and under no attraction to it, are such verbs as *bat, chat, pat, scat,* as well as *jot, rot, spot, trot,* with the wrong sort of vocalism; and *dart, fart, smart, start, thwart, snort, sort, halt, pant, rant, want* with nonprototypical vowel and consonant structure. Even in the core class, we find arbitrary exceptions: *flit, twit, knit* are all regular, as are *fret, sweat, whet,* and some uses of *wet*. Beside strong *cut* and *shut*, we find regular *butt, jut, strut*. Beside *hurt* we find *blurt, spurt*; beside *burst,* we find regular *bust*. The phonological constraints on the class far exceed anything relevant to degemination, but in the end they characterize rather than define the class, just as we have come to expect.

Morphological classification responds to fairly large-scale measures on word structure: is the word a monosyllable? does it rhyme with a key exemplar? does it alliterate (begin with a similar consonant cluster) as an exemplar? Phonological rules look for different and much more local configurations: is this segment an obstruent that follows a voiceless consonant? are these adjacent consonants nearly identical in articulation? In many ways, the two vocabularies are kept distinct: we are not likely to find a morphological subclass holding together because its members each contain somewhere inside them a pair of adjacent obstruents; nor will we find a rule of voicing-spread that applies only in rhyming monosyllables. If an analytical engine is to generalize effectively over language data, it can ill afford to look upon morphological classification and phonological rules as processes of the same formal type.

4.4.6. Default structure

We have found major differences between the strong system and the regular system, supporting the view that the strong system is a cluster of irregular patterns, with only the -*ing* forms and perhaps the no-change forms displaying some active life as partially generalizable subregularities in the adult language. Membership in the strong system is governed by several criteria: (1) monosyllabism; (2) nonderived verb root status; (3) for the subregularities, resemblance to key exemplars. This means that the system is largely closed, particularly because verb roots very rarely enter the language (new verbs are common enough, but are usually derived from nouns, adjectives, or onomatopoetic expressions). At a few points in history, there have been borrowed items that have met all the criteria: *quit* and *cost* are both from French, for example (Jespersen, 1942). The regular system is free from such constraint. No canonical structure is required—for example, 'not a monosyllable'. No information about derivational status is required, such as 'must not be derived from an adjective'. Phonetic similarity to an exemplar plays no role either. Furthermore, the behavior of regular verbs is entirely predictable on general grounds. The regular rule of formation is an extremely simple default with very few characteristics of its own—perhaps only one, as we suggest above: that the morpheme is a stop rather than a fricative.

The regular system also has an internal default structure that is worthy of note, since it contrasts with the RM model's propensities. The rule Past = stem + /d/ covers all possible cases. Under narrowly defined circumstances, some phonology takes place: a vowel intrudes to separate stem and affix, voicelessness propagates from the stem. Elsewhere—the default case—nothing happens. It appears that language learners are fond of such architectures, which appear repeatedly in languages. (Indeed, in the history of English all inflection heads in this direction.) Yet the RM network, unlike the rule theory, offers us no insight. The network is equally able to learn a set of scattered, nonlocal, phonetically unrelated subregularities: for example, "suffix *t* if the word begins with *b*; prefix *ik* if the word ends in a vowel; change all *s*'s to *r* before *ta*"; etc. The RM model treats the regular class as a kind of fortuitously overpopulated subregularity; indeed, as three such classes, since the *d-t-id* alternation is treated on a par with the choice between strong subclasses. The extreme and categorical uniformity of the regular system disappears from sight, and with it the hope of identifying such uniformity as a benchmark of linguistic generalization.

4.4.7. Why are the regular and strong systems so different?

We have argued that the regular and strong systems have very different properties: the regular system obeys a categorical rule that is stated in a form that can apply to any word and that is adjusted only by very general phonological regularities; whereas the strong system consists of a set of subclasses held together by phonologically-unpredictable hypersimilarities which are neither necessary nor sufficient criteria for membership in the classes.

Why are they so different? We think the answer comes from the common-sense characterization of the psychological difference between regular and strong verbs. The past tense forms of strong verbs must be memorized; the past tense forms of regular verbs can be generated by rule. Thus the irregular forms are roughly where grammar leaves off and memory begins. Whatever affects human memory in general will shape the properties of the strong class, but not the regular class, by a kind of Darwinian selection process, because only the easily-memorized strong forms will survive. The 10 most frequent verbs of English are strong, and it has long been noted that as the frequency of a strong form declines historically, the verb becomes more likely to regularize. The standard explanation is that you can only learn a strong past by hearing it and only if you hear it often enough are you likely to remember it. However, it is important to note that the bulk of the strong verbs are of no more than middling frequency and some of them are actually rare, raising the question of how they managed to endure. The hypersimilarities and graded membership structure of the strong class might provide an answer. Rosch and Mervis (1975) note that conceptual categories, such as vegetables or tools, tend to consist of members with family resemblances to one another along a set of dimensions and graded membership determined by similarity to a prototype. They also showed in two experiments that it is easier for subjects to memorize the members of an artificial category if those members display a family resemblance structure than if they are grouped into categories arbitrarily. Since strong verbs, like Rosch and Mervis's artificial exemplars, must be learned one by one, it is reasonable to expect that the ones that survive, particularly in the middle and low frequencies, will be those displaying a family resemblance structure. In order words, the reason that strong verbs are either frequent or members of families is that strong verbs are memorized and frequency and family resemblance assist memorization.

The regular system must answer to an entirely different set of requirements: the rule must allow the user to compute the past tense form of any regular verb and so must be generally applicable, predictable in its output, and so on.

While it is possible that connectionist models of category formation (e.g. McClelland & Rumelhart, 1985) might offer insights into why family resemblance fosters category formation, it is the difference between fuzzy families of memorized exemplars and formal rules that the models leave unexplained.[20] Rumelhart and McClelland's failure to distinguish between mnemonics and productive morphology leads to the lowest-common-denominator 'uniformity' of accomplishing all change through arbitrary Wickelfeature replacement, and thus vitiates the use of psychological principles to explain linguistic regularities.

5. How good is the model's performance?

The bottom-line and most easily grasped claim of the RM model is that it succeeds at its assigned task: producing the correct past tense form. Rumelhart and McClelland are admirably open with their test data, so we can evaluate the model's achievement quite directly.

Rumelhart and McClelland submitted 72 new regular verbs to the trained model and submitted each of the resulting activated Wickelfeature vectors to the unconstrained whole-string binding network to obtain the analog of freely-generated responses. The model does not really 'decide' on a unique past tense form and stick with it thereafter; several candidates get strength values assigned to them, and Rumelhart and McClelland interpret those strength values as being related roughly monotonically to the likelihood the model would output those candidates. Since there is noise in some of the processes that contribute to strength values, they chose a threshold value (.2 on the 0–1 scale) and if a word surpassed that criterion, it was construed as being one of the model's guesses for the past tense form for a given stem. By this criterion, 24 of the 72 probe stems resulted in a strong tendency to incorrect responses—33% of the sample. Of these, 6 (*jump, pump, soak,*

---

[20]See Armstrong, Gleitman, and Gleitman (1983) for an analogous argument applied to conceptual categories.

warm, trail, glare) had no response at threshold. Though it is hard to reconstruct the reasons for this, two facts are worth noting. First, these verbs have no special resemblance to the apparently quasi-productive strong verb types—the factor that affects human responses. Second, the no-response verbs tend to cluster in phonetic similarity space either with one another (*jump, pump*) or with other verbs that the model erred on, discussed below (*soak/smoke; trail/mail; glare/tour*). This suggests that the reason for the model's muteness is that it failed to learn the relevant transformations; i.e. to generalize appropriately about the regular past. Apparently the steps taken to prevent the model from bogging down in insufficiently general case-by-case learning, such as blurring the Wickelfeatures and using noisy probabilistic output units during learning, did not work well enough.

But it also reveals one of the *inherent* deficits of the model we have alluded to: there is no such thing as a *variable* for *any* stem, regardless of its phonetic composition, and hence no way for the model to attain the knowledge that you can add /d/ to a "stem" to get its past. Rather, all the knowledge of the model consists of responses trained to the *concrete features in the training set*. If the new verbs happen not to share enough of these features with the words in the training set, or happen to possess features to which competing and mutually incompatible outputs had been associated, the model can fail to output any response significantly stronger than the background noise. The regular rule in symbolic accounts, in contrast, doesn't care what's in the word or how often its contents were submitted previously for training; the concept of a stem itself is sufficient. We return to this point when discussing some of the limitations of connectionist architecture in general.

Of the remaining 18 verbs for which the model did not output a single correct choice, 4 yielded grossly bizarre candidates:

(28) a.   squat - squakt
     b.   mail - membled
     c.   tour - toureder
     d.   mate - maded

Three other candidates were far off the systematic mark:

(29) a.   hug - hug
     b.   smoke - smoke
     c.   brown - brawned

Seven more showed a strong or exclusive tendency to double marking with the regular past tense morpheme (later we examine whether children make errors of this sort):

(30) a. type - typeded
    b. step - steppeded
    c. snap - snappeded
    d. map - mappeded
    e. drip - drippeded
    f. carp - carpeded
    g. smoke - smokeded

Note that the model shows an interesting tendency to make ill-advised vowel changes:

(31) a. shape - shipt
    b. sip - sept
    c. slip - slept
    d. brown - brawned
    e. mail - membled

Well before it has mastered the richly exemplified regular rule, the pattern-associator appears to have gained considerable confidence in certain incorrectly-grasped, sparsely exemplified patterns of feature-change among the vowels. This implies that a major "induction problem"—latching onto the productive patterns and bypassing the spurious ones—is not being solved successfully.

In sum, for 14 of the 18 stems yielding incorrect forms, the forms were quite removed from the confusions we might expect people to make. Taking these with the 6 no-shows, we have 20 out of the 72 test stems resulting in seriously wrong forms, a 28% failure rate. This is the state of the model after it has been trained 190–200 times on each item in a vocabulary of 336 regular verbs.

What we have here is not a model of the mature system.

6. On some common objections to arguments based on linguistic evidence

We have found that many psychologists and computer scientists feel uncomfortable about evidence of the sort we have discussed so far, concerning the ability of a model to attain the complex organization of a linguistic system in its mature state, and attempt to dismiss it for a variety of reasons. We consider the evidence crucial and decisive, and in this section we reproduce some of the objections we have heard and show why they are groundless.

"Those philosophical arguments are interesting, but it's really the empirical data that are important." All of the evidence we have discussed is empirical.

It is entirely conceivable that people could go around saying *What'z the answer?* or *He high-stuck the goalie* or *The canary pept* or *I don't know how she bore him* or *Yesterday we chat for an hour*, or that upon hearing such sentences, people could perceive them as sounding perfectly normal. In every case it is an empirical datum about the human brain that they don't. Any theory of the psychology of language must account for such data.

"*Rule-governed behaviors indeed exist, but they are the products of schooling or explicit instruction, and are deployed by people only when in a conscious, reflective, problem-solving mode of thought that is distinct from the intuitive processes that PDP models account for*" (see, for example, Smolensky, in press). This is completely wrong. The rule adding /d/ to a stem to form the past is not generally taught in school (it doesn't have to be!) except possibly as a rule of spelling, which if anything obscures its nature: for one thing, the plural morpheme, which is virtually identical to the past morpheme in its phonological behavior, is spelled differently ("s" versus "ed"). The more abstract principles we have discussed, such as distinctions between morphology and phonology, the role of roots in morphology, preservation of stem and affix identity, phonological processes that are oblivious to morphological origin, disjoint conditions for the application of morphological and phonological changes, distinct past tenses for homophones, interactions between the strong and regular systems, and so on, are consciously inaccessible and not to be found in descriptive grammars or language curricula. Many have only recently been adequately characterized; traditional prescriptive grammars tend to be oblivious to them or to treat them in a ham-fisted manner. For example, H.L. Mencken (1936) noted that people started to use the forms *broadcasted* and *joy-rided* in the 1920s (without consciously knowing it, they were adhering to the principle that irregularity is a property of verb roots, hence verbs formed from nouns are regular). The prescriptive guardians of the language made a fruitless attempt to instruct people explicitly to use *broadcast* and *joy-rode* instead, based on its similarity to *cast-cast* and *ride-rode*.

In fact, the objection gets the facts exactly backwards. One of the phenomena that the RM model is good at handling is unsystematic analogy formation based on its input history with subregular forms (as opposed to the automatic application of the regular rule where linguistically mandated). The irregular system, we have noted, is closely tied to memory as well as to language, so it turns out that people often have metalinguistic awareness of some of its patterns, especially since competing regular and irregular past tense forms carry different degrees of prestige and other socioeconomic connotations. Thus some of the fine points of use of the irregulars depend on exposure to standard dialects, on normative instruction, and on conscious reflection. Thus people, when in a reflective, conscious, problem-solving mode, will seem to act more like the RM model: the overapplication of subregularities that the model is prone to can be seen in modes of language use that bear all the hallmarks of self-conscious speech, such as jocularity (e.g. *spaghettus, I got schrod at Legal Seafood, The bear shat in the woods*), explicit instruction within a community of specialists (e.g. *VAXen* as the plural of *VAX*), pseudoerudition (*rhinoceri, axia* for *axioms*), and hypercorrection such as the anti-*broadcasted* campaign documented by Mencken (similarly, we found that some of our informants offered *Hurst no-hitted the Blue Jays* as their first guess as to the relevant past form but withdrew it in favor of *no-hit* which they "conceded" was "more proper").

"We academics speak in complex ways, but if you were to go down to [name of nearest working-class neighborhood] *you'd find that people talk very differently."* If anything is universal about language, it is probably people's tendency to denigrate the dialects of other ethnic or socioeconomic groups. One would hope that this prejudice is not taken seriously as a scientific argument; it has no basis in fact. The set of verbs that are irregular varies according to regional and socioeconomic dialect (see Mencken, 1936, for extensive lists), as does the character of the subregular patterns, but the principles organizing the system as a whole show no variation across classes or groups.

"Grammars may characterize some aspects of the ideal behavior of adults, but connectionist models are more consistent with the sloppiness found in children's speech and adult's speech errors, which are more 'psychological' phenomena." Putting aside until the next section the question of whether connectionist models really do provide a superior account of adult's or children's errors, it is important to recognize a crucial methodological asymmetry that this kind of objection fails to acknowledge. The ability to account for patterns of error is a useful criterion for evaluating competing theories *each of which can account for successful performance equally well*. But a theory that can *only* account for errorful or immature performance, with no account of why the errors are errors or how children mature into adults, is of limited value (Pinker, 1979, 1984; Wexler & Culicover, 1980; Gleitman & Wanner, 1982). (Imagine a "model" of the internal combustion engine that could mimic its ability to fail to start on cold mornings—by doing nothing—but could not mimic its ability to run, under any circumstances.)

Thus it is not legitimate to suggest, as Rumelhart and McClelland do, that "people—or at least children, even in early grade-school years—are not perfect rule-applying machines either. ... Thus we see little reason to believe that our model's 'deficiencies' are significantly greater than those of native speakers of comparable experience" (PDPII, p. 265–266). Unlike the RM model, no adult speaker is utterly stumped in an unpressured naturalistic situation when he or she needs to produce the past tense form of *soak* or *glare*, none vacillates between *kid* and *kidded*, none produces *membled* for *mailed* or *toureder* for *toured*. Although children equivocate in experimental tasks eliciting inflected nonce forms, these tasks are notorious for the degree to which they underestimate competence with the relevant phenomena (Levy, 1983; Maratsos et al., 1987; Pinker, Lebeaux, & Frost, 1987)—not to mention the fact that children do not remain children forever. The crucial point is that adults can speak without error and can realize that their errors are errors (by which we mean, needless to say, from the standpoint of the untaxed operation of their own system, not of a normative standard dialect). And children's learning culminates in adult knowledge. These are facts that any theory must account for.

7. The RM model and the facts of children's development

Rumelhart and McClelland stress that their model's ability to explain the developmental sequence of children's mastery of the past tense is the key point in favor of their model over traditional accounts. In particular, these facts are the "fine structure of the phenomena of language use and language acquisition" that their model is said to provide an exact account of, as opposed the traditional explanations which "leave out a great deal of detail", describing the phenomena only "approximately".

One immediate problem in assessing this claim is that there is no equally explicit model incorporating rules against which we can compare the RM model. Linguistic theories make no commitment as to how rules increase or decrease in relative strength during acquisition; this would have to be supplied by a learning mechanism that meshed with the assumptions about the representation of the rules. And theories discussed in the traditional literature of developmental psycholinguistics are far too vague and informal to yield the kinds of predictions that the RM model makes. There do exist explicit models of the acquisition of inflection, such as that outlined by Pinker (1984), but they tend to be complementary in scope to the RM model; the Pinker model, for example, attempts to account for how the child realizes that one word is the past tense version of another, and which of two competing past tense candidates is to be retained, which in the RM model is handled by the "teacher" or not at all, and relegates to a black box the process of abstracting the morphological and phonological changes relating past forms and stems, which is what the RM model is designed to learn.

The precision of the RM theory is surely a point in its favor, but it is still difficult to evaluate, for it is not obvious what features of the model give it its empirical successes. More important, it is not clear whether such features are consequences of the model's PDP architecture or simply attributes of fleshed-out processes that would function in the same way in any equally-explicit model of the acquisition process. In most cases Rumelhart and McClelland do not apportion credit or blame for the model's behavior to specific aspects of its operation; the model's output is compared against the data rather globally. In other cases the intelligence of the model is so distributed and its output mechanisms are so interactive that it is difficult for anyone to know what aspect of the model makes it successful. And in general, Rumelhart and McClelland do not present critical tests between competing hypotheses embodying minimally different assumptions, only descriptions of goodness of fit between their model and the data. In this section, we unpack the assumptions of the model, and show which ones are doing the work in accounting for the developmental facts—and whether the developmental facts are accounted for to begin with.

7.1. Unique and shared properties of networks and rule systems

Among the RM model's many properties, there are two that are crucial to its accounts of developmental phenomena. First, it has a learning mechanism that makes it *type-frequency sensitive*: the more verbs it encounters that embody a given type of morphophonological change, the stronger are its graded representations of that morphophonological change, and the greater is the tendency of the model to generalize that change to new input verbs. Furthermore, the different past tense versions of a word that would result from applying various regularities to it are computed in parallel and there is a *competition* among them for expression, whose outcome is determined mainly by the strength of the regularity and the goodness of the match between the regularity and the input. (In fact the outcome can also be a blend of competing responses, but the issue of response blending is complex enough for us to defer discussing it to a later section.)

It is crucial to realize that neither frequency-sensitivity nor competition is unique to PDP models. Internal representations that have graded strength values associated with them are probably as old as theories of learning in psychology; in particular, it is commonplace to have greater strength values assigned to representations that are more frequently exemplified in the input during learning, so that strength of a representation basically corresponds to degree of confidence in the hypothesis represented. Competition among candidate operations that partially match the input is also a ubiquitous assumption among symbol-processing models in linguistics and cognitive psychology. Spreading-activation models and production systems, which are prototypical symbol-processing models of cognition, are the clearest examples (see, e.g. Newell & Simon, 1972; Anderson, 1976, 1983; MacWhinney & Sokolov, 1987).

To show how these assumptions are part and parcel of standard rule-processing models, we will outline a simplified module for certain aspects of past tense acquisition, which searches for the correct past tense rule or rules, keeping several candidates as possibilities before it is done. We do not mean to propose it as a serious theory, but only as a demonstration that many of the empirical successes of the RM model are the result of assumptions about frequency-sensitivity and competition among output candidates that are independent of parallel distributed processing in networks of simple units.

A simple illustrative module of a rule-based inflection acquisition theory, incorporating assumptions about frequency-sensitivity and competition

Acquiring inflectional systems poses a number of tricky induction problems, discussed at length in Pinker (1984). When a child hears an inflected verb in a single context, it is utterly ambiguous what morphological category the inflection is signaling (the gender, number, person, or some combination of those agreement features for the subject? for the object? is it tense? aspect? modality? some combination of these?). Pinker (1984) suggested that the child solves this problem by "sampling" from the space of possible hypotheses defined by combinations of an innate finite set of elements, maintaining these hypotheses in the provisional grammar, and testing them against future uses of that inflection, expunging a hypothesis if it is counterexemplified by a future word. Eventually, all incorrect hypotheses about the category features encoded by that affix will be pruned, any correct one will be hypothesized, and only correct ones will survive.

The surviving features define the dimensions of a word-specific paradigm structure into whose cells the different inflected forms of a given verb are placed (for example, singular–plural or present–past–future). The system then seeks to form a productive general paradigm—that is, a set of rules for related inflections—by examining the patterns exhibited across the paradigms for the individual words. This poses a new induction problem because of the large number of possible generalizations consistent with the data, and it cannot be solved by examining a single word-specific paradigm or even a set of paradigms. For example, in examining *sleep/slept*, should one conclude that the regular rule of English laxes and lowers the vowel and adds a *t*? If so, does it do so for all stems or only for those ending in a stop, or only those whose stem vowel is *i*? Or is this simply an isolated irregular form, to be recorded individually with no contribution to the regular rule system? There is no way to solve the problem other than by trying out various hypotheses and seeing which ones survive when tested against the ever-growing vocabulary. Note that this induction problem is inherent to the task and cannot be escaped from using connectionist mechanisms or any other mechanisms; the RM model attempts to solve the problem in one way, by trying out a large number of hypotheses of a certain type in parallel.

A symbolic model would solve the problem using a mechanism that can formulate, provisionally maintain, test, and selectively expunge hypotheses about rules of various degrees of generality. It is this hypothesis-formation mechanism that the simplified module embodies. The module is based on five assumptions:

1. Candidates for rules are hypothesized by comparing base and past tense versions of a word, and factoring apart the changing portion, which serves as the rule operation, from certain morphologically-relevant phonological components of the stem, which serve to define the class of stems over which the operation can apply.[21] Specifically, let us assume that when the addition of material to the edge of a base form is noted, the added material is stored as an affix, and the provisional definition of the morphological class will consist of the features of the edge of the stem to which the affix is attached. When a vowel is noted to change, the change is recorded, and the applicable morphological class will be provisionally defined in terms of the features of the adjacent consonants. (In a more realistic model, global properties defining the "basic words" of a language, such as monosyllabicity in English, would also be extracted.)

2. If two rule candidates have been coined that have the same change operation, a single collapsed version is created, in which the phonological features distinguishing their class definitions are eliminated.

3. Rule candidates increase in strength each time they have been exemplified by an input pair.

4. When an input stem has to be processed by the system in its intermediate stages, an input is matched in parallel against all existing rule candidates, and if it falls into several classes, several past tense forms may be generated.

5. The outcome of a competition among the past tense forms is determined by the strength of the relevant rule and the proportion of a word's features that were matched by that rule.

___

[21]More accurately, the changing portion is examined subsequent to the subtraction of any phonological and phonetic changes that have been independently acquired.

The model works as follows. Imagine its first input pair is *speak/spoke*. The changing portion is $i \rightarrow o$. The provisional definition of the class to which such a rule would apply would be the features of the adjacent consonants, which we will abbreviate as p_k. Thus the candidate rule coined is (32a), which can be glossed as "change *i* to *o* for the class of words containing the features of /p/ before the vowel and containing the features of /k/ after the vowel". Of course, the candidate rule has such a specific class definition in the example that it is almost like listing the pair directly. Let us make the minimal assumptions about the strength function, and simply increase it by 1 every time a rule is exemplified. Thus the strength of this rule candidate is 1. Say the second input is *get/got*. The resulting rule candidate, with a strength of 1, is (32b). A regular input pair, *tip/tipped*, would yield (32c). Similarly, *sing/sang* would lead to (32d), and *hit/hit* would lead to (32e), each with unit strength,

(32) a.   Change: $i \rightarrow o$
            Class: p_k
      b.   Change: $e \rightarrow \mathfrak{o}$
            Class: g_t
      c.   Suffix: t
            Class: $p\#$
      d.   Change: $i \rightarrow æ$
            Class: $s\_ŋ$
      e.   Suffix: $\emptyset$
            Class: $t\#$
            Change: $i \rightarrow i$
            Class: h_t.[22]

Now we can examine the rule-collapsing process. A second regular input, *walk/walked*, would inspire the learner to coin the rule candidate (33a) which, because it shares the change operation of rule candidate (32c), would be collapsed with it to form a new rule (33b) of strength 2 (summing the strengths of its contributing rules, or equivalently, the number of times it has been exemplified).

---

[22]Let us assume that it is unclear to the child at this point whether there is a null vowel change or a null affix, so both are stored. Actually, we don't think either is accurate, but it will do for the present example.

(33) a.   Suffix: t
           Class: k#

     b.   Suffix: t
           Class: C   #
                       [-voiced]
                       [-continuant]
                       [-sonorant]

The context-collapsing operation has left the symbol "C" (for consonant) and its three phonological features as the common material in the definitions of the two previously distinct provisional classes.

Now consider the results of a third regular input, *pace/paced*. First, a fairly word-specific rule (34a) would be coined; then it would be collapsed with the existing rule (33) with which it shares a change operation, yielding a rule (34b) with strength 3.

(34) a.   Suffix: t
           Class: s#

     b.   Suffix; t
           Class: C   #
                       [-voiced]

Rule candidates based on subregularities would also benefit from the increases in strength that would result from the multiple input types exemplifying it. For example, when the pair *ring/rang* is processed, it would contribute (35a), which would then be collapsed with (32d) to form (35b). Similar collapsing would strengthen other subregularities as tentative rule candidates, such as the null affix.

(35) a.   Change: i → a
           Class: r_ŋ
     b.   Change: i → a
           Class: C_ŋ

Though this model is ridiculously simple, one can immediately see that it has several things in common with the RM model. First, regularities, certain subregularities, and irregular alternations are extracted, to be entertained as possible rules, by the same mechanism. Second, mechanisms embodying the different regularities accrue strength values that are monotonically related to the number of inputs that exemplify them. Third, the model can generalize to new inputs that resemble those it has encountered in the past; for example, *tick*, which terminates in an unvoiced stop, matches the context of rule (34b), and the rule can add a /t/ to the end of it as a result to form *ticked*. Fourth, a new input can match several rules at the same time. For example, *bet* will match one rule candidate because it ends in an unvoiced stop and it will match another because it ends in *t*. The exact strengths of the competing alternatives will depend on the strengths of the candidate rules and on the goodness of match between the stem and the class definitions associated with the rules.[23]

This candidate-hypothesization module can only be part of the mechanism that acquires the past tense system. Other mechanisms or principles, such as those discussed in Pinker (1984), must evaluate the rule candidates and eliminate the incorrect ones, such as those that simply characterize lists of similar strong forms, and must retain any genuine rules in a general paradigm. As noted in Section 4.4, regular rules are distinguished by applying in the default or "elsewhere" case. One can imagine the following learning strategy, which can be called the "Nonexceptional Exceptions to Exceptions Strategy", that would discover regular rules using this criterion. Comparing the acquired stem-past pairs whose first member contains *eep*, the child would notice that there are many exceptions to the tentative *eep* → *ept* rule candidate and that most of the exceptions to it themselves follow the pattern holding of verbs whose present forms do not contain *eep* (*seeped, peeped, steeped, beeped*, etc.). Furthermore, exceptions to other subregularities such as *bend/bent*–*lend/lent* will also largely obey the pattern holding of verbs lacking *end* (*end/ended, fend/fended, mend/mended*, etc.). Thus, within the child's lexicon one regularity, the addition of /d/, knows no phonological bounds, and can potentially apply to any base form, whereas this is not true of any other regularity. In this way, some regularities can be enshrined as permanent productive rules whereas others can be discarded or treated differently.

Other constraints contributed by other principles and components of grammar would also influence the extraction and sorting of putative rules. For example, the syntax and lexicon would segregate derived forms out of these

---

[23]Note also that the strongest output among competing candidates for the past form of a given verb could change as a function of the input history of the model. For example, during the first five inputs the only output for *speak* would be its irregular past *spoke*. After the sixth input, the regularized past version *speaked* would also be provided, by rule (34b), though the strength of this output would be low because the regular rule would not be strong enough to overcome the strength of the irregular form resulting from its very close match to (32a). If candidate strength is equal to [proportion of stem features matched × strength of matching rule], the irregular output would have a strength of (.75 × 1) = .75, whereas the regular rule would have, say (.2 × 2) = .4 (the exact numbers are not crucial here). However, after a number of inputs, the regular rule has increased in strength to 4, and so the strength of *speaked* would be (.2 × 4) = .8, making it stronger than the irregular form *hit*. In this way, a rule-finding module could overgeneralize in its intermediate stages, erring on verbs that it previously handled properly, for similar reasons that the phenomenon occurs in the RM model. Later we examine whether this is the correct explanation for children's behavior.

calculations, and the phonology would subtract out modifications abstracted from consonant clusters of simple words and perhaps from sets of morphologically unrelated rules. Finally, the general regular paradigm would be used when needed to fill out empty cells of word-specific paradigms with a unique entry, while following the constraint that irregular forms in memory block the product of the regular rule, and only a single form can be generated for a specific stem when more than one productive rule applies to it (multiple entries can exist only when the irregular form is too weakly represented, or when both multiple forms are witnessed in the input; see Pinker, 1984).

Though both our candidate-hypothesization module and the RM model share certain properties, let us be clear about the differences. The RM model is designed to account for the entire process that maps stems to past tense forms, with no interpretable subcomponents, and few constraints on the regularities that can be recorded. The candidate-hypothesization module, on the other hand, is meant to be a part of a larger system, and its outputs, namely rule candidates, are symbolic structures that can be examined, modified or filtered out by other components of grammar. For example, the phonological acquisition mechanism can note the similarities between t/d/ɨd and s/z/ɨz and pull out the common phonological regularities, which would be impossible if those allomorphic regularities were distributed across a set of connection weights onto which countless other regularities were superimposed.

It is also important to note that, as we have mentioned, the candidate-hypothesization module is motivated by a requirement of the learnability task facing the child. Specifically, the child at birth does not know whether English has a regular rule, or if it does, what it is or whether it has one or several. He or she must examine the input evidence, consisting of pairs of present and past forms acquired individually, to decide. But the evidence is locally ambiguous in that the nonproductive exceptions to the regular rule are not a random set but display some regularities for historical reasons (such as multiple borrowings from other languages or dialects, or rules that have ceased to be productive) and psychological reasons (easily-memorized forms fall into family resemblance structures). So the child must distinguish real from apparent regularities. Furthermore, there is the intermediate case presented by languages that have several productive rules applying to different classes of stems. The "learnability problem" for the child is to distinguish these cases. Before succeeding, the child must entertain a number of candidates for the regular rule or rules, because it is only by examining large sets of present-past pairs that the spurious regularities can be ruled out and the partially-productive ones assigned to their proper domains; small samples are always ambiguous in this regard. Thus a child who has not yet solved the problem of distinguishing general productive rules from restricted productive rules from accidental patterns will have a number of candidate regularities still open as hypotheses. At this stage there will be competing options for the past tense form of a given verb. The child who *has not yet figured out* the distinction between regular, subregular, and idiosyncratic cases will display behavior that is similar to a system that is *incapable of making* the distinction—the RM model.

In sum, any adequate rule-based theory will have to contain a module that extracts multiple regularities at several levels of generality, assign them strengths related to their frequency of exemplification by input verbs, and let them compete in generating a past tense form for a given verb. In addition, such a model can attain the adult state by feeding its candidates into paradigm-organization processes, which, following linguistic constraints, distinguish real generalizations from spurious ones. With this alternative model in mind, we can now examine which aspects of the developmental data are attributable to specific features of the RM model's parallel distributed processing architecture—specifically, to its collapsing of linguistic distinctions—and those which are attributable to its assumptions of graded strength, type-frequency sensitivity, and competition which it shares with symbolic alternatives.

7.2. Developmental phenomena claimed to support the Rumelhart–McClelland model

The RM model is, as the authors point out, very rich in its empirical predictions. It is a strong point of their model that it provides accounts for several independent phenomena, all but one of them unanticipated when the model was designed. They consider four phenomena in detail: (1) the U-shaped curve representing the overregularization of strong verbs whose regular pasts the child had previously used properly; (2) The fact that verbs ending in *t* or *d* (e.g. *hit*) are regularized less often than other verbs; (3) The order of acquisition of the different classes of irregular verbs manifesting different subregularities; (4) The appearance during the course of development of [past + *ed*] errors such as *ated* in addition to [stem + *ed*] errors such as *eated*.

7.2.1. Developmental sequence of productive inflection (the "U"-shaped curve)

It is by now well-documented that children pass through two stages before attaining adult competence in handling the past tense in English. In the first stage, they use a variety of correct past tense forms, both irregular and regular, and do not readily apply the regular past tense morpheme to nonce words presented in experimental situations. In the second stage, they apply the past tense morpheme productively to irregular verbs, yielding overregularizations such as *hitted* and *breaked* for verbs that they may have used exclusively in their correct forms during the earlier stage. Correct and overregularized forms coexist for an extended period of time in this stage, and at some point during that stage, children demonstrate the ability to apply inflections to nonce forms in experimental settings. Gradually, irregular past tense forms that the child continues to hear in the input drive out the overregularized forms he or she has created productively, resulting in the adult state where a productive rule coexists with exceptions (see Berko, 1958; Brown, 1973; Cazden, 1968; Ervin, 1964; Kuczaj, 1977, 1981).

A standard account of this sequence is that in the first stage, with no knowledge of the distinction between present and past forms, and no knowledge of what the regularities are in the adult language that relate them, the child is simply memorizing present and past tense forms directly from the input. He or she correctly uses irregular forms because the overregularized forms do not appear in the input and there is no productive rule yet. Regular past tenses are acquired in the same way, with no analysis of them into a stem plus an inflection. Using mechanisms such as those sketched in the preceding section, the child builds a productive rule and can apply it to any stem, including stems of irregular verbs. Because the child will have had the opportunity to memorize irregular pasts before relating stems to their corresponding pasts and before the evidence for the regular relationship between the two has accumulated across inputs, correct usage can in many cases precede overregularization. The adult state results from a realization, which may occur at different times for different verbs, that overregularized and irregular forms are both past tense versions of a given stem, and by the application of a Uniqueness principle that, roughly, allows the cells of an inflectional paradigm for a given verb to be filled by no more and no less than one entry, which is the entry witnessed in the input if there are competing nonwitnessed rule-generated forms and witnessed irregulars (see Pinker, 1984).

The RM model also has the ability to produce an arbitrary past tense form for a given present when they have been exemplified in the input, and to generate regular past tense forms for the same verbs by adding -*ed*. Of course, it does so without distinct mechanisms of rote and rule. In early stages, the links between the Wickelfeatures of a base irregular form and the Wickelfeatures of its past form are given higher weights. However, as a diverse set of regular forms begins to stream in, links are strengthened between a large set of input Wickelfeatures and the output Wickelfeatures containing features of the regular past morpheme, enough to make the regularized form a stronger output than the irregular form. During the overregularization stage, "the past tenses of similar verbs they are learning show such a consistent pattern that the generalization from these similar verbs outweighs the relatively small amount of learning that has occurred on the irregular verb in question" (PDPII, p. 268). The irregular form eventually returns as the strongest output because repeated presentations of it cause the network to tune the connection weights so that the Wickelfeatures that are specific to the irregular stem form (and to similar irregular forms manifesting the same kind of stem-past variation) are linked more and more strongly to the Wickelfeatures specific to their past forms, and develop strong negative weights to the Wickelfeatures corresponding to the regular morpheme. That is, the prevalence of a general pattern across a large set of verbs trades off against the repeated presentation of a single specific pattern of a single verb presented many times (with subregularities constituting an intermediate case). This gives the model the ability to be either conservative (correct for an irregular verb) or productive (overregularizing an irregular verb) for a given stem, depending on the mixture of inputs it has received up to a given point.

Since the model's tendency to generalize lies on a continuum, any sequence of stages of correct irregulars or overregularized irregulars is possible in principle, depending on the model's input history. How, then, is the specific shift shown by children, from correct irregular forms to a combination of overregularized and correct forms, mimicked by the model? Rumelhart and McClelland divide the training sequence presented to the model into two stages. In the first, they presented 10 high-frequency verbs to the model, 2 of them regular, 10 times each. In the second, they added 410 verbs to this sample, 334 of them regular, and presented the sample of 420 verbs 190 times. The beginning of the downward arm of the U-shaped plot of percent correct versus time, representing a worsening of performance for the irregular verbs, occurs exactly at the boundary between the first set of inputs and the second. The sudden influx of regular forms causes the links capturing the regular pattern to increase in strength; prior to this influx, the regular pattern was exemplified by only two input forms, not many more than those exemplifying any of the idiosyncratic or subregular patterns. The shift from the first to the second stage of the model's behavior, then, is a direct consequence of a shift in the input mixture from a heterogeneous collection of patterns to a collection in which the regular pattern occurs in the majority.

It is important to realize the theoretical claim inherent in this demonstration. *The model's shift from correct to overregularized forms does not emerge from any endogenous process; it is driven directly by shifts in the environment.* Given a different environment (say, one in which heterogeneous irregular forms suddenly start to outnumber regular forms), it appears that the model could just as easily go in the opposite direction, regularizing in its first stage and then becoming accurate with the irregular forms. In fact, since the model always has the potential to be conservative or rule-governed, and continuously tunes itself to the input, it appears that just about any shape of curve at all is possible, given the right shifts in the mixture of regular and irregular forms in the input.

Thus if the model is to serve as a theory of children's language acquisition, Rumelhart and McClelland must attribute children's transition between the first and second stage to a prior transition of the mixture of regular and irregular inputs from the external environment. They conjecture that such a transition might occur because irregular verbs tend to be high in frequency. "Our conception of the nature of [the child's] experience is simply that the child learns first about the present and past tenses of the highest frequency verbs; later on, learning occurs for a much larger ensemble of verbs, including a much larger proportion of regular forms" (p. 241). They concede that there is no abrupt shift in the input to the child, but suggest that children's acquisition of the present tense forms of verbs serves as a kind of filter for the past tense learning mechanism, and that this acquisition of base forms undergoes an explosive growth at a certain stage of development. Because the newly-acquired verbs are numerous and presumably lower in frequency than the small set of early-acquired verbs, it will include a much higher proportion of regular verbs. Thus the shift in the proportion of regular verbs in the input to the model comes about as a consequence of a shift from high frequency to medium frequency verbs; Rumelhart and McClelland do not have to adjust the leanness or richness of the input mixture by hand.

The shift in the model's input thus is not entirely ad hoc, but is it realistic? The use of frequency counts of verbs in written samples in order to model children's vocabulary development is, of course, tenuous.[24] To determine whether the input to children's past tense learning shifts in the manner assumed by Rumelhart and McClelland, we examined Roger Brown's unpublished grammars summarizing samples of 713 utterances of the spontaneous speech of three children observed at five stages of development. The stages were defined in terms of equally spaced intervals of the children's Mean Length of Utterance (MLU). Each grammar includes an exhaustive list of the child's verbs in the sample, and an explicit discussion of whether the child

---

[24]For example, in the Kucera and Francis (1967) counts used by Rumelhart and McClelland, medium frequencies are assigned to the verbs *flee*, *seek*, *mislead* and *arise*, which are going to be absent from a young child's vocabulary. On the other hand *stick* and *tear*, which play a significant role in the ecology of early childhood, are ranked as low-frequency. *Be* and *do* are not in the high-frequency group, where they belong— *do* belongs because of its ubiquity in questions, a fact not reflected in the written language. *Be* appears to be out of the study, perhaps because Rumelhart and McClelland count the frequency of the *-ing* forms.

was overregularizing the past tense rule.[25] In addition, we examined the vocabulary of Lisa, the subject of a longitudinal language acquisition study at Brandeis University, in her one-word stage. Two of the children, Adam and Eve, began to overregularize in the Stage III sample; the third child, Sarah, began to overregularize only in the State V sample except for the single form *heared* appearing in Stage II which Brown noted might simply be one of Sarah's many cases of unusual pronunciations. We tabulated the size of each child's verb vocabulary and the proportion of verbs that were regular at each stage.[26]

The results, shown in Table 1 and Figure 2, are revealing. The percentage of the children's verbs that are regular is remarkably stable across children and across stages, never veering very far from 50%. (This is also true in parental speech itself: Slobin, 1971, showed that the percentage of regular verbs in Eve's parents' speech during the period in which she was overregularizing was 43%.) In particular, there is no hint of a consistent increase in the proportion of regular verbs prior to or in the stage at which regularizations first occur. Note also that an explosive growth in vocabulary does not invariably precede the onset of regularization. This stands in stark contrast to the assumed input to the RM model, where the onset of overregularization occurs subsequent to a sudden shift in the proportion of regular forms in the input from 20% to 80%. Neither the extreme rarity of regular forms during the conservative stage, nor the extreme prevalence of regular forms during the overproductive stage, nor the sudden transition from one input mixture to another, can be seen in human children. The explanation for their developmental sequence must lie elsewhere.

We expect that this phenomenon is quite general. The plural in English, for example, is overwhelmingly regular even among high-frequency nouns:[27] only 4 out of the 25 most frequent concrete count nouns in the Francis and Kucera (1982) corpus are irregular. Since there are so few irregular plurals, children are never in a stage in which irregulars strongly outnumber regulars

---

[25]For details of the study, see Brown (1973); for descriptions of the unpublished grammars, see Brown (1973) and Pinker (1984). Verification of some of the details reported in the grammars, and additional analyses of children's speech to be reported in this paper, were based on on-line transcripts of the speech of the Brown children included in the Child Language Data Exchange System; MacWhinney & Snow (1985).

[26]A verb was counted whether it appeared in the present, progressive, or past tense form, and was counted only once if it appeared in more than one form. Since most of the verbs were in the present, this is of little consequence. We counted a verb once across its appearances alone and with various particles since past tense inflection is independent of these differences. We excluded modal pairs such as *can/could* since they only occasionally encode a present/past contrast for adults. We excluded catenative verbs that encode tense and mood in English and hence which do not have obvious past tenses such as in *going to*, *come on*, and *gimme*.

[27]We are grateful to Maryellen McDonald for this point.

Table 1.   *Proportion of children's verbs that have regular past tense forms*

		Stage				
	1-Word	I	II	III	IV	V
Adam	–	.45(31)	.43(44)*	.55(83)	.46(83)	.54(78)
Eve	–	.55(31)	.51(49)*	.45(53)	.48(58)	.44(45)
Sarah	–	.61(18)	.37(49)	.52(44)	.43(58)	.51(84)*
Lisa	.53(53)	–	–	–	–	–
Mean for Adam, Eve, & Sarah		.54	.44	.51	.46	.50

Note: Size of verb vocabulary is listed in parentheses. An asterisk indicates the stage at which the child began overregularizing.

Figure 2.   *The percentage of verbs that are regular in four children's vocabularies at different stages (as defined by Brown, 1973). The predictions of the Rumelhart–McClelland model are shown for comparison purposes, under the assumption that regularization begins in Stage III.* Key: —*— Adam, —⊖— Eve, —⊟— Sarah, —△— Lisa, —— Rumelhart–McClelland Model.

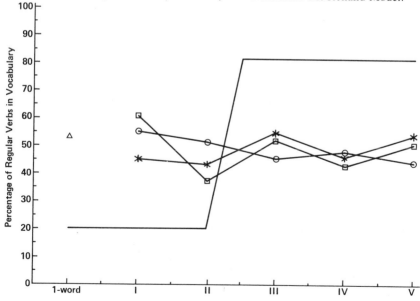

in the input or in their vocabulary of noun stems. Nonetheless, the U-shaped developmental sequence can be observed in the development of plural inflection in the speech of the Brown children: for example, Adam said *feet* nine times in the samples starting at age 2;4 before he used *foots* for the first time at age 3;9; Sarah used *feet* 18 times starting at 2;9 before uttering *foots* at 5;1; Eve uttered *feet* a number of times but never *foots*.

Examining *token* frequencies only underlines the unnaturally favorable assumptions about the input used in the RM model's training run. Not only does the transition from conservatism to overregularization correspond to a shift from a 20/80 to an 80/20 ratio of regulars to irregulars, but in the first, conservative phase, high-frequency irregular pairs such as *go/went* and *make/ made* were only presented 10 times each, whereas in the overregularizing phase the hundreds of regular verbs were presented 190 times each. In contrast, irregular verbs are always much higher in token frequency in children's environment. Slobin (1971) performed an exhaustive analysis of the verbs heard by Eve in 49 hours of adults' speech during the phase in which she was overregularizing and found that the ratio of irregular to regular tokens was 3:1. Similarly, in Brown's smaller samples, the ratios were 2.5:1 for Adam's parents, 5:1 for Eve's parents, and 3.5:1 for Sarah's parents. One wonders whether presenting the RM model with 10 high-frequency verbs, say, 190 times each in the first phase could have burned in the 8 irregulars so strongly that they would never be overregularized in Phase 2.

If children's transition from the first to the second phase is not driven by a change in their environments or in their vocabularies, what causes it? One possibility is that a core assumption of the RM model, that there is no psychological reality to the distinction between rule-generated and memorized forms, is mistaken. Children might have the capacity to memorize independent present and past forms from the beginning, but a second mechanism that coins and applies rules might not go into operation until some maturational change put it into place, or until the number of verbs exemplifying a rule exceeded a threshold. Naturally, this is not the only possible explanation. An alternative is that the juxtaposition mechanism that relates each stem to its corresponding past tense form has not yet succeeded in pairing up memorized stems and past forms in the child's initial stage. No learning of the past tense regularities has begun because there are no stem-past input pairs that can be fed into the learning mechanism; individually acquired independent forms are the only possibility.

Some of the evidence supports this alternative. Brown notes in the grammars that children frequently used the present tense form in contexts that clearly called for the past, and in one instance did the reverse. As the children developed, past tense forms were used when called for more often, and evidence for an understanding of the function of the past tense form and the tendency to overregularize both increase. Kuczaj (1977) provides more precise evidence from a cross-sectional study of 14 children. He concluded that once children begin to regularize they rarely use a present tense form of an irregular verb in contexts where a past is called for.

The general point is that in either case *the RM model does not explain children's developmental shift from conservatism to regularization. It attempts to do so only by making assumptions about extreme shifts in the input to rule learning that turn out to be false.* Either rules and stored forms are distinct, or some process other than extraction of morphophonological regularity explains the developmental shift. The process of coming to recognize that two forms constitute the present and past tense variants of the same verb, that is, the juxtaposition process, seems to be the most likely candidate.

Little needs to be said about the shift from the second stage, in which regularization and overregularization occurs, to the third (adult) stage, in which application of the regular rule and storage of irregular pasts cooccur. Though the model does overcome its tendency to overregularize previously acquired irregular verbs, we have shown in a previous section that it never properly attains the third stage. This stage is attained, we suggest, not by incremental strength changes in a pattern-finding mechanism, but by a mechanism that makes categorical decisions about whether a hypothesized rule candidate is a genuine productive rule and about whether to apply it to a given verb.

On the psychological reality of the memorized/rule-generated distinction. In discussing the developmental shift to regularization, we have shown that there can be developmental consequences of the conclusion that was forced upon us by the linguistic data, namely that rule-learning and memorization of individual forms are separate mechanisms. (In particular, we pointed out that one might mature before the other, or one requires prior learning—juxtaposing stems and past forms—and the other does not.) This illustrates a more general point: the psychological reality of the memorized/rule-generated distinction predicts the possibility of finding dissociations between the two processes, whereas a theory such as Rumelhart and McClelland's that denies that reality predicts that such dissociations should not be found. The developmental facts are clearly on the side of there being such a distinction.

First of all, children's behavior with irregular past forms during the first, pre-regularization phase bears all the signs of rote memorization, rather than a tentatively overspecific mapping from a specific set of stem features to a specific set of past features. Brown notes, for example, that Adam used *fell-down* 10 times in the Stage II sample without ever using *fall* or *falling*, so his production of *fell-down* cannot be attributed to any sort of mapping at all from stem to past. Moreover there is no hint in this phase of any interaction or transfer of learning across phonetically similar individual irregular forms: for example, in Sarah's speech, *break/broke* coexisted with *make/made* and neither had any influence on *take*, which lacked a past form of any sort in her speech over several stages. Similar patterns can be found in the other children's speech.

A clear example of a dissociation between rote and rule over a span in which they coexist comes from Kuczaj (1977), who showed that children's mastery of irregular past tense forms was best predicted by their chronological age, but their mastery of regular past tense forms was best predicted by their Mean Length of Utterance. Brown (1973) showed that MLU correlates highly with a variety of measures of grammatical sophistication in children acquiring English. Kuczaj's logic was that irregular pasts are simply memorized, so the sheer number of exposures, which increases as the child lives longer, is the crucial factor, whereas regular pasts can be formed by the application of a rule, which must be induced as part of the child's developing grammar, so overall grammatical development is a better predictor. Thus the linguistic distinction between lists of exceptions and rule-generated forms (see Section 4.4) is paralleled by a developmental distinction between opportunities for list-learning and sophistication of a rule system.

Another possible dissociation might be found in individual differences. A number of investigators of child language have noted that some children are conservative producers of memorized forms whereas others are far more willing to generalize productively. For example, Cazden (1968) notes that "Adam was more prone to overgeneralizations than Eve and Sarah" (p. 447), an observation also made by Brown in his unpublished grammars. More specifically, Table 1 shows that Sarah began to regularize the past tense two stages later than the other two children despite comparable verb vocabularies. Maratsos et al. (1987) documented many individual differences in the willingness of children to overgeneralize the causative alternation. If such differences do not reflect differences in the children's environments or vocabularies (they don't in the case of the past tense), presumably they result from the generalizing mechanism of some children being stronger or more developed than that of others, without comparable differences in their ability to record forms directly from the input. The RM model cannot easily account for any of these dissociations (other than by attributing crucial aspects of the generalization phenomena to mechanisms entirely outside their model), because memorized forms and generalizations are handled by a single mechanism—recall that the identity map in the network must be learned by adjusting a large set of connection weights, just like any of the stem alterations; it is not there at the outset, and is not intrinsically easy to learn.

The question is not closed, but the point is that the different theories can in principle be submitted to decisive empirical tests. It is such tests that should be the basis for debate on the psychological issue at hand. Simply demonstrating that there exist contrived environments in which a network model can be made to mimic some data, especially in the absence of comparisons to alternative models, tells us nothing about the psychology of the child.

7.2.2. Performance with no-change verbs

A class of English verbs does not change in form between stem and past: *beat, cut, put, hit*, and others. All of these verbs end in a *t* or *d*. Bybee and Slobin (1982) suggest that this is no coincidence. They suggest that learners generate a schema for the form of past tense verbs on the basis of prevalent regular forms which states that past tense verbs end in *t* or *d*. A verb whose stem already ends in *t* or *d* spuriously appears to have already been inflected for past tense, and the child is likely to assume that it *is* a past tense form. As a result, it can be entered as the past version of the verb in the child's paradigm, blocking the output of the regular rule. Presumably this tendency could result in the unchanged verb surviving into adulthood, causing the no-change verbs to have entered in the language at large in some past generation and to be easily relearned thereafter. We will call this phenomenon *misperception*.[28]

In support of this hypothesis, Bybee and Slobin found in an elicitation experiment that for verbs ending in *t* or *d*, children were more likely to produce a past tense form identical to the present than a regularized form, whereas for verbs not ending in a *t* or *d*, they were more likely to produce a regularized form than an unchanged form. In addition, Kuczaj (1978) found in a judgment task that children were more likely to accept correct no-change forms for nonchanging verbs than correct past tense forms for other irregular verbs such as *break* or *send*, and less likely to accept overregularized versions of no-change verbs than overregularized versions of other irregular verbs. Thus not only do children learn that verbs ending in *t/d* are likely to be unchanged, but this subregularity is easier for them to acquire than the kinds of changes such as the vowel alternations found in other classes of irregular verbs.

Unlike the three-stage developmental sequence for regularization, chil-

---

[28]Bybee and Slobin do not literally propose that the child mis*analyzes* *t/d*-final verbs as (nonexistent) stems inflected by a rule. Rather, they postulate a static template which the child matches against unanalyzed forms during word perception to decide whether the forms are in the past tense or not.

dren's sensitivity to the no-change subregularity for verbs ending in t/d played no role in the design of the RM model or of its simulation run. Nonetheless, Rumelhart and McClelland point out that during the phase in which the model was overregularizing, it produced stronger regularized past tense candidates for verbs not ending in t/d than for verbs ending in t/d, and stronger unchanged past candidates for verbs ending in t/d than for verbs not ending in t/d. This was true not only across the board, but also within the class of regular verbs, and within the classes of irregular verbs that do change in the past tense, for which no-change responses are incorrect. Furthermore, when Rumelhart and McClelland examined the total past tense response of the network (that is, the set of Wickelfeatures activated in the response pool) for verbs in the different irregular subclasses, they found that the no-change verbs resulted in fewer incorrectly activated Wickelfeatures than the other classes of irregulars. Thus both aspects of the acquisition of the no-change pattern fall out of the model with no extra assumptions.

Why does the model display this behavior? Because the results of its learning are distributed over hundreds of thousands of connection weights, it is hard to tell, and Rumelhart and McClelland do not try to tease apart the various possible causal factors. Misperception cannot be the explanation because the model always received correct stem-past pairs. There are two other possibilities. One is that connections from many Wickelfeatures to the Wickelfeatures for word-final t, and the thresholds for those Wickelfeatures, have been affected by the many *regular* stem-past pairs fed into the model. The response of the model is a blend of the operation of all the learned subregularities, so there might be some transfer from regular learning in this case. For example, the final Wickelphone in the correct past tense form of *hit*, namely *it#*, shares many of its Wickelfeatures with those of the regular past tense allomorphs such as *id#*. Let us call this effect *between-class transfer*.

It is important to note that much of the between-class transfer effect may be a consequence—perhaps even an artifact—of the Wickelfeature representation and one of the measures defined over it, namely percentage of incorrect Wickelfeatures activated in the output. Imagine that the model's learning component actually treated no-change verbs and other kinds of verbs identically, generating Wickelfeature sets of equal strength for *cutted* and *taked*. Necessarily, *taked* must contain more incorrect Wickelfeatures than *cutted*: most of the Wickelfeatures that one would regard as "incorrect" for *cutted*, such as those that correspond to the Wickelphone *tid* and *id#*, happen to characterize the *stem* perfectly (StopVowelStop, InterruptedFrontInterrupted, etc.), because *cut* and *ted* are featurally very similar. On the other hand, the incorrect Wickelfeatures for *taked* (those corresponding to Wickelphones *Akt* and *kt#*) will not characterize the correct output form *took*. This

effect is exaggerated further by the fact that there are many more Wickelfeatures representing word boundaries than representing the same phonemes
string-internally, as Lachter and Bever (1988) point out (recall that the Wickelfeature set was trimmed so as to exclude those whose two context
phonemes belonged to different phonological dimensions—since the word-
boundary feature # has no phonological properties, such a criterion will leave
all Wickelfeatures of the form XY# intact). This difference is then carried
over to the current implementation of the response-generation component,
which puts response candidates at a disadvantage if they do not account for
activated Wickelfeatures. The entire effect (a consequence of the fact that
the model does not keep track of which features go in which positions) can
be viewed either as a bug or a feature. On the one hand, it is one way of
generating the (empirically correct) phenomenon that no-change responses
are more common when stems have the same endings as the affixes that
would be attached to them. On the other hand, it is part of a family of
phonological confusions that result from the Wickelphone/Wickelfeature representations in general (see the section on Wickelphonology) and that hobble
the model's ability even to reproduce strings verbatim. If the stem-affix feature confusions really are at the heart of the model's no-change responses,
then it should also have recurring problems, unrelated to learning, in generating forms such as *pitted* or *pocketed* where the same Wickelfeatures occur in
the stem and affix or even twice in the same stem but they must be kept
distinct. Indeed, the model really does seems prone to make these undesirable errors, such as generating a single CVC sequence when two are necessary, as in the no-change responses for *hug, smoke*, and *brown*, or the con-
verse, in overmarking errors such as *typeded* and *steppeded*.

A third possible reason that no-change responses are easy for t/d-final
stems is that unlike other classes of irregulars in English, the no-change class
has a single kind of change (that is, no change at all), and all its members
have a phonological property in common: ending with a t or d. It is also the
largest irregular subclass. The model has been given relatively consistent
evidence of the contingency that verbs ending in t or d tend to have unchanged past tense forms, and it has encoded that contingency, presumably
in large part by strengthening links between input Wickelfeatures representing word-final t/ds and identical corresponding output Wickelfeatures. Basically, the model is potentially sensitive to any statistical correlation between
input and output feature sets, and it has picked up that one. That is, the
acquisition of the simple contingency "end in $t/d \rightarrow$ no change" presumably
makes the model mimic children. We can call this the *within-class uniformity*
effect. As we have mentioned, the simplified rule-hypothesization mechanism
presented in a previous section can acquire the same contingency (add a null

affix for verbs ending in a nonsonorant noncontinuant coronal), and strengthen it with every no-change pair in the input. If, as we have argued, a rule-learning model considered many rules exemplified by input pairs before being able to determine which of them was the correct productive rule or rules for the language, this rule would exist in the child's grammar and would compete with the regular *d* rule and with other rules, just as competing outputs are computed in the RM model.

Finally, there is a fourth mechanism that was mentioned in our discussion of the strong verb system. Addition of the regular suffix *d* to a form ending in *t* or *d* produces a phonologically-illicit consonant cluster: *td* or *dd*. For regular verbs, the phonological rule of vowel insertion places an *i* between the two consonants. Interestingly, no irregular past ends in *id*, though some add a *t* or *d*. Thus we find *tell/told* and *leave/left*, but we fail to find *bleed/bledded* or *get/gotted*. A possible explanation is that a phonological rule, degemination, removes an affix after it is added as an alternative means of avoiding adjacent coronals in the strong class. The no-change verbs would then just be a special case of this generalization, where the vowel doesn't change either. Basically, the child would capitalize on a phonological rule acquired elsewhere in the system, and might overgeneralize by failing to restrict the degemination rule to the strong verbs.

Thus we have an overlapping set of explanations for the early acquisition and overgeneralization of the no-change contingency. Bybee and Slobin cite misperception, Rumelhart and McClelland cite between-class transfer and within-class uniformity, and rule-based theories can cite within-class uniformity or overgeneralized phonology. What is the evidence concerning the reasons that children are so sensitive to this contingency?

Unfortunately, a number of confounds in English make the theories difficult to distinguish. No-change verbs have a diagnostic phonological property in common with one another. They also share a phonological property with regular inflected past tense forms. Unfortunately, they are the same property: ending with *t/d*. And it is the sharing of that phonological property that triggers the putative phonological rule. So this massive confound prevents one from clearly distinguishing the accounts using the English past tense rule; one cannot say that the Rumelhart–McClelland model receives clear support from its ability to mimic children in this case.

In principle, a number of more diagnostic tests are possible. First, one must explain *why* the no-change class is confounded. The within-class uniformity account, which is one of the factors behind the RM model's success, cannot do this: if it were the key factor, we would surmise that English could just as easily have contained a no-change class defined by *any* easily-characterized within-class property (e.g. begin with *j*, end with *s*). Bybee and Slobin note that across languages, it is very common for no-change stems to contain the very ending that a rule would add. While ruling out within-class uniformity as the *only* explanation, this still leaves misperception, transfer, and phonology as possibilities, all of which foster learning of no-change forms for stems resembling the relevant affix.

Second, one can look at cases where possessing the features of the regular ending is not confounded with the characteristics of the no-change class. For example, the nouns that do not change when pluralized in English such as *sheep* and *cod* do not in general end in an *s* or *z* sound. If children nonetheless avoid pluralizing nouns like *ax* or *lens* or *sneeze*, it would support one or more of the accounts based on stem-affix similarity. Similarly, we might expect children to be reluctant to add *-ing* to form verbs like *ring* or *hamstring* or *rethink*.

If such effects were found, differences among verbs all of which resemble the affix in question could discriminate the various accounts that exploit the stem-affix similarity effect in different ways. Transfer, which is exploited by the RM model, would, all other things being equal, lead to equally likely no-change responses for all stems with a given degree of similarity to the affix. Phonology would predict that transfer would occur only when the result of adding an affix led to adjacent similar segments; thus it would predict more no-change responses for the plural of *ax* than the progressive of *sting*, which is phonologically acceptable without the intervention of any further rule.

Returning now to a possible unconfounded test of the within-class uniformity effect (implicated by Rumelhart and McClelland and by the rule-hypothesization module), one could look for some phonological property in common among a set of no-change stems that was independent of the phonological property of the relevant affix and see whether children were more likely to yield both correct and incorrect no-change responses when a stem had that property. As we have pointed out, monosyllabicity is a property holding of the irregular verbs in general, and of the no-change verbs in particular; presumably it is for this reason that the RM model, it turns out, is particularly susceptible to leaving regular verbs ending in *t/d* erroneously unchanged when they are monosyllabic. As Rumelhart and McClelland point out, if children are less likely to leave verbs such as *decide* or *devote* unchanged than verbs such as *cede* or *raid* it would constitute a test of this aspect of their theory; this test is not confounded by effects of across-class transfer.[29]

---

[29]Actually, this test is complicated by the fact that monosyllabicity and irregularity are not independent: in English, monosyllabicity is an important feature in defining the domain of many morphological and syntactic rules (e.g. *nicer/*intelligenter, give/*donate the museum a painting*; see Pinker, 1984), presumably because in English a monosyllable constitutes the minimal or basic word (McCarthy & Prince, forthcoming). As we have pointed out, all the irregular verbs in English are monosyllables or contain monosyllabic roots, (likewise for →

A possible test of the misperception hypothesis is to look for other kinds of evidence that children misperceive certain stems as falling into a morphological category that is characteristically inflected. If so, then once the regular rule is acquired it could be applied in reverse to such misperceived forms, resulting in back-formations. For no-change verbs, this would result in errors such as *bea* or *blas* for *beat* or *blast*. We know of no reports of such errors among past tense forms (many would be impossible for phonological reasons) but have observed in Lisa's speech *mik* for *mix*, and in her noun system *clo (thes), len (s), sentent* (cf. *sentence*), *Santa Clau (s), upstair (s), downstair (s), bok* (cf. *box*), *trappy* (cf. *trapeze*), and *brefek* (cf. *brefeks* = 'breakfast').[30]

Finally, the process by which Rumelhart and McClelland exploit stem-affix similarity, namely transfer of the strength of the output features involved in regular pairs to the no-change stems, can be tested by looking at examples of blends of regular and subregular alternations that involve classes of verbs other than the no-change class. One must determine whether children produce such blends and whether it is a good thing or a bad thing for the RM theory that their model does so. We examine this issue in the next two sections.

In sum, the class of English verbs that do not change in the past tense involves a massive confound of within-class phonological uniformity and stem-affix similarity, leading to a complex nexus of predictions as to why children are so sensitive to the properties of the class. The relations between different models of past tense acquisition, predictions of which linguistic variables should have an effect on languages and on children, and the classes of verbs instantiating those variables, is many-to-many-to-many. Painstaking testing of the individual predictions using unconfounded sets of items in a variety of inflectional classes in English and other languages could tease the

nouns), a fact related in some way to irregularity being restricted to roots and monosyllables being prototypical English roots. So if children know that only roots can be irregular and that roots are monosyllables, (see Gordon, 1986, for evidence that children are sensitive to the interaction between roothood and morphology, and Gropen & Pinker, 1986, for evidence that they are sensitive to monosyllabicity), they may restrict their tendency to no-change responses to monosyllables even if it is not the product of their detecting the first-order correlation between monosyllabicity and unchanged pasts. Thus the ideal test would have to be done for some other language, in which a no-change class had a common phonological property independent of the definition of a basic root in the language, and independent of the phonology of the regular affix.

[30]Note that the facts of English do not comport well with any strong misperception account that would have the child invariably misanalyze irregular pasts as pseudo-stems followed by the regular affix: the majority of no-change verbs either have lax vowels and hence would leave phonologically impossible pseudo-stems after the affix was subtracted, such as *hi* or *cu*, or end in vowel-*t* sequences, which never occur in regular pasts and only rarely (e.g. *bought*) in irregulars. For the same reason it is crucial to Bybee and Slobin's account that children be constrained to form the schema $\langle past: ...t/d\#\rangle$ rather than several schemas matching the input more accurately, such as $\langle past: ...[unvoiced] \ t \ \#\rangle]$ and $\langle past: ...[voiced] \ d \ \#\rangle$. If they did, they would never misperceive *hit* and *cut* as past tense forms.

effects apart. At present, however, a full range of possibilities are all consistent with the data, ranging from the RM model explaining much of the phenomenon to its being entirely dispensable. The model's ability to duplicate children's performance, in and of itself, tells us relatively little.

7.2.3. Frequency of overregularizing irregular verbs in different vowel-change subclasses

Bybee and Slobin examined eight different classes of irregular past tense verbs (see the Appendix for an alternative, more fine-grained taxonomy). Their Class I contains the no-change verbs we have just discussed. Their Class II contains verbs that change a final *d* to *t* to form the past tense, such as *send/sent* and *build/built*. The other six classes involve vowel changes, and are defined by Bybee and Slobin as follows:

- Class III. Verbs that undergo an internal vowel change and also add a final /t/ or /d/, e.g. *feel/felt, lose/lost, say/said, tell/told*.
- Class IV. Verbs that undergo an internal vowel change, delete a final consonant, and add a final /t/ or /d/, e.g. *bring/brought, catch/caught*. [Bybee and Slobin include in this class the pair *buy/bought* even though it does not involve a deleted consonant. *Make/made* and *have/had* were also included even though they do not involve a vowel change.]
- Class V. Verbs that undergo an internal vowel change whose stems end in a dental, e.g. *bite/bit, find/found, ride/rode*.
- Class VI. Verbs that undergo a vowel change of /I/ to /æ/ or /ʌ/, e.g. *sing/sang, sting/stung*.
- Class VII. All other verbs that undergo an internal vowel change, e.g. *give/gave, break/broke*.
- Class VIII. All verbs that undergo a vowel change and that end in a diphthongal sequence, e.g. *blow/blew, fly/flew*. [*Go/went* is also included in this class.]

Bybee and Slobin noted that preschoolers had widely varying tendencies to overregularize the verbs in these different classes, ranging from 10% to 80% of the time (see the first column of Table 2). Class IV and III verbs, whose past tense forms receive a final *t/d* in addition to their vowel changes, were overregularized the least; Class VII and V verbs, which have unchanged final consonants and a vowel change, were overregularized somewhat more often; Class VI verbs, involving the *ing-ang-ung* regularity, were regularized more often than that; and Class VIII verbs, which end in a diphthong sequence which is changed in the past, were overregularized most often. Bybee and Slobin again account for this phenomenon by appealing to factors affecting the process of juxtaposing corresponding present and past forms. They suggest that the presence of an added t/d facilitates the child's recognition that Class III and IV past forms *are* past forms, and that the small percentage of shared segments between Class VIII present and past versions (e.g., one for *see/saw* or *know/knew*) hinders that recognition process. As the likelihood of successful juxtaposition of present and past forms decreases, the likelihood of the regular rule to operate, unblocked by an irregular past form, increases and overregularizations become more common.

Rumelhart and McClelland suggest, as in their discussion of no-change verbs, that their model as it stands can reproduce the developmental phenomenon. Since the Bybee and Slobin subjects range from $1\frac{1}{2}$ to 5 years, it is not clear which stage of performance of the model should be compared with that of the children, so Rumelhart and McClelland examined the output of the model at several stages. These stages corresponded to the model's first five trials with the set of medium-frequency, predominantly regular verbs, the next five trials, the next ten trials, and an average over those first twenty trials (these intervals constitute the period in which the tendency of the model to overregularize was highest). The average strength of the over-regularized forms within each class was calculated for each of these four intervals.

The fit between model and data is good for the interval comprising the first five trials, which Rumelhart and McClelland concentrate on. We calculate the rank-order correlation between degree of overregularization by children and model across classes as .77 in that first interval; however it then declines to .31 and .14 in the next two intervals and is .31 for the average response over all three intervals. The fact that the model is only successful at accounting for Bybee and Slobin's data for one brief interval (less than 3% of the training run) selected post hoc, whereas the data themselves are an average over a span of development of $3\frac{1}{2}$ years, should be kept in mind in evaluating the degree of empirical confirmation this study gives the model. Nonetheless, the tendency of Class VIII verbs (*fly/flew*) to be most often regularized, and for Class III verbs (*feel/felt*) to be among those least often regularized, persists across all three intervals.

The model, of course is insensitive to any factor uniquely affecting the juxtaposition of present and past forms because such juxtaposition is accomplished by the "teacher" in the simulation run. Instead, its fidelity to children's overregularization patterns at the very beginning of its own over-regularization stage must be attributed to some other factor. Rumelhart and McClelland point to differences among the classes in the frequency with which their characteristic vowel changes are exemplified by the verb corpus as a whole. Class VIII verbs have vowel shifts that are relatively idiosyncratic to the individual verbs in the class; the vowel shifts of other classes, on the other hand, might be exemplified by many verbs in many classes. Further-more, Class III and IV verbs, which require the addition of a final *t*/*d*, can benefit from the fact that the connections in the network that effect the addition of a final *t*/*d* have been strengthened by the large number of regular verbs. The model creates past tense forms piecemeal, by links between stem and past Wickelfeatures, and with no record of the structure of the individual words that contributed to the strengths of those links. Thus vowel shifts and consonant shifts that have been exemplified by large numbers of verbs can be applied to different parts of a base form even if the exact combination of such shifts exemplified by that base form is not especially frequent.

How well could the simplified rule-finding module account for the data? Like the RM model, it would record various subregular rules as candidates for a regular past tense rule. Assuming it is sensitive to type frequency, the rule candidates for more-frequently exemplified subregularities would be stronger. And the stronger an applicable subregular rule candidate is, the less is the tendency for its output to lose the competition with the overregularized form contributed by the regular rule. Thus if Rumelhart and McClelland's explanation of their model's fit to the data is correct, a rule-finding model sensitive to type-frequency presumably would fit the data as well.

This conjecture is hard to test because Bybee and Slobin's data are tabu-lated in some inconvenient ways. Each class is heterogeneous, containing verbs governed by a variety of vowel-shifts and varying widely as to the number of such shifts in the class and the number of verbs exemplifying them within the class and across the classes. Furthermore, there are some quirks in the classification. *Go*/*went*, the most irregular main verb in English, is assigned to Class VIII, which by itself could contribute to the poor perfor-mance of children and the RM model on that class. Conversely, *have* and *make*, which involve no vowel shift at all, are included in Class IV, possibly contributing to good average performance for the class by children and the model. (See the Appendix for an alternative classification.)

It would be helpful to get an estimate as to how much of the RM model's empirical success here might be due to the different frequencies of exemplifi-cation of the vowel-shift subregularities within each class, because such an effect carries over to a symbolic rule-finding alternative. To get such an estimate, we considered each vowel shift (e.g. $i \rightarrow æ$) as a separate candidate rule, strengthened by a unit amount with each presentation of a verb that exemplifies it in the Rumelhart–McClelland corpus of high- and medium-fre-quency verbs. To allow *have* and *make* to benefit from the prevalence of other verbs whose vowels do not change, we pooled the different vowel no-change rules ($a \rightarrow a;\ i \rightarrow i$, etc.) into a single rule (the RM model gets a similar benefit by using Wickelfeatures, which can code for the presence of vowels, rather than Wickelphones) whose strength was determined by the number of no-vowel-change verbs in Classes I and II.[31] Then we averaged the strengths of all the subregular rules included within each of Bybee and Slobin's classes. These averages allow a prediction of the ordering of over-regularization probabilities for the different subclasses, based solely on the number of irregular verbs in the corpus exemplifying the specific vowel alter-nations among the verbs in the class. Though the method of prediction is crude, it is just about as good at predicting the data as the output of the RM model during the interval at which it did best and much better than the RM model during the other intervals examined. Specifically, the rank-order cor-relation between number of verbs in the corpus exemplifying the vowel shifts in a class and the frequency of children's regularization of verbs in the class is .71. The data, predictions of the RM model, and predictions from our simple tabulations are summarized in Table 2.

What about the effect of the addition of *t/d* on the good performance on Class III and IV verbs? The situation is similar in some ways to that of the no-change verbs discussed in the previous section. The Class III and IV verbs

Table 2.   *Ranks of tendencies to overregularize irregular verbs involving vowel shifts*

		Children*	RM 1st set	RM 2nd set	RM 3rd set	RM average	Avg. freq. of vowel shift**
Verb subclass							
VIII	blow/blew	1 (.80)	1	1	1	1	1 (1.6)
VI	sing/sang	2 (.55)	4	4	4	4	3 (2.7)
V	bite/bit	3 (.34)	2	3	6	3	5 (3.9)
VII	break/broke	4 (.32)	3	6	3	6	2 (2.1)
III	feel/felt	5 (.13)	6	5	5	5	4 (3.8)
IV	seek/sought	6 (.10)	5	2	2	2	6 (4.5)
Rank order correlation with children's proportions			.77	.31	.14	.31	.71

* Actual proportions of regularizations by children are in parentheses.
** Mean number of verbs in the irregular corpus exemplifying the vowel shifts within a class are indicated in parentheses.

[31] In a sense, it would have been more accurate to calculate the strength of the no-vowel-change rule on the basis of all the verbs in the corpus, regular and irregular, rather than just the irregular verbs. But with our overly simple strength function, this would have greatly stacked the deck in favor of correctly predicting low regularization rates for Class IV verbs and so we only counted the exemplifications of no-vowel-change within the irregular verbs.

take some of the most frequently-exemplified vowel-changes (including no-change for *have* and *make*); they also involve the addition of *t* or *d* at the end causing them to resemble the past tense forms of regular verbs. Given this confound, good performance with these classes can be attributed to either factor and so the RM model's good performance with them does not favor it over the Bybee-Slobin account focusing on the juxtaposition problem.

The question of blended responses. An interesting issue arises, however, when we consider the possible effects of the addition of *t/d in combination with* the effects of a common vowel shift. Recall that the RM model generates its output piecemeal. Thus strong regularities pertaining to different parts of a word can affect the word simultaneously, producing a chimerical output that need not correspond in its entirety to previous frequent patterns. To take a simplified example, after the model encounters pairs such as *meet/met* it has strong links between *i* and *ε*; after it encounters pairs such as *play/played* it has strong links between final vowels and final vowel-*d* sequences; when presented with *flee* it could then generate *fled* by combining the two regularities, even if it never encountered an *ee/ed* alternation before. What is interesting is that this blending phenomenon is the direct result of the RM model's lack of word structure. In an alternative rule-finding account, there would be an $i \rightarrow \varepsilon$ rule candidate, and there would be a *d*-affixation rule candidate, but they would generate two distinct competing outputs, not a single blended output. (It is possible in principle that some of the subregular strong verbs such as *told* and *sent* involve the superposition of independent subregular rules, especially in the history of the language, but in modern English one cannot simply heap the effect of the regular rule on top of any subregular alternation, as the RM model is prone to do.) Thus it is not really fair for us to claim that a rule-hypothesization model can account for good performance with Class III and IV verbs because they involve frequently-exemplified vowel alternations; such alternations only result in correct outputs if they are blended with the addition of a *t/d* to the end of the word. In principle, this could give us a critical test between the network model and a rule-hypothesization model: unlike the ability to soak up frequent alternations, the automatic superposition of any set of them into a single output is (under the simplest assumptions) unique to the network model.

This leads to two questions: Is there independent evidence that children blend subregularities? And does the RM model itself really blend subregularities? We will defer answering the first question until the next section, where it arises again. As for the second, it might seem that the question of whether response blending occurs is perfectly straightforward, but in fact it is not. Say the model's active output Wickelfeatures in response to *flee* include those for medial ε and those for word-final *d*. Is the overt response of the model *fled*, a correct blend, or does it set up a competition between [*flid*] and [*flɛ*], choosing one of them, as the rule-hypothesization model would? In principle, either outcome is possible, but we are never given the opportunity to find out. Rumelhart and McClelland do not test their model against the Bybee and Slobin data by letting it output its favored response. Rather, they externally assemble alternatives corresponding to the overregularized and correct forms, and assess the relative strengths of those alternatives by observing the outcome of the competition in the restricted-choice whole-string binding network (recall that the output of the associative network, a set of activated Wickelfeatures, is the input to the whole-string binding network). These strengths are determined by the number of activated Wickelfeatures that each is consistent with. The result is that correct alternatives that also happen to resemble blends of independent subregularities are often the response chosen. But we do not know whether the model, if left to its own devices, would produce a blend as its top-ranked response.

Rumelhart and McClelland did not perform this test because it would have been too computationally intensive given the available hardware: recall that the only way to get the model to produce a complete response form on its own is by giving it (roughly) all possible output strings (that is, all permutations of segments) and having them compete against each other for active Wickelfeatures in an enormous "unconstrained whole-string binding network". This is an admitted kluge designed to give approximate predictions of the strengths of responses that a more realistic output mechanism would construct. Rumelhart and McClelland only ran the unconstrained whole-string binding network on a small set of new low-frequency verbs in a transfer test involving no further learning. It is hard to predict what will happen when this network operates because it involves a "rich-get-richer" scheme in the competition among whole strings, by which a string that can uniquely account for some Wickelfeatures (including Wickelfeatures incorrectly turned on as part of the noisy output function) gets disproportionate credit for the features that it and its competitors account for equally well, occasionally leading to unpredictable winners. In fact, the whole-string mechanism does yield blends such as *slip/slept*. But as mentioned, these blends are also occasionally bizarre, such as *mailed/membled* or *tour/toureder*. And this is why the question of overt blended outputs is foggy: it is unclear whether tuning the whole-string binding network, or a more reasonable output construction mechanism, so that the bizarre blends were eliminated, would also eliminate the blends that perhaps turn out to be the correct outputs for Class III and IV.[32]

---

[32]To complicate matters even further, even outright blends are possible in principle within the rule-based

In sum, the relative tendencies of children to overregularize different classes of vowel-change irregular verbs does not favor the RM model. The model for one brief stage selected post hoc shows a moderately high correlation with data on children's behavior in the strength it assigns to overregularized forms. Much of this correlation is simply due to the frequencies with which the vowel alternations in a given class have been exemplified by verbs in the corpus as a whole. A rule-hypothesization model would also be sensitive to these frequencies under even the simplest of assumptions. But the ability of the network model to blend independent subregularities into a single response follows naturally from its lack of word structure and could lead to tests distinguishing the models. Unfortunately, whether the network model would actually output blended responses in its best incarnation is unknown; whether children output blended responses is a question we will turn to shortly.

7.2.4. "Eated" versus "ated" errors

The final developmental phenomenon that Rumelhart and McClelland examine is the tendency of children to produce overregularization errors consisting of an irregular past affixed with *ed*, such as *ated* or *broked*. Such errors tend to occur considerably later in development than errors consisting of a base form affixed with *ed*, such as *eated* or *breaked* (Kuczaj, 1977). Rumelhart and McClelland compared the strength of *eated* and *ated* outputs for the irregular verbs in their corpus. They found that the strength of the *ated* form relative to the *eated* form increased over the course of training, thus mimicking the Kuczaj data.

What causes past + *ed* errors? There are two possibilities. One is that the child sometimes fails to realize that the irregular past is the past tense form of some base form. Thinking it is a base form itself, he or she feeds it into the past tense formation mechanism and gets a doubly-marked error. This cannot be the explanation for the model's behavior because correct present/ past pairs are always provided to it. The alternative is that the two different changes are applied to the correct base form and the results are blended to yield the double-marking. This is similar to one of the explanations for the model's relatively infrequent overregularization of Class III and IV verbs discussed in the previous section, and to one of the explanations for the

model. For example, children might have two subregular rules that both apply, as might have been appropriate in an earlier stage of English. Or, there may be a response buffer that receives the output of the competition process, and occasionally two candidates of approximately equal strength slip out of the competition mechanism and are blended in the response buffer. The result would be a blended speech error from the point of view of the "design" of the rule-application module but possibly an adventitious correct response. Though this account may not seem as natural as the blending inherent in the network model, the notion of a serially ordered response buffer distinct from a representation of target segments is part of standard explanations for anticipatory and perseverative speech errors (e.g., Shattuck-Hufnagel, 1979).

model's tendency to leave *t/d*-final stems unchanged discussed in the section before that. As in the previous discussions, the lack of a realistic response production mechanism makes it unclear whether the model would ever actually produce past + *ed* blends when it is forced to utter a response on its own, or whether the phenomenon is confined to such forms simply increasing in strength in the three-alternative forced-choice experiment because only the past + *ed* form by definition contains three sets of features all of them strengthened in the course of learning (its idiosyncratic features, the features output by subregularities, and the features of regularized forms). In Rumelhart and McClelland's transfer test on new verbs, they chose a minimum strength value of .2 as a criterion for when a form should be considered as being a likely overt response of the model. By this criterion, the model should be seen as rarely outputting past + *ed* forms, since such forms on the average never exceed a strength of .15. But let us assume for now that such forms would be output, and that blending is their source.

At first one might think that the model had an advantage in that it is consistent with the fact that *ated* errors increase relative to the *eated* errors in later stages, a phenomenon not obviously predicted by the misconstrued stem account.[33] However, many of the phenomena we discuss below that favor the misconstrued-stem account over the RM model appear during the same, relatively late period as the *ated* errors (Kuczaj, 1981), so lateness itself does not distinguish the accounts. Moreover, Kuczaj (1977) warns that the late-*ated* effect is not very robust and is subject to individual differences. In a later study (Kuczaj, 1978), he eliminated these sampling problems by using an experimental task in which children judged whether various versions of past tense forms sounded "silly". He found in two separate experiments that while children's acceptance of the *eated* forms declined monotonically their acceptance of *ated* forms showed an inverted U-shaped function, first increasing *but then decreasing* relative to *eated*-type errors. Since in the RM model the strengths of both forms monotonically approach an asymptote near zero, with the curves crossing only once, the model demonstrates no special ability to track the temporal dynamics of the two kinds of errors. In the discussion below we will concentrate on the reasons that such errors occur in the first place.

Once again, a confound in the materials provided by the English language confounds Rumelhart and McClelland's conclusion that their model accounts

[33]Kuczaj did suggest an interesting hypothesis: children might treat *went* as a base form that expresses pastness inherently, as part of its intrinsic meaning, rather than as the grammatical composition of *go + past* (Kuczaj, 1981, observed *was wenting* but never *is wenting*). The eventual realization that tense must be marked *grammatically*, and not just implicitly by the inherent meanings of verbs, is a later acquisition, and its effect is the regular inflection of irregular forms.

children's *ated*-type errors. Irregular past tense forms appear in the child's input and hence can be misconstrued as base forms. They also are part of the model's output for irregular base forms and hence can be blended with the regularized response. Until forms which have one of these properties and not the other are examined, the two accounts are at a stalemate.

Fortunately, the two properties can be unconfounded. Though the correct irregular past will usually be the strongest non-regularized response of the network, it is also sensitive to subregularities among vowel changes and hence one might expect blends consisting of a frequent and consistent but incorrect vowel change plus the regular *ed* ending. In fact the model does produce such errors for regular verbs it has not been trained on, such as *shape/shipped, sip/sepped, slip/slept,* and *brown/brawned.* Since the stems of these responses are either not English verbs or have no semantic relationship to the correct verb, such responses can never be the result of mistakenly feeding the wrong base form of the verb into the past tense formation process. Thus if the blending assumed in the Rumelhart and McClelland model is the correct explanation for children's past + *ed* overregularizations, we should see children making these and other kinds of blend errors. We might also expect errors consisting of a blend of a correct irregular alteration of a verb plus a frequent subregular alteration, such as *send/soant* (a blend of the $d \rightarrow t$ and $\varepsilon \rightarrow o$ subregularities) or *think/that* (a blend of the *ing* $\rightarrow$ *ang* and *final consonant cluster* $\rightarrow t$ subregularities). (As mentioned, though, these last errors are not ruled out in principle in all rule-based models, since superposition may have had a role in the creation of several of the strong past forms in the history of English, but indiscriminately adding the regular affix onto strong pasts is ruled out by most theories of morphology.)

Conversely, if the phenomenon is due to incorrect base input forms, we might expect to see other inflection processes applied to the irregular past, resulting in errors such as *wenting* and *broking* or *wents* and *brokes.* Since mechanisms for progressive or present indicative inflection would never be exposed to the idiosyncrasies or subregularities of irregular past tense forms under Rumelhart and McClelland's assumptions, such errors could not result from blending of outputs. Similarly, irregular pasts should appear in syntactic contexts calling for bare stems if children misconstrue irregular pasts as stems. In addition, we might expect to find cases where *ed* is added to incorrect base forms that are plausible confusions of the correct base form but implausible results of the mixing of subregularities.

Finally, we might expect that if children are put in a situation in which the correct stem of a verb is provided for them, they would not generate past + *ed* errors, since the source of such errors would be eliminated.

All five predictions work against the RM model and in favor of the explanation based on incorrect inputs. Kuczaj (1977) reports that his transcripts contained no examples where the child overapplied any subregularity, let alone a blend of two of them or of a subregularity plus the regular ending. Bybee and Slobin do not report any such errors in children's speech, though they do report them as adult slips of the tongue in a time-pressured speaking task designed to elicit errors. We examined the full set of transcripts of Adam, Eve, Sarah, and Lisa for words ending in -ed. We found 13 examples of irregular past + ed or en errors in past and passive constructions:

(36) Adam: ranned
         tooked
         stoled (twice)
         broked (participle)
         felled

    Eve: tored

    Sarah: flewed (twice)
           caughted
           stucked (participle)

    Lisa: torned (participle)
           tooken (twice) (participle)
           sawn (participle)

The participle forms must be interpreted with caution. Because English irregular participles sometimes consist of the stem plus en (e.g. take - took - taken) but sometimes consist of the irregular past plus en (e.g. break - broke - broken), errors like tooken could reflect the child overextending this regularity to past forms of verbs that actually follow the stem + en pattern; the actual stem or even the child's mistaken hypothesis about it may play no role.

What about errors consisting of a subregular vowel alternation plus the addition of ed? The only examples where an incorrect vowel other than that of the irregular form appeared with ed are the following:

(37) Adam: I think it's not fulled up to de top.
           I think my pockets gonna be all fulled up.
           I'm gonna ask Mommy if she has any more grain ... more stuff
           that she needs grained. [He has been grinding crackers in a meat
           grinder producing what he calls "grain".]

    Sarah: Oo, he hahted.

    Lisa: I brekked your work.

For Adam, neither vowel alternation is exemplified by any of the irregular verbs in the Rumelhart-McClelland corpus, but in both cases the stem is identical to a non-verb that is phonologically and semantically related to the target verb and hence may have been misconstrued as the base form of the verb or converted into a new base verb. Sarah's error can be attributed directly to phonological factors since she also pronounced *dirt*, involving no morphological change, as "dawt", according to the transcriber. This leaves Lisa's *brekked* as the only putative example; note that unlike her single-sub-regularity errors such as *bote* for *bit* which lasted for extended periods of time, this appeared only once, and the correct form *broke* was very common in her speech. Furthermore blending is not a likely explanation: among high and middle frequency verbs, the alternation is found only in *say/said* and to a lesser extent in pairs such as *sleep/slept* and *leave/left*, whereas in many other alternations the *e* sound is mapped onto other vowels (*bear/bore, wear/ wore, tear/tore, take/took*, and *shake/shook*). Thus it seems unlikely that the RM model would produce a blend in this case but not in the countless other opportunities for blending that the children avoided. Finally, we note that Lisa was referring to a pile of papers that she scattered, an unlikely example of *breaking* but a better one of *wrecking*, which may have been the target serving as the real source of the blend (and not a past tense subregularity) if it was a blend. In sum, except perhaps for this last example under an extremely charitable interpretation, the apparent blends seem far more suggestive of an incorrect stem correctly inflected than a blend between two past tense subregularities.

This conclusion is strengthened when we note that children do make errors such as *wents* and *wenting*, which could only result from inflecting the wrong stem. Kuczaj (1981) reports frequent use of *wenting, ating*, and *thoughting* in the speech of his son, and we find in Eve's speech *fells* and *wents* and in Lisa's speech *blow awayn, lefting, hidding* (= hiding), *stoling, to took, to shot*, and *might loss*. These last three errors are examples of a common phenomenon sometimes called 'overtensing', which because it occurs mostly with irregulars (Maratsos & Kuczaj, 1978), is evidence that irregulars are misconstrued as stems (identical to infinitives in English). Some examples from Pinker (1984) include *Can you broke those, What are you did?, She gonna fell out*, and *I'm going to sit on him and made him broken*. Note that since many of these forms occur at the same time as the *ated* errors, the relatively late appearance of *ated* forms may reflect the point at which stem extraction (and mis-extraction) in general is accomplished.

Finally, Kuczaj (1978) presents more direct evidence that past + *ed* errors are due to irregular pasts misconstrued as stems. In one of his tasks, he had children convert a future tense form (i.e. "X will + ⟨verb stem⟩") into a past tense form (i.e. "X already ⟨verb past⟩"). Past + *ed* errors virtually vanished (in fact they completely vanished for two of the three age groups). Kuczaj argues that the crucial factor was that children were actually given the proper base forms. This shows that children's derivation of the errors must be from *ate* to *ated*, not, as it is in the RM model, from *eat* to *ated*.

Yet another test of the source of apparently blended errors is possible when we turn our attention to the regular system. If the child occasionally misanalyzes a past form as a stem, he or she should do so for regular inflected past forms and not just irregular ones, resulting in errors such as *talkeded*. The RM model also produces such errors as blends, but for reasons that Rumelhart and McClelland do not explain, all these errors involve regular verbs whose stems end in *p* or *k*: *carpeded, drippeded, mappeded, smokeded, snappeded, steppeded*, and *typeded*, but not *browneded, warmeded, teareded* or *clingeded*, nor, for that matter, irregular stems of any sort: the model did not output *creepeded/crepted, weepeded/wepted, diggeded*, or *stickeded*. We suggest the following explanation for this aspect of the model's behavior. The phonemes *p* and *k* share most of their features with *t*. Therefore on a Wickelfeature by Wickelfeature basis, learning that *t* and *d* give you *id* in the output transfers to *p, b, g* and *k* as well. So there will be a bias toward *id* responses after all stops. Since there is also a strong bias toward simply adding *t*, there will be a tendency to blend the 'add *t*' and the 'add *id*' responses. Irregular verbs, as we have noted, never end in *id*, so to the extent that the novel irregulars resemble trained ones (see Section 4.4), the features of the novel irregulars will inhibit the response of the *id* Wickelfeatures and double-marking will be less common.

In any case, though Rumelhart and McClelland cannot explain their model's behavior in this case, they are willing to predict that children as well will double-mark more often for *p*- and *k*-final stems. In the absence of an explanation as to why the model behaved as it did, Rumelhart and McClelland should just as readily extrapolate the model's reluctance to double-mark irregular stems and test the prediction that children should double-mark only regular forms (if our hypothesis about the model's operation is correct, the two predictions stem from a common effect). Checking the transcripts, we did find *ropeded* and *stoppeded* (the latter uncertain in transcription) in Adam's speech, and *likeded* and *pickeded* in Sarah's, as Rumelhart and McClelland would predict. But Adam also said *tieded* and Sarah said *buyded* and *makeded* (an irregular). Thus the model's prediction that double-marking should be specific to stems ending with *p* and *d*, and then only when they are regular, is not borne out. In particular, note that *buyded* and *tieded* cannot be the result of a blend of subregularities, because there *is* no subregularity according to which *buy* or *tie* would tend to attract a *id* ending.[34]

Finally, Slobin (1985) notes that Hebrew contains two quite pervasive rules for inflecting the present tense, the first involving a vowel change, the second a consonantal prefix and a different vowel change. Though Israeli children overextend the prefix to certain verbs belonging to the first class, they never blend this prefix of the second class with the vowel change of the first class. This may be part of a larger pattern that children seem to respect the integrity of the word as a cohesive unit, one that can have affixes added to it and that can be modified by general phonological processes, but that cannot simply be composed as a blend of bits and pieces contributed by various regular and irregular inflectional regularities. It is suggestive in this regard that Slobin (1985), in his crosslinguistic survey, lists examples from the speech of children learning Spanish, French, German, Hebrew, Russian, and Polish, where the language mandates a stem modification plus the addition of an affix and children err by only adding the affix.

Once again we see that the model does not receive empirical support from its ability to mimic a pattern of developmental data. The materials that Rumelhart and McClelland looked at are again confounded in a way that leaves their explanation and the standard one focusing on the juxtaposition problem equally plausible given only the fact of *ated* errors. One can do better than that. By looking at unconfounded cases, contrasting predictions leading to critical tests are possible. In this case, six different empirical tests all go against the explanation inherent in the Rumelhart and McClelland model: absence of errors due to blending of subregularities, presence of *went-ing*-type errors, presence of errors where irregular pasts are used in nonpast contexts, presence of errors where the regular past ending is mistakenly applied to non-verb stems, drastic reduction of *ated*-errors when the correct stem is supplied to the child, and presence of errors where the regular ending is applied twice to stems that are irregular or that end in a vowel. These tests show that errors such as *ated* are the result of the child incorrectly feeding *ate* as a base form into the past tense inflection mechanism, and not the result of blending components of *ate* and *eated* outputs.

---

[34]One might argue that the misconstrued-stem account would fail to generate these errors, too, since it would require that the child first generate *maked* and *buyed* using a productive past tense rule and then forget that the forms really were in the past tense. Perhaps, the argument would go, some other kind of blending caused the errors, such as a mixture of the two endings *d* and *id* which are common across the language even if the latter is contraindicated for these particular stems. In fact, the misconstrued-stem account survives unscathed, because one can find errors not involving overinflection where child-generated forms are treated as stems: for example, Kuczaj (1976) reports sentences such as *They wouldn't haved a house* and *She didn't goed*.

7.3. Summary of how well the model fares against the facts of children's development

What general conclusions can we make from our examination of the facts of children's acquisition of the English past tense form and the ability of the RM model to account for them? This comparison has brought several issues to light.

To begin with, one must reject the premise that is implicit in Rumelhart and McClelland's arguments, namely that if their model can duplicate a phenomenon, the traditional explanation of that phenomenon can be rejected. For one thing, there is no magic in the RM model duplicating correlations in language systems: the model can extract any combination of over 200,000 atomic regularities, and many regularities that are in fact the consequences of an interaction among principles in several grammatical components will be detectable by the model as first-order correlations because they fall into that huge set. As we argued in Section 4, this leaves the structure and constraints on the phenomena unexplained. But in addition, it leaves many of the simple goodness-of-fit tests critically confounded. When the requirements of a learning system designed to attain the adult state are examined, and when unconfounded tests are sought, the picture changes.

First, some of the developmental phenomena can be accounted for by any mechanism that keeps records of regularities at several levels of generality, assigns strengths to them based on type-frequency of exemplification, and lets them compete in producing past tense candidate forms. These phenomena include children's shifts or waffling between irregular and overregularized past tense forms, their tendency not to change verbs ending in t/d, and their tendency to overregularize verbs with some kinds of vowel alternations less than others. Since there are good reasons why rule-hypothesization models should be built in this way, these phenomena do not support the RM model as a whole or in contrast with rule-based models in general, though they do support the more general (and uncontroversial) assumption of competition among multiple regularities of graded strength during acquisition.

Second, the lack of structures corresponding to distinct words in the model, one of its characteristic features in contrast with rule-based models, might be related to the phenomenon of blended outputs incorporating independent subregularities. However, there is no good evidence that children's correct responses are ever the products of such blends, and there *is* extensive evidence from a variety of sources that their *ated*-type errors are *not* the products of such blends. Furthermore, given that many blends are undesirable, it is not clear that the model should be allowed to output them when a realistic model of its output process is constructed.

Third, the three-stage or U-shaped course of development for regular and irregular past tense forms in no way supports the RM model. In fact, the model provides the wrong explanation for it, making predictions about changes in the mixture of irregular and regular forms in children's vocabularies that are completely off the mark.

This means that in the two hypotheses for which unconfounded tests are available (the cause of the U-shaped overregularization curve, and the genesis of *ated*-errors), both of the processes needed by the RM model to account for developmental phenomena—frequency-sensitivity and blending—have been shown to play no important role, and in each case, processes appealing to rules—to the child's initial hypothesization of a rule in one case, and to the child's misapplication of it to incorrect inputs in a second—have received independent support. And since the model's explanations in the two confounded cases (performance with no-change verbs, and order of acquisition of subclasses) appeal in part to the blending process, the evidence against blending in our discussion of the *ated* errors taints these accounts as well. We conclude that the developmental facts discussed in this section and the linguistic facts discussed in Section 4 converge on the conclusion that knowledge of language involves the acquisition and use of symbolic rules.

8. General discussion

Why subject the RM model to such painstaking analysis? Surely few models of any kind could withstand such scrutiny. We did it for two reasons. First, the conclusions drawn by Rumelhart and McClelland—that PDP networks provide exact accounts of psychological mechanisms that are superior to the approximate descriptions couched in linguistic rules; that there is no induction problem in their network model; that the results of their investigation warrant revising the way in which language is studied—are bold and revolutionary. Second, because the model is so explicit and its domain so rich in data, we have an unusual opportunity to evaluate the Parallel Distributed Processing approach to cognition in terms of its concrete technical properties rather than bland generalities or recycled statements of hopes or prejudices.

In this concluding section we do four things: we briefly evaluate Rumelhart and McClelland's strong claims about language; we evaluate the general claims about the differences between connectionist and symbolic theories of cognition that the RM model has been taken to illustrate; we examine some of the ways that the problems of the RM model are inherently due to its PDP architecture, and hence ways in which our criticisms implicitly extend to certain kinds of PDP models in general; and we consider whether the model could be salvaged by using more sophisticated connectionist mechanisms.

8.1. On Rumelhart and McClelland's strong claims about language

One thing should be clear. Rumelhart and McClelland's PDP model does not differ from a rule-based theory in providing a more exact account of the facts of language and language behavior. The situation is exactly the reverse. As far as the adult steady state is concerned, the network model gives a crude, inaccurate, and unrevealing description of the very facts that standard linguistic theories are designed to explain, many of them in classic textbook cases. As far as children's development is concerned, the model's accounts are at their best no better than those of a rule-based theory with an equally explicit learning component, and for two of the four relevant developmental phenomena, critical empirical tests designed to distinguish the theories work directly against the RM model's accounts but are perfectly consistent with the notion that children create and apply rules. Given these empirical failings, the ontological issue of whether the PDP and rule-based accounts are realist portrayals of actual mechanisms as opposed to convenient approximate summaries of higher-order regularities in behavior is rather moot.

There is also no basis for Rumelhart and McClelland's claim that in their network model, as opposed to traditional accounts, "there is no induction problem". The induction problem in language acquisition consists, among other things, of finding sets of inputs that embody generalizations, extracting the right kinds of generalizations from them, and deciding which generalizations can be extended to new cases. The model does not deal at all with the first problem, which involves recognizing that a given word encodes the past tense and that it constitutes the past tense version of another word. This juxtaposition problem is relegated to the model's environment (its "teacher"), or more realistically, some unspecified prior process; such a division of labor would be unproblematic if it were not for the fact that many of the developmental phenomena that Rumelhart and McClelland marshall in support of their model may be intertwined with the juxtaposition process (the onset of overregularization, and the source of *ated* errors, most notably). The second part of the induction problem is dealt with in the theory the old-fashioned way: by providing it with an innate feature space that is supposed to be appropriate for the regularities in that domain. In this case, it is the distinctive features of familiar phonological theories, which are incorporated into the model's Wickelfeature representations (see also Lachter & Bever, 1987). Aspects in which the RM model differs from traditional accounts in how it uses distinctive features, such as representing words as unordered pools of feature trigrams, do not clearly work to the advantage of the model, to put it mildly. Finally, the theory deals very poorly with the crucial third aspect of the induction problem, when to generalize to new items. It cannot make proper phonological generalizations or respect the morphosyntactic constraints on the domain of application of the regular rule, and in its actual performance it errs in two ways, both overestimating the significance of the irregular subgeneralizations and underestimating the generality of the regular rule.

The third claim, that the success of their model calls for a revised understanding of language and language acquisition, is hardly warranted in light of the problems we have discussed. To give credit where it is due, we do not wish to deny the extent to which Rumelhart and McClelland's work has increased our understanding of language acquisition. The model has raised intriguing questions about the role of the family resemblance structure of subregularities and of their frequency of exemplification in overregularization, the blending of independent subregularities in generating overt outputs, effects of the mixture of regular and irregular forms in the input on the tradeoffs between rote and generalization, and the causes of transitions between developmental stages, in particular, the relative roles of the present-past juxtaposition process and the pattern-extraction process. But the model does not give superior or radically new answers for the questions it raises.

8.2. Implications for the metatheory and methodology of connectionism

Often the RM model is presented as a paradigm case not only of a new way to study language, but of a new way to understand what a cognitive theory is a theory of. In particular, a persistent theme in connectionist metatheory affirms that 'macro-level' symbolic theories can at best provide an approximate description of the domain of inquiry; they may be convenient in some circumstances, the claim goes, but never exact or real:

> Subsymbolic models accurately describe the microstructure of cognition, while symbolic models provide an approximate description of the macrostructure. (Smolensky, in press, p. 21)

> We view macrotheories as approximations to the underlying microstructure which the distributed model presented in our paper attempts to capture. As approximations they are often useful, but in some situations it will turn out that an examination of the microstructure may bring much deeper insight. (Rumelhart & McClelland, PDPI, p. 125)

> ... these [macro-level] models are approximations and should not be pushed too far. (Rumelhart & McClelland, p. 126; bracketed material ours here and elsewhere)

In such discussions the relationship between Newtonian physics and Quantum Mechanics typically surfaces as the desired analogy.

One of the reasons that connectionist theorists tend to reserve no role for higher-level theories as anything but approximations is that they create a dichotomy that, we think, is misleading. They associate the systematic, rule-based analysis of linguistic knowledge with what they call the "explicit inaccessible rule" view of psychology, which

> ... holds that the rules of language are stored in explicit form as propositions, and are used by language production, comprehension, and judgment mechanisms. These propositions cannot be described verbally [by the untutored native speaker]. (Rumelhart and McClelland, PDPII, p. 217)

Their own work is intended to provide "an alternative to explicit inaccessible rules ... a mechanism in which there is no explicit representation of a rule" (p. 217). The implication, or invited inference, seems to be that a formal rule is an eliminable descriptive convenience unless inscribed somewhere and examined by the neural equivalent of a read-head in the course of linguistic information processing.

In fact, there is no necessary link between realistic interpretation of rule theories and the "explicit inaccessible" view. Rules *could* be explicitly inscribed and accessed, but they *also* could be implemented in hardware in such a way that every consequence of the rule-system holds. If the latter turns out to be the case in a cognitive domain, there is a clear sense in which the rule-theory is validated—it is exactly true—rather than faced with a competing alternative or relegated to the status of an approximate convenience.[35]

Consider pattern-associators like Rumelhart and McClelland's, which gives symbolic output from symbolic input. Under a variety of conditions, it will function as a rule-implementer. To take only the simplest, suppose that all connection weights are 0 except those from the input node for feature f_i to the output node for f_i, which are set to 1. Then the network will implement the identity map. There is no read-head, write-head, or executive overseeing the operation, yet it is legitimate and even enlightening to speak of it in terms of rules manipulating symbols.

More realistically, one can abstract from the RM pattern associator an implicit theory implicating a "representation" consisting of a set of unordered Wickelfeatures and a list of "rules" replacing Wickelfeatures with other Wic-

---

[35]Note as well that many of the examples offered to give common-sense support to the desirability of eliminating rules are seriously misleading because they appeal to a confusion between attributing a *rule-system* to an entity and attributing the *wrong* rule-system to an entity. An example that Rumelhart and McClelland cite, in which it is noted that bees can create hexagonal cells in their hive with no knowledge of the rules of geometry, gains its intuitive force because of this confusion.

kelfeatures. Examining the properties of such rules and representations is quite revealing. We can find out what it takes to add /d/ to a stem; what it takes to reverse the order of phonemes in an input; whether simple local modifications of a string are more easily handled than complex global ones; and so on. The results we obtain carry over without modification to the actual pattern associator, where much more complex conditions prevail. The deficiencies of Wickelphone/Wickelfeature transformation are as untouched by the addition of thresholds, logistic probability functions, temperatures, and parameters of that ilk as they are by whether the program implementing the model is written in Fortran or C.

An important role of higher-level theory, as Marr for one has made clear, is to delineate the basic assumptions that lower level models must inevitably be built on. From this perspective, the high-level theory is not some approximation whose behavior offers a gross but useful guide to reality. Rather, the relation is one of embodiment: the lower-level theory embodies the higher level theory, and it does so with exactitude. The RM model has a theory of linguistic knowledge associated with it; it is just that the theory is so unorthodox that one has to look with some care to find it. But if we want to understand the model, dealing with the embodied theory is not a convenience, but a necessity, and it should be pushed as far as possible.

8.2.1. When does a network implement a rule?

Nonetheless, as we pointed out in the Introduction, it is not a logical necessity that a cognitive model implement a symbolic rule system, either a traditional or a revisionist one; the "eliminative" or rule-as-approximation connectionism that Rumelhart, McClelland, and Smolensky write about (though do not completely succeed in adhering to in the RM model) is a possible outcome of the general connectionist program. How could one tell the difference? We suggest that the crucial notion is the *motivation* for a network's structure.

In a radical or eliminative connectionist model, the overall properties of the rule-theory of a domain are not only caused by the mechanisms of the micro-theory (that is, the stipulated properties of the units and connections) but follow in a natural way from micro-assumptions that are well-motivated on grounds that have nothing to do with the structure of the domain under macro-scrutiny. The rule-theory would have second-class status because its assumptions would be epiphenomena: if you really want to understand why things take the shape they do, you must turn not to the axioms of a rule-theory but to the micro-ecology that they follow from. The intuition behind the symbolic paradigm is quite different: here rule-theory drives micro-theory; we expect to find many characteristics of the micro-level which make no micro-sense, do not derive from natural micro-assumptions or interactions, and can only be understood in terms of the higher-level system being implemented.

The RM pattern associator again provides us with some specific examples. As noted, it is surely significant that the regular past-tense morphology leaves the stem completely unaltered. Suppose we attempt to encode this in the pattern associator by pre-setting it for the identity map; then for the vast majority of items (perhaps more than 95% on the whole vocabulary), most connections will not have to be changed at all. In this way, we might be able to make the learner pay (in learning time) for divergences from identity. But such a setting has no justification from the micro-level perspective, which conduces only to some sort of uniformity (all weights 0, for example, or all random); the labels that we use from our perspective as theorists are invisible to the units themselves, and the connections implementing the identity map are indistinguishable at the micro-level from any other connections. Wiring it in is an implementational strategy driven by outside considerations, a fingerprint of the macro-theory.

An actual example in the RM model as it stands is the selective blurring of Wickelfeature representations. When the Wickelfeature ABC is part of an input stem, extra Wickelfeatures XBC and ABY are also turned on, but AXC is not: as we noted above (see also Lachter & Bever, 1988), this is motivated by the macro-principles that individual phonemes are the significant units of analysis and that phonological interactions when they occur generally involve adjacent pairs of segments. It is not motivated by any principle of micro-level connectionism.

Even the basic organization of the RM model, simple though it is, comes from motives external to the micro-level. Why should it be that the stem is mapped to the past tense, that the past tense arises from a modification of the stem? Because a sort of intuitive proto-linguistics tells us so. It is easy to set up a network in which stem and past tense are represented only in terms of their semantic features, so that generalization gradients are defined over semantic similarity (e.g. *hit* and *strike* would be subject to similar changes in the past tense), with the unwelcome consequence that no phonological relations will 'emerge'. Indeed, the telling argument against the RM pattern associator as a model of linguistic knowledge is that its very design forces it to blunder past the major generalizations of the English system. It is not unthinkable that many of the design flaws could be overcome, resulting in a connectionist network that learns more insightfully. But subsymbolism or eliminative connectionism, as a radical metatheory of cognitive science, will not be vindicated if the principal structures of such hypothetical improved models turn out to be dictated by higher-level theory rather than by micro-necessities. To the extent that connectionist models are not mere isotropic node tangles, they will themselves have properties that call out for explanation. We expect that in many cases, these explanations will constitute the macro-theory of the rules that the system would be said to implement.

Here we see, too, why radical connectionism is so closely wedded to the notion of blank slates, simple learning mechanisms, and vectors of "teaching" inputs juxtaposed unit-by-unit with the networks' output vectors. If you *really* want a network not to implement *any* rules at all, the properties of the units and connections at the micro-level must suffice to organize the network into something that behaves intelligently. Since these units are too simple and too oblivious to the requirements of the computational problem that the entire network will be required to solve to do the job, the complexity of the system must derive from the complexity of the set of environmental inputs causing the units to execute their simple learning functions. One explains the organization of the system, then, only in terms of the structure of the environment, the simple activation and learning abilities of the units, and the tools and language of those aspects of statistical mechanics apropos to the aggregate behavior of the units as they respond to environmental contingencies (as in Hinton & Sejnowski, 1986; Smolensky, 1986)—the rules genuinely would have no role to play.

As it turns out, the RM model requires both kinds of explanation—implemented macrotheory and massive supervised learning—in accounting for its asymptotic organization. Rumelhart and McClelland made up for the model's lack of proper rule-motivated structure by putting it into a teaching environment that was unrealistically tailored to produce much of the behavior they wanted to see. In the absence of macro-organization the environment must bear a very heavy burden.

Rumelhart and McClelland (1986a, p. 143) recognize this implication clearly and unflinchingly in the two paragraphs they devote in their volumes to answering the question "Why are People Smarter than Rats?":

> Given all of the above [the claim that human cognition and the behavior of lower animals can be explained in terms of PDP networks], the question does seem a bit puzzling. ... People have much more cortex than rats do or even than other primates do; in particular they have very much more ... brain structure not dedicated to input/output—and presumably, this extra cortex is strategically placed in the brain to subserve just those functions that differentiate people from rats or even apes. ... But there must be another aspect to the difference between rats and people as well. This is that the human environment includes other people and the cultural devices that they have developed to organize their thinking processes.

We agree completely with one part: that the plausibility of radical connectionism is tied to the plausibility of this explanation.

8.3. On the properties of parallel distributed processing models

In our view the more interesting points raised by an examination of the RM
model concern the general adequacy of the PDP mechanisms it uses, for it
is this issue, rather than the metatheoretical ones, that will ultimately have
the most impact on the future of cognitive science. The RM model is just one
early example of a PDP model of language, and Rumelhart and McClelland
make it clear that it has been simplified in many ways and that there are many
paths for improvement and continued development within the PDP framework. Thus it would be especially revealing to try to generalize the results of
our analysis to the prospects for PDP models of language in general. Although the past tense rule is a tiny fragment of knowledge of language, many
of its properties that pose problems for the RM model are found in spades
elsewhere. Here we point out some of the properties of the PDP architecture
used in the RM model that seem to contribute to its difficulties and hence
which will pose the most challenging problems to PDP models of language.

8.3.1. Distributed representations

PDP models such as RM's rely on 'distributed' representations: a large-
scale entity is represented by a pattern of activation over a set of units rather
than by turning on a single unit dedicated to it. This would be a strictly
implementational claim, orthogonal to the differences between connectionist
and symbol-processing theories, were it not for an additional aspect: the units
have semantic content; they stand for (that is, they are turned on in response
to) specific properties of the entity, and the entity is thus represented solely
in terms which of those properties it has. The links in a network describe
strengths of association between properties, not between individuals. The
relation between features and individuals is one-to-many in both directions:
Each individual is described as a collection of many features, and each feature
plays a role in the description of many individuals.

Hinton et al. (1986) point to a number of useful characteristics of distributed representations. They provide a kind of content-addressable memory,
from which individual entities may be called up through their properties.
They provide for automatic generalization: things true of individual X can be
inherited by individual Y inasmuch as the representation of Y overlaps that
of X (i.e. inasmuch as Y shares properties with X) and activation of the
overlapping portion during learning has been correlated with generalizable

properties. And they allow for the formation of new concepts in a system via new combinations of properties that the system already represents.

It is often asserted that distributed representation using features is uniquely available to PDP models, and stands as the hallmark of a new paradigm of cognitive science, one that calculates not with symbols but with what Smolensky (in press) has dubbed 'subsymbols' (basically, what Rumelhart, McClelland, and Hinton call 'microfeatures'). Smolensky puts it this way:

> (18) Symbols and Context Dependence.
> In the symbolic paradigm, the context of a symbol is manifest around it, and consists of other symbols; in the subsymbolic paradigm, the context of a symbol is manifest inside it, and consists of subsymbols.

It is striking, then, that one aspect of distributed representation—featural decomposition—is a well-established tool in every area of linguistic theory, a branch of inquiry securely located in (perhaps indeed paradigmatic of) the 'symbolic paradigm'. Even more striking, linguistic theory calls on a version of distributed representation to accomplish the very goals that Hinton et al. (1986) advert to. Syntactic, morphological, semantic, and phonological entities are analyzed as feature complexes so that they can be efficiently content-addressed in linguistic rules; so that generalization can be achieved across individuals; so that 'new' categories can appear in a system from fresh combinations of features. Linguistic theory also seeks to make the correct generalizations inevitable given the representation. One influential attempt, the 'evaluation metric' hypothesis, proposed to measure the optimality of linguistic rules (specifically phonological rules) in terms of the number of features they refer to; choosing the most compact grammar would guarantee maximal generality. Compare in this regard Hinton et al.'s (1986, p. 84) remark about types and instances:

> ... the relation between a type and an instance can be implemented by the relationship between a set of units [features] and a larger set [of features] that includes it. Notice that the more general the type the smaller the set of units [features] used to encode it. As the number of terms in an intensional [featural] description gets smaller, the corresponding extensional set [of individuals] gets larger.

This echoes exactly Halle's (1957, 1962) observation that the important general classes of phonemes were among those that could be specified by small sets of features. In subsequent linguistic work we find thorough and continuing exploration of a symbol-processing content-addressing automatically-generalizing rule-theory built, in part, on featural analysis. No distinction-in-principle between PDP and all that has gone before can be linked to the presence or absence of featural decomposition (one central aspect of distributed representation) as the key desideratum. Features analyze the structure of paradigms—the way individuals contrast with comparable individuals—and any theory, macro, micro, or mini, that deals with complex entities can use them.

Of course, distributed representation in PDP models implies more than just featural decomposition: an entity is represented as *nothing but* the features it is composed of. Concatenative structure, constituency, variables, and their binding—in short, syntagmatic organization—are virtually abandoned. This is where the RM model and similar PDP efforts really depart from previous work, and also where they fail most dramatically.

A crucial problem is the difficulty PDP models have in representing *individuals* and *variables* (this criticism is also made by Norman, 1986, in his generally favorable appraisal of PDP models). The models represent individual objects as sets of their features. Nothing, however, represents the fact that a collection of features corresponds to an existing individual: that it is distinct from a twin that might share all its features, or that an object similar to a previously viewed one is a single individual that has undergone a change as opposed to two individual objects that happen to resemble one another, or that a situation has undergone a change if two identical objects have switched positions.[36] In the RM model, for example, this problem manifests itself in the inability to supply different past tenses for homophonous verbs such as *wring* and *ring*, or to enforce a categorical distinction between morphologically disparate verbs that are given similar featural representations such as *become* and *succumb*, to mention just two of the examples discussed in Section 4.3.

As we have mentioned, a seemingly obvious way to handle this problem—just increase the size of the feature set so that more distinctions can be encoded—will not do. For one thing, the obvious kinds of features to add, such as semantic features to distinguish homophones, gives the model too much power, as we have mentioned: it could use any semantic property or combination of semantic and phonological properties to distinguish inflectional rules, whereas in fact only a relatively small set of features are ever encoded inflectionally in the world's languages (Bybee, 1985; Talmy, 1985). Furthermore, the crucial properties governing choice of inflection are not semantic at all but refer to abstract morphological entities such as basic lexical itemhood or roothood. Finally, this move would commit one to the prediction that semantically-related words are likely to have similar past tenses, which is just not true (compare, e.g. *hit/hit* versus *strike/struck* versus *slap/slapped*

---

[36]We thank David Kirsh for these examples.

(similar meanings, different kinds of past tenses) or *stand/stood* versus *understand/understood* versus *stand out/stood out* (different meanings, same kind of past tense). Basically, increasing the feature set is only an approximate way to handle the problem of representing individuals; by making finer distinctions it makes it less likely that individuals will be confused but it still does not encode individuals as individuals. The relevant difference between *wring* and *ring* as far as the past tense is concerned is that they are different words, pure and simple.[37]

A second way of handling the problem is to add arbitrary features that simply distinguish words. In the extreme case, there could be a set of *n* features over which *n* orthogonal patterns of activation stand in one-to-one correspondence with *n* lexical items. This won't work, either. The basic problem is that distributed representations, when they are the *only* representations of objects, face the conflicting demands of keeping individuals distinct and providing the basis for generalization. As it stands, Rumelhart and McClelland must walk a fine line between keeping similar words distinct and getting the model to generalize to new inputs—witness their use of Wickelfeatures over Wickelphones, their decision to encode a certain proportion of incorrect Wickelfeatures, their use of a noisy output function for the past tense units, all designed to blur distinctions and foster generalization (as mentioned, the effort was only partially successful, as the model failed to generalize properly to many unfamiliar stems). Dedicating some units to representing wordhood would be a big leap in the direction of nongeneralizability. With orthogonal patterns representing words, in the extreme case, word-specific output features could be activated accurately in every case and the discrepancy between computed-output and teacher-supplied-input needed to strengthen connections from the relevant stem *features* would never occur. Intermediate solutions, such as having a relatively small set of word-distinguishing features available to distinguish homophones with distinct endings, might help. But given the extremely delicate balance between discriminability and generalizability, one won't know until it is tried, and in any case, it would at best be a hack that did not tackle the basic problem at hand: individuating individuals, and associating them with the abstract predicates that govern the permissible generalizations in the system.

The lack of a mechanism to bind sets of features together as individuals causes problems at the output end, too. A general problem for coarse-coded

---

[37]Of course, another problem with merely increasing the feature set, especially if the features are conjunctive, is that the network can easily grow too large very quickly. Recall that Wickelphones, which in principle can make finer distinctions than Wickelfeatures, would have required a network with more than two billion connections.

distributed representations is that when two individuals are simultaneously represented, the system can lose track of which feature goes with which individual—leading to "illusory conjunctions" where, say, an observer may be unable to say whether he or she is seeing a blue circle and a red triangle or a red triangle and a blue circle (see Hinton et al., 1986; Treisman & Schmidt, 1982). The RM model simultaneously computes past tense output features corresponding to independent subregularities which it is then unable to keep separate, resulting in incorrect blends such as *slept* as the past tense of *slip*—a kind of self-generated phonological illusory conjunction. The current substitute for a realistic binding mechanism, namely the "whole-string binding network", does not do the job, and we are given no reason to believe that a more realistic and successful model is around the corner. The basic point is that the binding problem is a core deficiency of this kind of distributed representation, not a minor detail whose solution can be postponed to some later date.

The other main problem with features-only distributed representations is that they do not easily provide *variables* that stand for sets of individuals regardless of their featural decomposition, and over which quantified generalizations can be made. This dogs the RM model in many places. For example, there is the inability to represent certain reduplicative words, in which the distinction between a feature occurring once versus occurring twice is crucial, or in learning the general nature of the rule of reduplication, where a morpheme must be simply copied: one needs a variable standing for an *occurrence* of a morpheme independent of the particular features it is composed of. In fact, even the English regular rule of adding /d/ is never properly learned (that is, the model does not generalize it properly to many words), because in essence the real rule causes an affix to be added to a "word", which is a variable standing for *any* admissible phone sequence, whereas the model associates the family of /d/ features with a list of *particular* phone sequences it has encountered instead. Many of the other problems we have pointed out can also be traced to the lack of variables.

We predict that the kind of distributed representation used in the two layer pattern-associators like the one in the RM model will cause similar problems anywhere they are used in modeling middle- to high-level cognitive processes.[38] Hinton, McClelland, and Rumelhart (p. 82) themselves provide an example that (perhaps inadvertently) illustrates the general problem:

---

[38]Within linguistic semantics, for example, a well-known problem is that if semantic representation is a set of features, how are propositional connectives defined over such feature sets? If P is a set of features, what function of connectionist representation will give the set for ~P?

People are good at generalizing newly acquired knowledge. ... If, for example, you learn that chimpanzees like onions you will probably raise your estimate of the probability that gorillas like onions. In a network that uses distributed representations, this kind of generalization is automatic. The new knowledge about chimpanzees is incorporated by modifying some of the connection strengths so as to alter the causal effects of the distributed pattern of activity that represents chimpanzees. The modification automatically changes the causal effects of all similar activity patterns. So if the representation of gorillas is a similar activity pattern over the same set of units, its causal effects will be changed in a similar way.

This venerable associationist hypothesis about inductive reasoning has been convincingly discredited by contemporary research in cognitive psychology. People's inductive generalizations are not automatic responses to similarity (in any non-question-begging sense of similarity); they depend on the reasoner's unconscious "theory" of the domain, and on any theory-relevant fact about the domain acquired through any route whatsoever (communicated verbally, acquired in a single exposure, inferred through circuitous means, etc.), in a way that can completely override similarity relations (Carey, 1985; de Jong & Mooney, 1986; Gelman & Markman, 1986; Keil, 1986; Osherson, Smith, & Shafir, 1986; Pazzani, 1987). To take one example, knowledge of how a set of perceptual features was caused, or knowledge of the "kind" that an individual is an example of, can override any generalizations inspired by the object's features themselves: for example, an animal that looks exactly like a skunk will nonetheless be treated as a raccoon if one is told that the stripe was painted onto an animal that had raccoon parents and raccoon babies (see Keil, 1986; who demonstrates that this phenomenon occurs in children and is not the result of formal schooling). Similarly, even a basketball ignoramus will not be seduced by the similarity relations holding among the typical starting players of the Boston Celtics and those holding among the starting players of the Los Angeles Lakers, and thus will not be tempted to predict that a yellow-shirted blond player entering the game will run to the Celtics' basket when he gets the ball just because all previous blond players did so. (Hair color, nonetheless, might be used in qualitatively different generalizations, such as which players will be selected to endorse hair care products.) The example, from Pazzani and Dyer (1987), is one of many that have led to artificial intelligence systems based on "explanation-based learning" which has greater usefulness and greater fidelity to people's common-sense reasoning than the "similarity-based learning" that Hinton et al.'s example system performs automatically (see, e.g., de Jong & Mooney, 1986). Osherson et al. (1987), also analyse the use of similarity as a basis for generalization and show its inherent problems; Gelman and Markman (1986) show how preschool children shelve similarity relations when making inductive generalizations about natural kinds.

The point is that people's inductive inferences depend on variables assigned to sets of individuals that pick out some properties and completely ignore others, differently on different occasions, depending in knowledge-specific ways on the nature of the inductive inference to be made on that occasion. Furthermore the knowledge that can totally alter or reverse an inductive inference is not just another pattern of trained feature correlations, but depends crucially on the structured propositional content of the knowledge: learning that all gorillas are exclusively carnivorous will lead to a different generalization about their taste for onions than learning that some or many are exclusively carnivorous or that it is not the case that all gorillas are exclusively carnivorous, and learning that a *particular* gorilla who happens to have a broken leg does not like onions will not necessarily lead to *any* tendency to project that distaste onto other injured gorillas and chimpanzees. Though similarity surely plays a role in domains of which people are entirely unfamiliar, or perhaps in initial gut reactions, full-scale intuitive inference is not a mere reflection of patterns of featural similarity that have been intercorrelated in the past. Therefore one would not want to use the automatic-generalization properties of distributed representations to provide an account of human inductive inference in general. This is analogous to the fact we have been stressing throughout, namely that the past tense inflectional system is not a slave to similarity but it is driven in precise ways by speakers' implicit "theories" of linguistic organization.

In sum, featural decomposition is an essential feature of standard symbolic models of language and cognition, and many of the successes of PDP models simply inherit these advantages. However what is unique about the RM model and other two-layer pattern associators is the claim that individuals and types are represented as nothing but activated subsets of features. This impoverished mechanism is viable neither in language nor in cognition in general. The featural decomposition of an object must be available to certain processes, but can only be one of the records associated with the object and need not enter into all the processes referring to the object. Some symbol referring to the object qua object, and some variable types referring to task-relevant classes of objects that cut across featural similarity, are required.

8.3.2. Distinctions among subcomponents and abstract internal representations

The RM model collapses into a single input–output module a mapping that in rule-based accounts is a composition of several distinct subcomponents feeding information into one another, such as derivational morphology and inflectional morphology, or inflectional morphology and phonology. This, of course, is what gives it its radical look. If the subcomponents of a traditional account were kept distinct in a PDP model, mapping onto distinct subnetworks or pools of units with their own inputs and outputs, or onto distinct layers of a multilayer network, one would naturally say that the network simply implemented the traditional account. But it is just the factors that differentiate Rumelhart and McClelland's collapsed one-box model from the traditional accounts that causes it to fail so noticeably.

Why do Rumelhart and McClelland have to obliterate the traditional decomposition to begin with? The principal reason is that when one breaks a system down into components, the components must communicate by passing information—internal representations—among themselves. But because these are *internal* representations the environment cannot "see" them and so cannot adjust them during learning via the perceptron convergence procedure used in the RM model. Furthermore, the internal representations do not correspond directly to environmental inputs and outputs and so the criteria for matches and mismatches necessary to drive the convergence procedure are not defined. In other words the representations used in decomposed, modular systems are *abstract*, and many aspects of their organization cannot be learned in any obvious way. (Chomsky, 1981, calls this argument from "poverty of the stimulus".) Sequences of morphemes resulting from factoring out phonological changes are one kind of abstract representation used in rule systems; lexical entries distinct from phonetic representations are another; morphological roots are a third. The RM model thus is composed of a single module mapping from input directly to output in part because there is no realistic way for their convergence procedure to learn the internal representations of a modular account properly.

A very general point we hope to have made in this paper is that symbolic models of language were not designed for arbitrary reasons and preserved as quaint traditions; the distinctions they make are substantive claims motivated by empirical facts and cannot be obliterated unless a new model provides equally compelling accounts of those facts. Designing a model that can record hundreds of thousands of first-order correlations can simulate some but not all of this structure and is unable to explain it or to account for the structures that do not occur across languages. Similar conclusions, we predict, will emerge from other cognitive domains that are rich in data and theory. It is unlikely that any model will be able to obliterate distinctions among subcomponents and their corresponding forms of abstract internal representations that have been independently motivated by detailed study of a domain of cognition. This alone will sharply brake any headlong movement away from the kinds of theories that have been constructed within the symbolic framework.

8.3.3. Discrete, categorical rules

Despite the graded and frequency-sensitive responses made by children and by adults in their speech errors and analogical extensions in parts of the strong verb system, many aspects of knowledge of language result in categorical judgments of ungrammaticality. This fact is difficult to reconcile with any mechanism that at asymptote leaves a number of candidates at suprathreshold strength and allows them to compete probabilistically for expression (Bowerman, 1987, also makes this point). In the present case, adult speakers assign a single past tense form to words they represent as being "regular" even if subregularities bring several candidates to mind (*e.g. brought/*brang/* bringed*); and subregularities that may have been partially productive in childhood are barred from generating past tense forms when verbs are derived from other syntactic categories (e.g. *pang; *high-stuck*) or are registered as being distinct lexical items from those exemplifying subregularities (e.g. *I broke the car*). Categorical judgments of ungrammaticality is a common (though not all-pervasive) property of linguistic judgments of novel words and strings, and cannot be predicted by semantic interpretability or any prior measure or "similarity" to known words or strings (e.g. *I put; *The child seems sleeping; *What did you see something?*). Obviously PDP models can display categorical judgments by various kinds of sharpening and threshold circuits; the question is whether models can be built—other than by implementing standard symbolic theories—in which the quantitatively strongest output prior to the sharpening circuit invariably corresponds to the unique qualitatively appropriate response.

8.3.4. Unconstrained correlation extraction

It is often considered a virtue of PDP models that they are powerful learners; virtually any amount of statistical correlation among features in a set of inputs can be soaked up by the weights on the dense set of interconnections among units. But this property is a liability if human learners are more constrained. In the case of the RM model, we saw how it can acquire rules that are not found in any language such as nonlocal conditioning of phonological changes or mirror-reversal of phonetic strings. This problem would get even worse if the set of feature units was expanded to represent other kinds of information in an attempt to distinguish homophonous or phonologically similar forms. The model also exploits subregularities (such as those of the irregular classes) that adults at best do not exploit productively (*slip/*slept* and *peep/*pept*) and at worst are completely oblivious to (e.g. lexical causatives like *sit/set—lie/lay—fall/fell—rise/raise*, which are never generalized to *cry/*cray*). The types of inflection found across human languages involves a highly constrained subset of the logically possible semantic features, feature combinations, phonological alterations, items admitting of inflection, and agreement relations (Bybee, 1985; Talmy, 1985). For example, to represent the literal meanings of the verbs *brake* and *break* the notion of a man-made mechanical device is relevant, but no language has different past tenses or plurals for a distinction between man-made versus natural objects, despite the cognitive salience of that notion. And the constrained nature of the variation in other components of language such as syntax has been the dominant theme of linguistic investigations for a quarter of a century (e.g. Chomsky, 1981). These constraints are facts that any theory of language acquisition must be able to account for; a model that can learn all possible degrees of correlation among a set of features is not a model of the human being.

8.4. Can the model be recast using more powerful PDP mechanisms?

The most natural response of a PDP theorist to our criticisms would be to retreat from the claim that the RM model in its current form is to be taken as a literal model of inflection acquisition. The RM model uses some of the simplest of the devices in the PDP armamentarium, devices that PDP theorists in general have been moving away from. Perhaps it is the limitations of these simplest PDP devices—two-layer pattern association networks—that cause problems for the RM model, and these problems would all diminish if more sophisticated kinds of PDP networks were used. Thus the claim that PDP networks rather than rules provide an exact and detailed account of language would survive.

In particular, two interesting kinds of networks, the Boltzmann Machine (Hinton & Sejnowski, 1986) and the Back-Propagation scheme (Rumelhart et al., 1986) have been developed recently that have "hidden units" or intermediate layers between input and output. These hidden units function as internal representations and as a result such networks are capable of computing functions that are uncomputable in two-layer pattern associators of the RM variety. Furthermore, in many interesting cases the models have been able to "learn internal representations". For example the Rumelhart et al. model changes not only the weights of the connections to its output units in response to an error with respect to the teaching input, but it propagates the error signal backwards to the intermediate units and changes their weights in the direction that alters their aggregate effect on the output in the right direction. Perhaps, then, a multilayered PDP network with back-propagation learning could avoid the problems of the RM model.

There are three reasons why such speculations are basically irrelevant to the points we have been making.

First, there is the gap between revolutionary manifestos and actual accomplishments. Rumelhart and McClelland's surprising claims—that language can be described only approximately by rules, that there is no induction problem in their account, and that we must revise our understanding of linguistic information processing—are based on the putative success of *their existing* model. Given that their existing model does not do the job it is said to do, the claims must be rejected. If a PDP advocate were to eschew the existing RM model and appeal to more powerful mechanisms, the only claim that could be made is that there may exist a model of unspecified design that may or may not account for past tense acquisition without the use of rules and that if it did, we should revise our understanding of language, treat rules as mere approximations, and so on. Such an assertion, of course, would have as little claim to our attention as any other claim about the hypothetical consequences of a nonexistent model.

Second, a successful PDP model of more complex design may be nothing more than an implementation of a symbolic rule-based account. The advantage of a multilayered model is precisely that it is free from the constraints that so sharply differentiate the RM model from standard ones, namely, the lack of internal representations and subcomponents. Multilayered networks, and other sophisticated models such as those that have one network that can gate the connections between two others or networks that can simulate semantic networks, production systems, or LISP primitive operations (Hinton, 1981; Touretzky, 1986; Touretzky & Hinton, 1985) are appealing because they have the ability to mimic or implement the standard operations and representations needed in traditional symbolic accounts (though perhaps with some twists). We do not doubt that it would be possible to *implement* a rule system in networks with multiple layers: after all, it has been known for over 45 years that nonlinear neuron-like elements can function as logic gates and that hence that networks consisting of interconnected layers of such elements can compute propositions (McCulloch & Pitts, 1943). Furthermore, given what we know about neural information processing and plasticity it seems likely that the elementary operations of symbolic processing will *have* to be implemented in a system consisting of massively interconnected parallel stochastic units in which the effects of learning are manifest in changes in connections. These uncontroversial facts have always been at the very foundations of the realist interpretation of symbolic models of cognition; they do not signal a departure of any sort from standard symbolic accounts. Perhaps a multilayered or gated multinetwork system could solve the tasks of inflection acquisition without simply implementing standard grammars intact (for example, they might behave discrepantly from a set of rules in a way that mimicked people's systematic divergence from that set of rules, or their intermediate layers might be totally opaque in terms of what they represent), and thus would call for a revised understanding of language, but there is no reason to believe that this will be true.

As we mentioned in a previous section, the really radical claim is that there are models that can *learn* their internal organization through a process that can be exhaustively described as an interaction between the correlational structure of environmental inputs and the aggregate behavior of the units as they execute their simple learning and activation functions in response to those inputs. Again, this is no more than a vague hope. An important technical problem is that when intermediate layers of complex networks have to learn anything in the local unconstrained manner characteristic of PDP models, they are one or more layers removed from the output layer at which discrepancies between actual and desired outputs are recorded. Their inputs and outputs no longer correspond in any direct way to overt stimuli and responses, and the steps needed to modify their weights are no longer transparent. Since differences in the setting of each tunable component of the intermediate layers have consequences that are less dramatic at the comparison stage (their effects combine in complex ways with the effects of weight changes of other units before affecting the output layer), it is harder to ensure that the intermediate layers will be properly tuned by local adjustments propagating backwards. Rumelhart et al. (1986) have dealt with this problem in clever ways with some interesting successes in simple domains such as learning to add two-digit numbers, detecting symmetry, or learning the exclusive-'or' operator. But there is always the danger in such systems of converging on incorrect solutions defined by local minima of the "energy landscape" defined over the space of possible weights, and such factors as the starting configuration, the order of inputs, several parameters of the learning function, the number of hidden units, and the innate topology of the network (such as whether all input units are connected to all intermediate units, and whether they are connected to all output units via direct paths or only through intervening links) can all influence whether the models will properly converge even in some of the simple cases. There is no reason to predict with certainty that these models will fail to acquire complex abilities such as mastery of the past tense system without wiring in traditional theories by hand—but there is even less reason to predict that they will.

These problems are exactly that, problems. They do not demonstrate that interesting PDP models of language are impossible in principle. At the same time, they show that there is no basis for the belief that connectionism will dissolve the difficult puzzles of language, or even provide radically new solutions to them. As for the present, we have shown that the paradigm example of a PDP model of language can claim nothing more than a superficial fidelity to some first-order regularities of language. More is known than just the first-order regularities, and when the deeper and more diagnostic patterns are examined with care, one sees not only that the PDP model is not a viable alternative to symbolic theories, but that the symbolic account is supported in virtually every aspect. Principled symbolic theories of language have achieved success with a broad spectrum of empirical generalizations, some of considerable depth, ranging from properties of linguistic structure to patterns of development in children. It is only such success that can warrant confidence in the reality and exactitude of our claims to understanding.

Appendix: English strong verbs

Here we provide, for the reader's convenience, an informally classified listing of all the strong verbs that we recognize in our own vocabulary (thus we omit, for example, Rumelhart & McClelland's *drag-drug*). The notation *?Verb* means that we regard *Verb* as somewhat less than usual, particularly as a strong form in the class where it's listed. The notation *??Verb* means that we regard *Verb* as obsolete (particularly in the past) but recognizable, the kind of thing one picks up from reading. The notation (+) means that the verb, in our judgment, admits a regular form. Notice that obsolescence does not imply regularizability: a few verbs simply seem to lack a usable past tense or past participle. We have found that judgments differ from dialect to dialect, with a cline of willingness-to-regularize running up from British English (south-of-London) to Canadian (Montreal) to American (general). When in doubt, we've taken the American way.

Prefixed forms are listed when the prefix-root combination is not semantically transparent.

The term 'laxing' refers to the replacement of a tense vowel or diphthong by its lax counterpart. In English, due to the Great Vowel Shift, the notion 'lax counterpart' is slightly odd: the tense-lax alternations are not *i-I, e-ε, u-U*, and so on, but rather *ay-I, i-ε, e-æ, o-ɔ/a, u-ɔ/a*. The term 'ablaut' refers to all other vowel changes.

I. T/D Superclass

1. T/D + ∅

hit, slit, split, quit, ?knit(+),[39] ?spit, ??shit, ??beshit
bid[40], rid, ?forbid
shed, spread, wed(+)[41]
let, set, beset[42], upset, wet(+)
cut, shut
put
burst, cast, cost, thrust(+)
hurt

2. T/D with laxing class

bleed, breed, feed, lead, mislead, read, speed(+), ?plead(+)
meet
hide(en), slide
bite(en), light(+), alight(+!)
shoot

3. Overt-T ending

3a. Suffix-t
burn, ??learn, ?dwell, ??spell, ???smell
?spill, ??spoil
3b. Devoicing
bend, send, spend, ?lend, ?rend
build
3c. -t with laxing
lose
deal, feel, ?kneel(+)
mean
?dream
creep, keep, leap(+), sleep, sweep(+), weep
leave

---

[39]*He knit a sweater* is possible, not?? *He knit his brows.*
[40]As in poker, bridge, or defense contracts.
[41]The adjective is only *wedded.*
[42]Mainly an adjective.

3d. x-ought - ought
buy, bring, catch, fight, seek, teach, think

4. Overt -D ending

4a. Satellitic laxing (cf. bleed *group)*
flee
say
hear
4b. Drop stem consonant
have
make
4c. With ablaut [ε - o - o]
sell, tell, foretell
4d. With unique vowel change and +n participle:
do

II. E-ɔ ablaut class

1. i/ε - o/ɔ - o/ɔ+n

freeze, speak, ??bespeak, steal, weave(+)[43], ?heave(+)[44]
get, forget, ??beget
??tread[45]
swear, tear, wear, ?bear, ??forbear, ??forswear

2. Satellitic x - o - o+n

awake, wake, break
choose

---

[43]Only in reference to carpets, etc. is the strong form possible. *The drunk wove down the road.* The adjective is *woven.*

[44]Only nautical *heave to/hove to.* *He hove his lunch.* Past participle not *hoven.*

[45]Though *trod* is common in British English, it is at best quaint in American English.

III. I - æ/ʌ - ʌ group

1. I - æ - ʌ

ring, sing, spring
drink, shrink, sink, stink
swim
begin

2. I - ʌ - ʌ

cling, ?fling, sling, sting, string, swing, wring
stick
dig
win, spin
?stink, ?slink

3. Satellites x - æ/ʌ - ʌ

run (cf. I - æ - ʌ)
hang, strike[46]
?sneak (cf. I - ʌ - ʌ)

IV. Residual clusters

1. x- u - x/o+n

blow, grow, know, throw
draw, withdraw
fly
?slay

2. e - U -e+n

take, mistake, forsake, shake, partake

---

[46]*Stricken* as participle as in 'from the record', otherwise as an adjective.

3. ay - aw - aw

bind, find, grind, wind

4. ay - o - X

4a. ay - o -I+n
rise, arise
write, ??smite
ride
drive, ?strive
4b. ay - o - ?
dive, shine[47]
?stride
??thrive

V. Miscellaneous

1. Pure suppletion

be
go, forgo, undergo

2. Backwards ablaut

fall, befall (cf. get–got)
hold, behold (cf. tell–told)
come, become

3. x - Y - x+n

eat
beat
see (possibly satellite of *blow*-class)
give, forgive
forbid, ??bid[48]

---

[47]Typically intransitive: *He shone his shoes.*

[48]As in 'ask or command to'. The past *bade* is very peculiar, *bidded* is impossible, and the past participle is obscure, though certainly not *bidden*.

4. Miscellaneous

sit, spit
stand, understand, withstand (possibly satellite of *I* - ʌ - ʌ class)
lie

5. Regular but for past participle

a. Add -n to stem (all allow -ed in participle)
sow, show, sew, prove, shear, strew
b. Add -n to ablauted stem
swell

A remark. A number of strong participial forms survive only as adjectives (most, indeed, somewhat unusual): *cleft, cloven, girt, gilt, hewn, pent, bereft, shod, wrought, laden, mown, sodden, clad, shaven, drunken, (mis)shapen.* The verb *crow* admits a strong form only in the phrase *the cock crew*; notice that *the rooster crew* is distinctly peculiar and *Melvin crew over his victory* is unintelligible. Other putative strong forms like *leant, clove, abode, durst, chid,* and *sawn* seem to us to belong to another language.

References

Anderson, J.A., & Hinton, G.E. (1981). Models of information processing in the brain. In G.E. Hinton & J.A. Anderson (Eds.), *Parallel models of associative memory.* Hillsdale, NJ: Erlbaum.
Anderson, J.R. (1976). *Language, memory and thought.* Hillsdale, NJ: Erlbaum.
Anderson, J.R. (1983). *The architecture of cognition.* Cambridge, MA: Harvard University Press.
Armstrong, S.L., Gleitman, L.R., & Gleitman, H. (1983). What some concepts might not be. *Cognition, 13,* 263–308.
Aronoff, M. (1976). *Word formation in generative grammar.* Cambridge, MA: MIT Press.
Berko, J. (1958). The child's learning of English morphology. *Word, 14,* 150–177.
Bloch, B. (1947). English verb inflection. *Language 23,* 399–418.
Bowerman, M. (1987). Discussion: Mechanisms of language acquisition. In B. MacWhinney (Ed.), *Mechanisms of language acquisition.* Hillsdale, NJ: Erlbaum.
Brown, R. (1973). *A first language: The early stages.* Cambridge, MA: Harvard University Press.
Bybee, J.L. (1985). *Morphology: a study of the relation between meaning and form.* Philadelphia: Benjamins.
Bybee, J.L., & Slobin, D.I. (1982). Rules and schemes in the development and use of the English past tense. *Language, 58,* 265–289.
Carey, S. (1985). *Conceptual change in childhood.* Cambridge, MA: Bradford Books/MIT Press.
Cazden, C.B. (1968). The acquisition of noun and verb inflections. *Child Development, 39,* 433–448.
Chomsky, N. (1957). *Syntactic structures.* The Hague: Mouton.
Chomsky, N. (1965). *Aspects of the theory of syntax.* Cambridge, MA: MIT Press.
Chomsky, N. (1981). *Lectures on government and binding.* Dordrecht, Netherlands: Foris.

Chomsky, N., & Halle, M. (1968). *The sound pattern of English.* New York: Harper and Row.

Curme, G. (1935). *A grammar of the English language II.* Boston: Barnes & Noble.

de Jong, G.F., & Mooney, R.J. (1986). Explanation-based learning: An alternative view. *Machine Learning, 1,* 145–176.

Ervin, S. (1964). Imitation and structural change in children's language. In E. Lenneberg (Ed.), *New directions in the study of language.* Cambridge, MA: MIT Press.

Feldman, J.A., & Ballard, D.H. (1982). Connectionist models and their properties. *Cognitive Science, 6,* 205–254.

Fodor, J.A. (1968). *Psychological explanation.* New York: Random House.

Fodor, J.A. (1975). *The language of thought.* New York: T.Y. Crowell.

Francis, N., & Kucera, H. (1982). *Frequency analysis of English usage: Lexicon and grammar.* Boston: Houghton Mifflin.

Fries, C. (1940). *American English grammar.* New York: Appleton-Century.

Gelman, S.A., & Markman, E.M. (1986). Categories and induction in young children. *Cognition, 23,* 183–209.

Gleitman, L.R., & Wanner, E. (1982). Language acquisition: The state of the state of the art. In E. Wanner and L.R. Gleitman (Eds.), *Language acquisition: The state of the art.* New York: Cambridge University Press.

Gordon, P. (1986). Level-ordering in lexical development. *Cognition, 21,* 73–93.

Gropen, J., & Pinker, S. (1986). Constrained productivity in the acquisition of the dative alternation. Paper presented at the 11th Annual Boston University Conference on Language Development, October.

Halle, M. (1957). In defense of the Number Two. In E. Pulgram (Ed.), *Studies presented to J. Whatmough.* Mouton: The Hague.

Halle, M. (1962). Phonology in generative grammar. *Word, 18,* 54–72.

Halwes, T., & Jenkins, J.J. (1971). Problem of serial behavior is not resolved by context-sensitive memory models. *Psychological Review, 78,* 122–29.

Hinton, G.E. (1981). Implementing semantic networks in parallel hardware. In G.E. Hinton & J.A. Anderson (Eds.), *Parallel models of associative memory.* Hillsdale, NJ: Erlbaum.

Hinton, G.E., McClelland, J.L., & Rumelhart, D.E. (1986). Distributed representations. In D.E. Rumelhart, J.L. McClelland, and the PDP Research Group, *Parallel distributed processing: Explorations in the microstructure of cognition. Volume 1: Foundations.* Cambridge, MA: Bradford Books/MIT Press.

Hinton, G.E., & Sejnowski, T.J. (1986). Learning and relearning in Boltzmann machines. In D.E. Rumelhart, J.L. McClelland, and the PDP Research Group, *Parallel distributed processing: Explorations in the microstructure of cognition. Volume 1: Foundations.* Cambridge, MA: Bradford Books/MIT Press.

Hoard, J., & C. Sloat (1973). English irregular verbs. *Language, 49,* 107–20.

Hockett, C. (1942). English verb inflection. *Studies in Linguistics, 1.2.,* 1–8.

Jespersen, O. (1942). *A modern English grammar on historical principles, VI.* Reprinted 1961: London: George Allen & Unwin Ltd.

Keil, F.C. (1986). The acquisition of natural kinds and artifact terms. In W. Demopoulos & A. Marras (Ed.), *Language learning and concept acquisition: Foundational issues.* Norwood, NJ: Ablex.

Kiparsky, P. (1982a). From cyclical to lexical phonology. In H. van der Hulst, & N. Smith (Eds.). *The structure of phonological representations.* Dordrecht, Netherlands: Foris.

Kiparsky, P. (1982b). Lexical phonology and morphology. In I.S. Yang (Ed.), *Linguistics in the morning calm.* Seoul: Hansin, pp. 3–91.

Kucera, H., & N. Francis (1967). *Computational analysis of present-day American English.* Providence: Brown University Press.

Kuczaj, S.A. (1976). Arguments against Hurford's auxiliary copying rule. *Journal of Child Language, 3,* 423–427.

Kuczaj, S.A. (1977). The acquisition of regular and irregular past tense forms. *Journal of Verbal Learning and Verbal Behavior, 16,* 589–600.

Kuczaj, S.A. (1978). Children's judgments of grammatical and ungrammatical irregular past tense verbs. *Child Development, 49,* 319–326.

Kuczaj, S.A. (1981). More on children's initial failure to relate specific acquisitions. *Journal of Child Language, 8,* 485–487.

Lachter, J., & Bever, T.G. (1988). The relation between linguistic structure and associative theories of language learning—A constructive critique of some connectionist learning models. *Cognition, 28,* 195–247 this issue.

Lakoff, G. (1987). Connectionist explanations in linguistics: Some thoughts on recent anti-connectionist papers. Unpublished electronic manuscript, ARPAnet.

Levy, Y. (1983). The use of nonce word tests in assessing children's verbal knowledge. Paper presented at the 8th Annual Boston University Conference on Language Development, October, 1983.

Liberman, M., & Pierrehumbert, J. (1984). Intonational invariance under changes in pitch range and length. In M. Aronoff & R. Oehrle (Eds.), *Language sound structure.* Cambridge, MA: MIT Press.

MacWhinney, B., & Snow, C.E. (1985). The child language data exchange system. *Journal of Child Language, 12,* 271–296.

MacWhinney, B., & Sokolov, J.L. (1987). The competition model of the acquisition of syntax. In B. MacWhinney (Ed.), *Mechanisms of language acquisition.* Hillsdale. NJ: Erlbaum.

Maratsos, M., Gudeman, R., Gerard-Nogo, P., & de Hart, G. (1987). A study in novel word learning: The productivity of the causative. In B. MacWhinney (Ed.), *Mechanisms of language acquisition.* Hillsdale, NJ: Erlbaum.

Maratsos, M., & Kuczaj, S.A. (1978). Against the transformationalist account: A simpler analysis of auxiliary overmarkings. *Journal of Child Language, 5,* 337–345.

Marr, D. (1982). *Vision,* San Francisco: Freeman.

McCarthy, J., & Prince, A. (forthcoming). *Prosodic morphology.*

McClelland, J.L., & Rumelhart, D.E. (1985). Distributed memory and the representation of general and specific information. *Journal of Experimental Psychology: General, 114,* 159–188.

McClelland, J.L., Rumelhart, D.E., & Hinton, G.E. (1986). The appeal of parallel distributed processing. In D.E. Rumelhart, J.L. McClelland, and the PDP Research Group, *Parallel distributed processing: Explorations in the microstructure of cognition. Volume 1: Foundations.* Cambridge, MA: Bradford Books/MIT Press.

McClelland, J.L., Rumelhart, D.E., & The PDP Research Group. (1986). *Parallel distributed processing: Explorations in the microstructure of cognition. Volume 2: Psychological and biological models.* Cambridge, MA: Bradford Books/MIT Press.

McCulloch, W.S., & Pitts, W. (1943). A logical calculus of the ideas immanent in nervous activity. *Bulletin of Mathematical Biophysics, 5,* 115–133.

Mencken, H. (1936). *The American language.* New York: Knopf.

Minsky, M. (1963). Steps toward artificial intelligence. In E.A. Feigenbaum & J. Feldman (Eds.), *Computers and thought.* New York: McGraw-Hill.

Newell, A., & Simon, H. (1961). Computer simulation of human thinking. *Science, 134,* 2011–2017.

Newell, A., & Simon, H. (1972). *Human problem solving.* Englewood Cliffs, NJ: Prentice-Hall.

Norman, D.A. (1986). Reflections on cognition and parallel distributed processing. In J.L. McClelland, D.E. Rumelhart, & The PDP Research Group, *Parallel distributed processing: Explorations in the microstructure of cognition. Volume 2: Psychological and biological models.* Cambridge, MA: Bradford Books/MIT Press.

Osherson, D.N., Smith, E.E., & Shafir, E. (1986). Some origins of belief. *Cognition, 24,* 197–224.

Palmer, H. (1930). *A grammar of spoken English on a strictly phonetic basis.* Cambridge: W. Heffer.

Pazzani, M. (1987). Explanation-based learning for knowledge-based systems. *International Journal of Man-Machine Studies, 26,* 413–433.

Pazzani, M., & Dyer, M. (1987). A comparison of concept identification in human learning and network learning with the generalized delta rule. Unpublished manuscript, UCLA.

Pierrehumbert, J., & Beckman, M. (1986). Japanese tone structure. Unpublished manuscript, AT&T Bell Laboratories, Murray Hill, NJ.

Pinker, S. (1979). Formal models of language learning. *Cognition, 7*, 217–283.

Pinker, S. (1984). *Language learnability and language development.* Cambridge, MA: Harvard University Press.

Pinker, S., Lebeaux, D.S., & Frost, L.A. (1987). Productivity and conservatism in the acquisition of the passive. *Cognition, 26*, 195–267.

Putnam, H. (1960). Minds and machines. In S. Hook (Ed.), *Dimensions of mind: A symposium.* New York: NYU Press.

Pylyshyn, Z.W. (1984). *Computation and cognition: Toward a foundation for cognitive science.* Cambridge, MA: Bradford Books/MIT Press.

Rosch, E., & Mervis, C.B. (1975). Family resemblances: Studies in the internal representation of categories. *Cognitive Psychology, 7*, 573–605.

Rosenblatt, F. (1962). *Principles of neurodynamics.* New York: Spartan.

Ross, J.R. (1975). Wording up. Unpublished manuscript, MIT.

Rumelhart, D.E., Hinton, G.E., & Williams, R.J. (1986). Learning internal representations by error propagation. In D.E. Rumelhart, J.L. McClelland, and the PDP Research Group, *Parallel distributed processing: Explorations in the microstructure of cognition. Volume 1: Foundations.* Cambridge, MA: Bradford Books/MIT Press.

Rumelhart, D.E., & McClelland, J.L. (1986a). PDP models and general issues in cognitive science. In D.E. Rumelhart, J.L. McClelland, and the PDP Research Group, *Parallel distributed processing: Explorations in the microstructure of cognition. Volume 1: Foundations.* Cambridge, MA: Bradford Books/MIT Press.

Rumelhart, D.E., & McClelland, J.L. (1986b). On learning the past tenses of English verbs. In J.L. McClelland, D.E. Rumelhart, and the PDP Research Group, *Parallel distributed processing: Explorations in the microstructure of cognition. Volume 2: Psychological and biological models.* Cambridge, MA: Bradford Books/MIT Press.

Rumelhart, D.E., & McClelland, J.L. (1987). Learning the past tenses of English verbs: Implicit rules or parallel distributed processing? In B. MacWhinney (Ed.), *Mechanisms of language acquisition.* Hillsdale, NJ: Erlbaum.

Rumelhart, D.E., McClelland, J.L., and the PDP Research Group. (1986). *Parallel distributed processing: Explorations in the microstructure of cognition. Volume 1: Foundations.* Cambridge, MA: Bradford Books/MIT Press.

Sampson, G. (1987). A turning point in linguistics. *Times Literary Supplement*, June 12, 1987, 643.

Savin, H., & Bever, T.G. (1970). The nonperceptual reality of the phoneme. *Journal of Verbal Learning and Verbal Behavior, 9*, 295–302.

Shattuck-Hufnagel, S. (1979). Speech errors as evidence for a serial-ordering mechanism in sentence production. In W.E. Cooper & E.C.T. Walker (Eds.), *Sentence processing: Psycholinguistic studies presented to Merrill Garrett.* Hillsdale, NJ: Erlbaum.

Sietsema, B. (1987). Theoretical commitments underlying Wickelphonology. Unpublished manuscript. MIT.

Sloat, C., & Hoard, J. (1971). The inflectional morphology of English. *Glossa, 5*, 47–56.

Slobin, D.I. (1971). On the learning of morphological rules: A reply to Palermo and Eberhart. In D.I. Slobin (Ed.), *The ontogenesis of grammar: A theoretical symposium.* New York: Academic Press.

Slobin, D.I. (1985). Crosslinguistic evidence for the language-making capacity. In D.I. Slobin (Ed.), *The crosslinguistic study of language acquisition. Volume II: Theoretical issues.* Hillsdale, NJ: Erlbaum.

Smolensky, P. (1986). Information processing in dynamical systems: Foundations of harmony theory. In D.E. Rumelhart, J.L. McClelland, and the PDP Research Group, *Parallel distributed processing: Explorations in the microstructure of cognition. Volume 1: Foundations.* Cambridge, MA: Bradford Books/MIT Press.

Smolensky, P. (in press). The proper treatment of connectionism. *Behavioral and Brain Sciences.*

Sommer, B.A. (1980). The shape of Kunjen syllables. In D.L. Goyvaerts (Ed.), *Phonology in the 80's.* Ghent: Story-Scientia.

Sweet, H. (1892). *A new English grammar, logical and historical.* Oxford: Clarendon.

Talmy, L. (1985). Lexicalization patterns: Semantic structure in lexical forms. In T. Shopen (Ed.), *Language typology and semantic description, Vol. 3: Grammatical categories and the lexicon.* New York: Cambridge University Press.

Touretzky, D. (1986). BoltzCONS: Reconciling connectionism with the recursive nature of stacks and trees. *Proceedings of the Eighth Annual Conference of the Cognitive Science Society.*

Touretzky, D., & Hinton, G.E. (1985). Symbols among the neurons: Details of a connectionist inference architecture. *Proceedings of the Ninth International Joint Conference on Artificial Intelligence.*

Treisman, A., & Schmidt, H. (1982). Illusory conjunctions in the perception of objects. *Cognitive Psychology, 14,* 107–141.

van der Hulst, H., & Smith, N. (Eds.) (1982). *The structure of phonological representations.* Dordrecht, Netherlands: Foris.

Wexler, K., & Culicover, P. (1980). *Formal principles of language acquisition.* Cambridge, MA: MIT Press.

Wickelgren, W.A. (1969). Context-sensitive coding, associative memory, and serial order in (speech) behavior. *Psychological Review, 76,* 1–15.

Williams, E. (1981). On the notions "lexically related" and "head of a word". *Linguistic Inquiry, 12,* 245–274.

The relation between linguistic structure and associative theories of language learning—A constructive critique of some connectionist learning models*

JOEL LACHTER
THOMAS G. BEVER
University of Rochester

> There's no safety in numbers ... or anything else
> (Thurber)

Abstract

Recently proposed connectionist models of acquired linguistic behaviors have linguistic rule-based representations built in. Similar connectionist models of language acquisition have arbitrary devices and architectures which make them mimic the effect of rules. Connectionist models in general are not well-suited to account for the acquisition of structural knowledge, and require predetermined structures even to simulate basic linguistic facts. Such models are more appropriate for describing the formation of complex associations between structures which are independently represented. This makes connectionist models potentially important tools in studying the relations between frequent behaviors and the structures underlying knowledge and representations. At the very least, such models may offer computationally powerful ways of demonstrating the limits of associationistic descriptions of behavior.

1. Rules and models

This paper considers the status of current proposals that connectionist systems of cognitive modelling can account for rule-governed behavior without directly representing the corresponding rules (Hinton & Anderson, 1981; Hanson

*We are grateful for comments on earlier drafts of this paper from Gary Dell, Jeff Elman, Jerry Feldman, Jerry Fodor, Lou Ann Gerken, Steve Hanson, George Lakoff, Steve Pinker, Alan Prince, Zenon Pylyshyn, Patrice Simard, Paul Smolensky, and Ginny Valian. Requests for reprints should be addressed to J. Lachter or T.G. Bever, Department of Psychology, University of Rochester, Rochester, NY 14627, U.S.A. This work was completed while the first author was supported by a National Science Foundation pre-doctoral fellowship.

& Kegl, 1987a, b; McClelland & Rumelhart, 1986; Rumelhart & McClelland, 1986; Smolensky, in press). We find that those models which seem to exhibit regularities defined by structural rules and constraints, do so only because of their ad hoc representations and architectures which are manifestly motivated by such rules. We conclude that, at best, connectionist models may contribute to our understanding of complex associations between independently defined structures.

For the purposes of our discussion, a rule is a function which maps one representation onto another. The status of rules within the field of cognitive modelling are at the center of a current war. For the past 20 years, the dominant approach to algorithmic modelling of intelligent behavior has been in terms of 'production systems' (for discussions and references see Anderson, 1983; Neches, Langley, & Klar, 1987). Production systems characteristically (but not criterially) utilize a set of statements and algorithmic steps which result in a behavior. Such models characteristically (but not criterially) operate linearly; that is, a model first consults a proposition, applies it if relevant, then goes on to the next proposition, and so on.

Recently, a different paradigm in cognitive modelling has been proposed, using information arranged in systems which can apply as a set of parallel constraint satisfactions. In these systems, a network of interconnected nodes represents the organization underlying the behavior. The relationship between each pair of nodes is an activation function which specifies the strength with which one node's activation level effects another. Such systems are touted as meeting many potential objections to production systems, in that the effect of the nodes on output behavior can be simultaneous, and the relationship to neuronal nets is transparent and enticing (Feldman & Ballard, 1982). Since the nodes are by definition interconnected, this paradigm for artificial intelligence has become known as 'connectionism' (Dell, 1986; Feldman & Ballard, 1982; Grossberg, 1987; Hinton & Sejnowski, 1983; Hopfield, 1982; McClelland & Rumelhart, 1981; for general references on connectionism, see Feldman et al., 1985; McClelland & Rumelhart, 1986).

Connectionist modelling defines sets of computational languages based on network structures and activation functions. In certain configurations, such languages can map any Boolean input/output function. Thus, connectionism is no more a psychological theory than is Boolean algebra. Its value for psychological theory in general can be assessed only in specific models. Language offers one of the most complex challenges to any theoretical paradigm. Accordingly, we concentrate our attention on some recent connectionist models devoted to the description of language behaviors. After some initial consideration of models of acquired language behavior, we turn to models which purport to learn language behaviors from analogues to normal input. Such models are most important because they might be ambitiously taken as solving the problem of how rule-governable behavior is induced from the environment without the invocation of rules.

What we shall demonstrate, roughly, is this: particular connectionist models for language indeed do not contain algorithmic rules of the sort used in production systems. Some of these models, however, work at their pre-defined tasks because they have special representations built in, which are connectionist-style implementations of rule-based descriptions of language (Dell, 1986; Hanson & Kegl, 1987; McClelland & Elman, 1986). Another model, touted because it does not contain rules, actually contains arbitrary computational devices which implement fragments of rule-based representations—we show that it is just these devices that crucially enable this model to simulate some properties of rule-based regularities in the input data (Rumelhart & McClelland, 1986b). Thus, none of these connectionist models succeed in explaining language behavior without containing linguistic representations, which in speakers are the result of linguistic rules.

2. Models of acquired language behaviors

We consider first some models of adult skill. The goal in these cases, is to describe a regular input/output behavior in a connectionist configuration. Dell's model of speech production serves as a case-in-point (based on Dell, 1986; personal communication; see Figure 1). There are two intersecting systems of interconnected nodes, one for linguistic representations and one for sequencing the output. In the linguistic representation, nodes are organized in four separate levels, words, syllables, phonemes, and phonological features. Each word describes a hierarchy specifying the order of component syllables, which in turn specify their component phonemes, which in turn specify bundles of phonetic features. The sequencing system activates elements in phonologically allowable orders. Each phone receives activation input both from the linguistic subsystem and the sequencing subsystem, which results in their being produced in a specified order. As each phoneme is activated, it in turn activates all the features and all the syllables to which it is connected, even irrelevant ones which are not in the current word; then those features, words and syllables can in turn activate other phonemes. This pattern of radiating activation automatically activates relatively strongly just those irrelevant words and syllables with structurally similar descriptions. Accordingly, the model predicts that errors can occur as a function of the activation of irrelevant phones, syllables and words, but primarily those in structurally similar positions. It is well known that these are just the kind of

Figure 1.

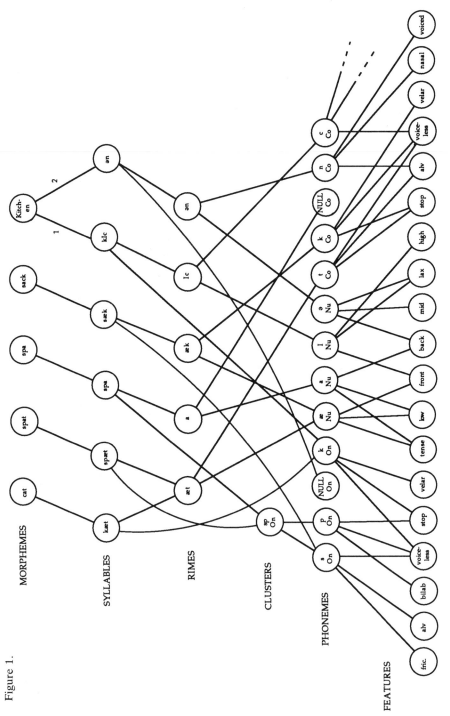

speech errors that occur, exchanges between sounds and words in structurally similar positions.

It is crucial that the nodes are arrayed at different levels of lexical and phonological representation. Each of these levels has some pre-theoretic intuitive basis, but actually the units at each level are consistently defined in terms of a theory with rules which range categorically over those units. Hence, if the model is taken as a psychological theory, it would support the validity of particular levels of representation which are uniquely defined in terms of a rule-governed structural theory. The model also makes certain assumptions about the prior availability of sequence instructions, absolute speed of activation, and speed of inhibition of just-uttered units. Thus, the model comprises a fairly complete outline of the sequencing of speech output, given prior linguistically defined information, and the prior specification of a number of performance mechanisms and parameters. The model is a talking mechanism for the normal flow of speech which can correctly represent errors because it has the linguistic units and the relations between them wired in.

Such models can represent perceptual as well as productive processes. For example, Elman, McClelland and Rumelhart have developed a series of models for word recognition (Elman & McClelland, 1986; McClelland & Elman, 1986; McClelland & Rumelhart, 1981; Rumelhart & McClelland, 1982). These models are similar to Dell's model in the sense that they have several levels of linguistic representation built into them. For example, TRACE (McClelland & Elman, 1986) recognizes words based on a stylized acoustic feature sequential input. The model utilizes three kinds of detector nodes, for acoustic features, phonemes and words. Feature nodes are grouped into 11 sets, each corresponding to a successive 'time slice' of the acoustic input. Each slice presents the value of each of seven feature dimensions; each dimension has 9 possible values. Accordingly, at the input level of this model, each 'phoneme' is represented in terms of a feature/value/time-slice matrix which defines 693 separate nodes. The centers of each set of time slices from a phoneme are spaced 6 slices apart, to simulate the acoustic overlap that real phones have in speech. Every three time slices, there is centered a set of connections to 15 phoneme detector nodes, with each phoneme node receiving input from 11 time slices. This means that a three-phoneme word activates 1993 feature/value/time-slice nodes and 165 phoneme units. Finally, there are 211 word nodes appropriately linked to their constituent phonemes.

TRACE builds in several levels of linguistic analysis. This is not merely an external observation about the model, it is reflected in its internal architecture. All nodes at the same level of representation inhibit each other, while nodes at adjacent levels of representation excite each other. The within-level inhibition serves the function of reducing the active nodes at each level to those that are 'most' active; the across-level facilitation serves the function of increasing the effect of one level on another. The within-level inhibition in TRACE is set at distinct values for each level, as are the levels of excitation between different levels. The result is that the model exhibits qualitatively distinct sets of nodes, grouped and layered in the same way as the corresponding linguistic levels of representation. With all this built-in linguistic apparatus, TRACE can model a number of interesting aspects of lexical access by humans. First, it can recognize words from mock acoustic feature input. Second, it can generate a variety of effects involving interference relations between levels of representation: for example, a family of 'word superiority' effects, in which properties of words influence the perception of particular phonemes and features. Such effects occur because nodes at the different levels of representation are interconnected. We take this to be one of the obvious features of connectionist algorithms: insofar as there are interactions between levels of representation—especially influence from higher to lower levels—a parallel system with multiple simultaneous connections both within and between levels is indicated. Indeed, it is difficult to see how a production-system set of rules could be elegantly configured to capture such phenomena.

3. A model which seems to learn past tense rules

The previous models embed an already established linguistic analysis into a model of adult behavior: these models demonstrate that the connectionist framework allows for the implementation of linguistic structure in computationally effective ways. If we take such models as psychologically instructive, they inform us that once one knows what the internal structure of a language is, it can be encoded in such a system in a way which predicts linguistic behavior.

A more ambitious goal is to construct a connectionist model which actually *learns* from regularities in normal input, and generates behavior which conforms to the real behavior. In this way, the model can aspire to explain the patterns characteristic of the behavior. Consider the recent model proposed by Rumelhart and McClelland (1986b, R&M) which seems to learn the past tense rules of English verbs without learning any explicit rules. This model has been given considerable attention in a current review article, especially with reference to its empirical and principled failings and how such failings follow from the choice of computational architecture (Pinker & Prince, 1988). Our approach is complementary: we examine the R&M model internally, in order to understand *why* it works. We argue that the model seems to work for two kinds of reasons; first, it contains arbitrary devices which make it relatively sensitive to those phonological structures which are involved in the past-tense rules; second, it stages the input data and internal learning functions so that it simulates child-like learning behavior. We first describe the past-tense phenomena in rule-governed terms, and then examine how the R&M model conforms to the consequent regularities in the child's stages of acquisition.

The principles of the past tense formation in English involve a regular ending ('ed') for most verbs, and a set of internal vowel changes for a minority of verbs. In our discussion we are interested in a particular kind of structural rule, typical of linguistic phenomena: one which performs categorical operations on categorical symbols. In this sense, linguistic rules admit of no exceptions. That is, they are not probabilistically sensitive to inputs, and their effects are not probabilistic. We can see how they work in the formation of the regular past tense from the present in English verbs. The regularities are:

mat ... mattED
need ... needED   If the verb ends in "t" or "d", add "ed"

push ... pushT   If the verb ends in sounds,
pick ... pickT   "sh", "k", "p", "ch", ... add "t"

buzz ... buzzD
bug ... bugD   If the verb ends in "z", "g", "b", "j" or a vowel ... add "d"
ski ... skiD

These facts are described with rules which draw on and define a set of phonological 'distinctive features', attributes which co-occur in each distinct phoneme. Features are both concrete and abstract: they are concrete in the sense that they define the phonetic/acoustic content of speech; they are abstract in the sense that they are the objects of phonological rules, which in turn can define levels of representation which are not pronounced or pronounceable in a given language. The description of the rules of past tense formation exemplify these characteristics. (Note that any particular description is theory dependent. We have chosen a fairly neutral form (basically that in Halle, 1962), although we recognize that phonological theory is continually in convulsions. The generalizations we draw are worded to hold across a wide range of such theories.)

1a. Add a phoneme which has all the features in common to T and D, with the voicing dimension unspecified.

1b. Insert a neutral vowel, 'e', between two word-final consonants that have identical features, ignoring voicing.

1c. Assimilate the voicing of the T/D to that of the preceding segment.

These rules define distinct internal representations of each past form:

	Rule
Push	
PushT/D	1a
PushT	1b

Pit	
PitT/D	1a
PiteT/D	1b
PiteD	1c

There are models in which such rules are interpreted as simultaneous distinct constraints (Goldsmith, 1976) or as applying in strict order (Halle, 1962). Either way, the effects on the output form are categorical, each rule involving a distinct, but abstract phonetic form. The specific shape of the rules also clarifies the sense in which distinctive features are symbolic. For example, rule (1b) refers to sequences of consonants which are made in the same manner and place, regardless of their voicing status. This rule also applies to break up sequences of 's, z, sh, ch' created by affixing the plural and present tense S/Z to nouns ('glitches') and verbs ('botches'): the voicing assimilation rule (1c) applies in those cases as well. The generality of the application of such rules highlights the fact that they apply to abstract subsets of features, not to actual phonetic or acoustic objects.

The depth of abstract representations becomes clear when we consider how these rules are embedded within a fuller set of optional phonological processes involved in describing English sound systems in general (Chomsky & Halle, 1968). Consider the verbs 'mound' and 'mount'; in one of their allowed past tense pronunciations, they appear as 'mo¯̃uDed' (long nasalized vowel preceding a tongue flap) and 'mõuDed' (short nasalized vowel preceding a tongue flap). These two words can end up being differentiated acoustically only in terms of the length of the first vowel, even though the underlying basis for the difference is in the voicing or absence of it in the final d/t of the stem (see Chomsky, 1964). The rules involved in arriving at these pronunciations include,

1d. nasalize a vowel before a nasal
1e. drop a nasal before a homorganic stop
1f. lengthen a vowel before a voiced consonant
1g. change t or d to a tongue flap, D, between vowels

Each of these rules has independent application in other parts of English pronunciation patterns, so they are distinct. If these rules are separated so that they can apply to isolated cases, they must apply in order when combined. For example, since (1d) requires a nasal, (1e) cannot have applied; if (1f) is to apply differentially to 'mound', and not to 'mount', then (1e) must have applied; if the vowel length is to reflect the difference between 'mound' and 'mount', (1f) must apply before (1g). Thus, whether the intermediate stages are serially or logically ordered, the inputs, mound+past, mount+past, have a very abstract relation to their corresponding outputs:

mound+past		mount+past
mound D/T	(rule 1a)	mount D/T
mound eD/T	(rule 1b)	mount eD/T
mound ed	(rule 1c)	mount ed
m˜ounded	(rule 1d)	m˜ounted
m˜ouded	(rule 1e)	m˜outed
m˜˜ouded	(rule 1f)	(can't apply)
m˜˜ouDed	(rule 1g)	m˜ouDed

That the rules can be optional does not make them probabilistic within the model: they state what is allowed, not how often it happens (indeed, for many speakers, deleting nasals can occur more easily before unvoiced homorganic stops, than before voiced stops). Optionality in a rule is a way of expressing the fact that the structure can occur with and without a corresponding property.

The fact that linguistic rules apply to their appropriate domain 'without exception' does not mean that the appropriate domain is defined only in terms of phonological units. For example, in English there is a particular set of 'irregular' verbs which are not subject to the three past-tense formation rules described above. Whether a verb is irregular or not depends on its lexical representation: certain verbs are and others are not 'regular'. For example, one has to know which 'ring' is meant to differentiate the correct from incorrect past tenses below (see Pinker & Prince, 1988 for other cases).

2a. The Indians ringed (*rang) the settler's encampment.
2b. The Indians rang (*ringed) in the new year.

There are about 200 irregular verbs in modern English. They are the detritus of a more general rule-governed system in Old English (which have an interesting relation to the Indo-European e/o ablaut, see Bever & Langendoen, 1963). They fall into a few groups; those involving no change (which characteristically already end in t or d (beat, rid); those which add t (or d) (send); those lowering the vowel (drink, give); those involving a reversal of the vowel color between front and back (find, break; come); those which both lower and change vowel color (sting); those which involve combinations of all three kinds of change (bring, feel, tell). The point for our purposes is that almost all of the 'irregular' verbs draw on a small set of phonological processes. Only a few involve completely suppletive forms (e.g., go/went).

This brief analysis of the past tense formation in terms of features and rules, reveals several properties of the structural system. First, the relevant grouping of features for the rules is vertical, with features grouped into phonemic segments. This property is not formally necessary. For example, rules could range over isolated features collected from a series of phones: apparently, it is a matter of linguistic fact that the phoneme is a natural domain of the phonological processes involved in the past tense formation (note that there may be suprasegmental processes as well, but these tend to range over different locations of values on the same feature dimension). Second, it is the segment at the end of the verb stem that determines the ultimate features of the regular past tense ending. This, too, is a fact about the English past system, not a logically necessary property.

4. The R&M model: A general picture of PDP models of learning

Rumelhart and McClelland (1986b; R&M) implemented a model which learns to associate past tense with the present tense of both the majority and minority verb types. The first step in setting up this model is to postulate a description of words in terms of individual feature units. Parallel distributed connectionist models are not naturally suited to represent serially ordered representations, since all components are to be represented simultaneously in one matrix. But phonemes, and their corresponding bundles of distinctive features, clearly are ordered. R&M solve this problem by invoking a form of phonemic representation suggested by Wickelgren (1969), which recasts ordered phonemes into 'Wickelphones', which can be ordered in a given word in only one way. Wickelphones appear to avoid the problem of representing serial order by differentiating each phoneme as a function of its immediate phonemic neighborhood. For example, 'bet' would be represented as composed of the following Wickelphones.

eT#, bEt, #Be

Each Wickelphone is a triple, consisting of the central phoneme, and a representation of the preceding and following phonemes as well. As reflected in the above representation, such entities do not have to be represented in memory as ordered: they can be combined in only one way into an actual sequence, if one follows the rule that the central phone must correspond to the prefix of the following unit and the postfix of the preceding unit. That rule leads to only one output representation for the above three Wickelphones, namely 'b...e...t'. Of course, the number of Wickelphones in a language is much larger than the number of phonemes—roughly the third power. But such a representational scheme seems to circumvent the need for a direct representation of order itself (at least, so long as the vocabulary is restricted so that a given Wickelphone never occurs more than once in a word—see Pinker & Prince, 1988).

Figure 2. *Categorization of phonemes on four simple dimensions*

		Place					
		Front		Middle		Back	
		V/L	U/S	V/L	U/S	V/L	U/S
Interrupted	*Stop*	b	p	d	t	g	k
	Nasal	m	–	n	–	N	–
Cont. Consonant	*Fric.*	v/D	f/T	z	s	Z/j	S/C
	Liq/SV	w/l	–	r	–	y	h
Vowel	*High*	E	i	O	ʌ	U	u
	Low	A	e	I	a/α	W	*/o

Key: N = ng in *sing*; D = th in *the*; T = th in *with*; Z = z in *azure*; S = sh in *ship*; C = ch in *chip*; E = ee in *beet*; i = i in *bit*; O = oa in *boat*; ʌ = u in *but* or schwa; U = oo in *boot*; u = oo in *book*; A = ai in *bait*; e = e in *bet*; I = i_e in *bite*; a = a in *bat*; α = a in *father*; W = ow in *cow*; * = aw in *saw*; o = o in *hot*.

R&M assign a set of phonemic distinctive features to each phone within a Wickelphone. There are 4 feature dimensions, two with two values and two with three, yielding 10 individual feature values (see Figure 2). This allows them to represent Wickelphones in feature matrices: for example the /E/ in 'bet' would be represented as shown below.

Dimension 1	Interrupted	Vowel	Interrupted
Dimension 2	Stop	Low	Stop
Dimension 3	Voiced	Short	Unvoiced
Dimension 4	Front	Front	Middle
	f1	f2	f3

The verb learning model represents each Wickelphone in a set of 'Wickelfeatures'. These consist of a triple of features, [f1, f2, f3], the first taken from the prefix phone, the second from the central phone and the third from the post-fix phone. Accordingly, some of the Wickelfeatures for the 'bet' would be the following:

f1	f2	f3
[end,	interrupted,	vowel]
[end,	interrupted,	low]
[stop,	low,	stop]
[voiced,	low,	unvoiced]

There are about 1000 potential Wickelfeatures (10 prefix values × 10 central phone values × 10 post-fix values)—(the potential number is somewhat higher because of the treatment of word boundaries; we describe below how the actual number is limited).

There are two layers at which the Wickelfeature representations of the words occur, the input and the output. Each layer consists of a separate node for each of the Wickelfeatures: all of the nodes at each layer are connected to all of the nodes at the other, as depicted in Figure 3. The machine is taught in the following way: the input is provided in the form of a conventional phonemic notation, and transformed into a corresponding set of Wickelfeatures. The input layer of Wickelfeatures is activated by the input. Each input node is connected to each output node with a specific weight. On each trial, the weights of these connections determine the influence of the activation of the input node on the activation of the output node it is connected to. If the weight between an input node and an output node is 0, then the state of the

Figure 3. *(Reproduced from Rumelhart and McClelland, 1986b, p. 222, with permission of the publisher, Bradford Books/MIT Press.)*

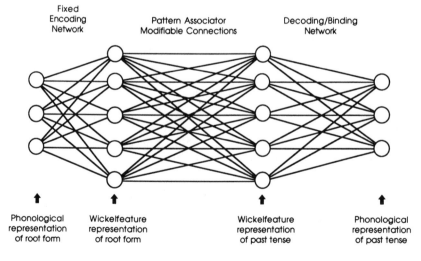

input node does not affect the state of the output node. If the weight is positive, and if the input node is activated by the present-tense input, the output node is also activated by the connection between them; if the weighting is negative then the output node would be inhibited by that connection. Each output node also has a threshold, which the summed activation input from all input nodes must exceed for the output node to become active (we note below that the threshold is itself interpreted as a probabilistic function).

On each training trial, the machine is given the correct output Wickelfeature set as well as the input set. This makes it possible to assess the extent to which each output Wickelfeature node which should be activated, is, and conversely. The machine then uses a variant on the standard perceptron learning rule (Rosenblatt, 1962), which changes the weights between the active input nodes and the output nodes which were incorrect on the trial: lower the weight and raise the threshold for all nodes that were incorrectly activated; do the opposite for nodes that were incorrectly inactivated.

The machine was given a set of 200 training sessions, with a number of verbs in each session. At the end of this training, the system could take new verbs, that it had not processed before, and correctly associate their past tense in most cases. Hence, the model appears to learn, given a finite input, how to generalize to new cases. Furthermore, the model appears to go through several stages of acquisition which correspond to the stages of learning the past tense of verbs which children go through as well (Brown, 1973; Bybee & Slobin, 1982). During an early phase, the model (and children) produce the correct past tense for a small number of verbs, especially a number of the minority forms (went, ran, etc.). Then, the model (and children) 'overgeneralize' the attachment of the majority past form, 'ed' and its variants, so that they then make errors on forms on which they had been correct before (goed, wented, runned, etc.). Finally, the model (and children) produce the correct minority and majority forms. It would seem that the model has learned the rule-governed behaviors involved in forming the past tense of novel verbs. Yet, as R&M point out, the model does not 'contain' rules, only matrices of associative strengths between nodes. They argue that the success of the system in learning the rule-governed properties, and in simulating the pattern of acquisition, shows that rules may not be a necessary component of the description of acquisition behavior.

Whenever a model is touted to be as successful as theirs, it is hard to avoid the temptation to take it as a replacement for a rule-governed description and explanation of the phenomena. That is, we can go beyond R&M and take this model as a potential demonstration that the appearance that behavior is rule-governed is an illusion, and that its real nature is explained by nodes and the associative strengths between networks of nodes. A number of linguistic commentators have drawn this conclusion about connectionist models, in particular because of the apparently successful performance of R&M's past-tense learning model (Langackre, 1987; Sampson, 1987). Below, we examine the model in this light: we find no evidence that the model replaces linguistic rules; rather, it has internal architecture which is arranged to be particularly sensitive to aspects of data that conform to the rules. Thus, the model may (or may not) be a successful algorithmic description of learning; but, insofar as it works, it actually confirms the existence of rules as the basis for natural language.

5. The model's TRICS (The Representations It Crucially Supposes)

We now turn to some special characteristics of the model which contribute to making it work. In each case, we note that apparently arbitrary decisions, often presented as 'simplifications' of the model, actually could be explained as accommodations to the rule-governed properties of the system and the resulting behavior. We should note that, by and large, it did not require much detective work to isolate the arbitrary properties—in most cases, R&M are explicit about them. There are two kinds of TRICS, those that reconstitute crucial aspects of the linguistic system, and those which create the over-generalization pattern exhibited by children.

5.1.

A set of properties of the model serve to re-focus on the phoneme-by-phoneme clustering of features, and to emphasize the clarity of the information at the end of the verb. That is, the arbitrary decisions about the details of the model are transparently interpretable as making most reliable for associative learning, the information relevant to the rule-governed description of the formation of the past tense. Our forensic method is the following: we examine each arbitrary decision about the model with the rule system in mind, and ask about each decision: would this facilitate or inhibit the behavioral emergence of data which looks like that governed by the past tense rules? Without exception, we find that the decision would facilitate the emergence of such behavior.

5.1.1.

The first simplification of the model involves reducing the number of within-word Wickelfeatures from about 1000 to 260. One way to do this, would be to delete randomly some Wickelfeatures, and rely on the overall redundancy of the system to carry the behavioral regularities. Another option is to use a principled basis for dropping certain Wickelfeatures. For example, one could drop all Wickelfeatures whose component subfeatures are on different dimensions—this move alone would reduce the number of features considerably. Such reduction would occur if Wickelfeatures were required to have at least two sub-features on the same dimension. R&M do something like this, but in an eccentric way: they require that all Wickelfeatures have the same dimension for f1 and f3: f2 can range fully across all feature dimensions and values. Accordingly, the potential Wickelfeatures for the vowel /E/ in 'bet' on the left below are possible, those on the right are not.

[interrupted, vowel, interrupted]	[interrupted, vowel, stop]
[voiced, mid, unvoiced]	[stop, vowel, unvoiced]
[front, short, middle]	[front, short, unvoiced]

This apparently arbitrary way of cutting down on the number of Wickel-features has felicitous consequences for the relative amount of rule-based information contained within each sub-feature. It has the basic effect of reducing the information contained within f1 and f3, since they are heavily predictable—that is the actually employed Wickelphones are "centrally informative." This heightens the relative importance of information in f2, since it can be more varied. This move is entirely arbitrary from the standpoint of the model; but it is an entirely sensible move if the goal were to accommodate to a structural rule account of the phenomena: the rules imply that the relevant information in a phoneme is in f2. The use of centrally informative Wickelphones automatically emphasizes f2.

5.1.2.

Word boundaries present a special descriptive problem. By virtue of being boundaries, most feature values are irrelevant. In standard phonology, word boundary is often treated as an environmental feature, without phonetic content of its own. The difficulty for a Wickelfeature notation is that word-boundary phones have an f1 or f3 which designates the word boundary. This requires that some sort of Wickelfeature status be given to f1, 2, 3 triples which have either f1 or f3 as a word boundary. A theoretically neutral solution to this would be to treat word-boundary as a bi-polar feature, and allow it to combine with other features into Wickelfeatures. R&M do something like this, but again in an eccentric way. They set up a completely separate set of 200 Wickelfeatures just for phones at word boundaries. Consider word-final phones. R&M allow the available Wickelfeatures to be the cross product of all possible values of f1 and f2, so long as f3 is the boundary. For example, all the features below are among the possible features for the /t/ in /bEt/.

[vowel, interrupted, end]   [low, unvoiced, end]
[front, stop, end]   [short, middle, end]

We can see that this gives a privileged informational status to phones at the word boundary, compared with any other ordinally defined position within the word: the phones at the boundary are the only ones with their own unique set of Wickelfeatures. This makes the information at the boundary uniquely recognizable. That is, the Wickelfeature representation of the words exhibits the property of 'boundary sharpening'.

This arbitrary move accommodates another property we noted in the rule-governed account of the past tense. The phone at the word boundary determines the shape of the regular past. Here, too, we see that an apparently arbitrary decision was just the right one to make in order to make sure that the system would accommodate to the rule-governed regularities.

5.1.3.
R&M allow certain input Wickelfeatures to be activated even when only some of the constituent sub-features are present. One theoretically arbitrary way to do this would be to allow some Wickelphone nodes to be activated sometimes when any 1 out of 3 subfeatures does not correspond to the input. R&M do something like this, but yet again, in an eccentric way—the model allows a Wickelphone node to be activated if either f1 or f3 is incorrect, but not if f2 is incorrect. That is, the fidelity of the relationship between an input Wickelphone and the nodes which are actually activated, is subject to 'peripheral blurring'. This effect is not small: the blurring was set to occur with a probability of .9 (this value was determined by R&M after some trial and error with other values). That is, a given Wickelnode is activated 90 percent of the time when either the input does not correspond to its f1 or f3. But it can always count on f2. This dramatic feature of the model is unmotivated within the connectionist framework. But it has the same felicitous result from the standpoint of the structure of the phenomenon as discussed in 5.1.1. It heightens (in this case, drastically) the relative reliability of the information in f2, and tends to destroy the reliability of information in f1 and f3. This further reflects the fact that the structurally relevant information is in f2.

Blurring, however, has to be kept under careful control. Clearly, if blurring occurred on 100 percent of the features with incorrect f1 or f3, the crucial information will be lost as to how to sequentially order the phones. For this reason, R&M had to institute an arbitrary choice of which Wickelfeatures could be incorrectly activated, so that for each input feature there are some reliable cues to Wickelphone order. This necessitates blurring the Wickelfeatures with less than 100 percent of the false options.

5.1.4.

The use of phonological features is one of the biggest TRICS of all. Features are introduced as an encoding device which reduces the number of internodal connections—the number of connections between two layers of 30,000 Wickelphones is roughly one billion. Some kind of encoding was necessary to reduce this number. Computationally, any kind of binary encoding could solve the problem: R&M chose phonological features as the encoding device because that is the only basis for the model to arrive at appropriate generalizations. Furthermore, the four distinctive features do not all correspond to physically definable dimensions. In order to simplify the number of encoded features, R&M create some feature hybrids. For example b,v,EE are grouped together along one 'dimension' in opposition to m,l,EY. While such a grouping is not motivated by either phonetics or linguistic theory, it is neither noxious nor helpful to the model, so far as we can tell. However, the other major arbitrary feature grouping lumps together long vowels and voiced consonants in opposition to short vowels and unvoiced consonants. All verbs which end in vowels, end in long vowels: accordingly, that particular grouping of features facilitates selective learning of the verbs that end in a segment which must be followed by /d/, namely the verbs ending in vowels and in voiced consonants.

5.1.5.

It is interesting to ponder how successful the devices of central informativeness, peripheral blurring and boundary sharpening are in reconstituting traditional segmental phonemic information. Phonemic representations of words offer a basis for representing similarity between them. One of the properties of Wickelphones is that they do not represent shared properties of words. For example, 'slowed' and 'sold' are no more similar in Wickelphones than 'sold' and 'fig'. This is obviously an inherent characteristic of Wickelphonology (Pinker & Prince, 1988; Savin & Bever, 1970) which would extend to Wickelfeature representations if there were no TRICS. But there are, and they turn out to go a long way to restoring the similarity metric represented directly in normal phonemic notations. One way to quantify this is to examine how many shared input Wickelfeatures there are for words which do and do not share phonemes. This is difficult to do in detail, because R&M do not give complete accounts of which features were chosen for blurring. Two arbitrarily chosen words without shared phonemes will also share few Wickelfeatures—our rough calculation for a pair of arbitrarily chosen 4 letter words is about 10 percent. Words which share initial or final phonemes, will have a noticeable number of shared features because of boundary sharpening. Blurring plays an especially important role in reconstituting similarity among words with shared internal phonemes, such as 'slowed' and 'sold'. Roughly, our calculations show that two such words go from about 20 percent shared features without blurring to around 65 percent with it. In terms of correlating the chances of a node being activated in each word, this represents a rise from about .1 to about .5. The corresponding proportions for phonemically distinct words are 10 and 30 percent—the correlation in that case, stays at 0, even with blurring. The technical reason for this proportional difference is that the blurring has a radiating effect on just the right Wickelfeatures to create an overlap when there are common phonemes. Thus, the model does not correctly reconstitute the phonemic representation, but it does replicate some of its effects.

5.2.

There are two major behavioral properties of the model. First, it seems to learn (i.e., it changes its behavior); second, it goes through a period of over-generalizing the regular rule. The fact that the model learns at all has the same formal basis as the fact that the model can represent the present → past mapping. Any mapping a perceptron can carry out, it can 'learn' to carry out, using the kind of learning rule described above (Rosenblatt, 1962). Basically, the model is composed of 460 perceptrons which converge on the appropriate mapping representation. In fact, in simple perceptrons, the convergence can be quite efficient. On each trial, the learning rule adjusts a threshold discrimination function such that only the correct output units are activated. What is striking about R&M's complex perceptron is that it takes so long to learn the mapping. The function for regular verbs is extremely simple, and might well be reasonably arrived at with just one training cycle. Thereafter, a few cycles would suffice to straighten out the errors on the irregular forms, especially because, as we pointed out above, most irregular verbs follow a restricted set of rules. In this case, there would be little intermediate performance characteristic of learning, and no period during which the regular endings over-generalized to previously correct irregular verbs.

The reason that the model in fact does exhibit considerable intermediate performance and overgeneralization is due to another one of the TRICS, which imposes a probabilistic function on the output. The probability of an output unit being active is a sigmoid function of its net activation (weighted input minus threshold): this function represents the fact that even when the input is correctly assigned, there are output errors. Such a move qualitatively improves the generalizations made by the system once it has been trained. This is because, in general, as the number of error-correcting trials increases, the difference between activations resulting from inputs for which the unit is supposed to have positive output and those for which it is supposed to have negative output, grows more rapidly than the difference among the inputs of each type. This enhances the clarity of the generalization and also makes the learning proceed more slowly. As R&M put it, its use here is motivated by the fact that it "causes the system to learn more slowly so the effect of regular verbs on the irregulars continues over a much longer period of time." (R&M, p. 224).

The period of overgeneralization of the regular past at the 11th cycle of trials also depends on a real trick, not a technically defined one. For the first 10 cycles, the machine is presented with only 10 verbs, 8 irregular and 2 regular ones. On the 11th cycle it is presented with an additional 410 verbs of which about 80 percent are regular. Thus, even on the 11th cycle alone, the model is given more instances of regular verbs than the training trials it has received on the entire preceding 10 cycles: it is no wonder that the regular past ending immediately swamps the previously acquired regularities. R&M defend this arbitrary move by suggesting that children also experience a sudden surge of regular past tense experience. We know of no acquisition data which show anything of the sort (see Pinker & Prince, 1988, who compile evidence to the contrary). Furthermore, if there were a sudden increase in the number of verbs a child knows at the time he learns the regular past tense rule, it would be ambiguous evidence between acquiring the rule, and acquiring a lot of verbs. The rule allows the child to memorize half as many lexical-items for each verb, and learn twice as many verbs from then on. Therefore, even if it were true that children show a sudden increase in the number of verbs they know at the same time that they start overgeneralizing, it would be very difficult to decide which was the cause and which the effect.

5.3. *TRICS aren't for kids*

It is clear that a number of arbitrary decisions made simply to get the model up and working, were made in ways that would facilitate learning the structural regularities inherent to the presented data. To us it seems fairly clear what went on: Wickelphones were the representation of choice because they seem to solve the problem of representing serial order (though they do so only for a restricted vocabulary, see Pinker & Prince, 1988; Savin & Bever, 1970). But Wickelphones also give equal weight to the preceding and following phone, while it is the central phone which is the subject of rule-governed regularities. Accordingly, a number of devices are built into the model to reduce the information and reliability of the preceding and following subphones in the Wickelphone. Further devices mark phones at word-boundary as uniquely important elements, as they are in rule-governed accounts of some phonological changes which happen when morphemes are adjoined. Finally, the behavioral learning properties of the model were insured by making the model learn slowly, and flooding it with regular verbs at a particular point.

The most important claim for the R&M model is that it conforms to the behavioral regularities described in rule-governed accounts, but without any rules. We have not reported on the extent to which the model actually captures the behavioral regularities. Pinker & Prince (1988) demonstrate that, in fact, the model is not adequate, even to the basic facts: hence, the first claim for the model is not correct. We have shown further, that even if the model *were* empirically adequate, it would be because the model's architecture is designed to extract rule-based regularities in the input data. The impact of the rules for the past tense learning, is indirectly embedded in the form of representation and the TRICS: even Wickelfeatures involve a linguistic theory with acoustic segments and phonological features within them; the work of the TRICS is to render available the segmental phoneme, and emphasize boundary phonemes in terms of segmental features. That is, garbage in/garbage out: regularities in/regularities out. How crucial the TRICS really are is easy to find out: simply run the model without them, and see what it does. We expect that if the TRICS were replaced with theoretically neutral devices, the new model would not learn with even the current limited 'success', if at all; nor would it exhibit the same behaviors.

If a slightly improved set of TRICS does lead to successful performance, one could argue that this new model is a theory of the innate phonological devices available to children. On this interpretation, the child would come to the language learning situation with uncommitted connectionist networks supported by TRICS of the general kind built into the R&M model. The child operates on the feedback it receives from its attempts to produce phonologically correct sequences, and gradually builds up a network which exhibits rule-like properties, but without any rules, as R&M claim. It is difficult to consider the merits of such a proposal in the abstract: clearly, if the TRICS were sufficiently structured so that they were tantamount to an implementation of universal phonological constraints in rule-governed accounts, then such a theory would be the equivalent of one that is rule-based (see Fodor & Pylyshyn, 1988, for a discussion of connectionist models as potential implementation systems). The theory in R&M self-avowedly and clearly falls short of representing the actual rules. So, we must analyze the nature of the TRICS in the model at hand, to assess their compatibility with a plausible universal theory of phonology.

None of the TRICS fares well under this kind of scrutiny. Consider first the limitation on Wickelfeatures which makes them 'centrally informative':

this requires that f1 and f3 be marked for the same feature dimension (although the values on that dimension may be different). Certain phonological processes depend on information about the phone preceding and following the affected segment. For example, the rule which transforms /T or D/ to a voiced tongue flap, applies only when both the preceding and following segments are vowels. The 'central-informativeness' TRIC neatly accommodates a process like this, since it makes available a set of Wickelfeatures with f1 and f3 marked as 'vowel'. Unfortunately, the same TRIC makes it hard to learn processes in which f1 and f3 are marked for different dimensions. Since such processes are also quite common, the universal predictions this makes are incorrect.

The second set of representational TRICS has the net result of sharpening the reliability of information at word boundaries: this is well-suited to isolate the relevant information in the regular past-tense formation in English, and would seem like a natural way to represent the fact that morphological processes effect segments at the boundaries of morphemes when they are combined. Unfortunately, such processes do not seem to predominate over within-word processes, such as the formation of the tongue-flap between vowels, or the restrictions on nasal deletion. Furthermore, there are numerous languages which change segments within morphemes as they are combined, as in the many languages with vowel harmony. Thus, there is no empirical support for a system which unambiguously gives priority to phonological processes at morpheme boundaries.

R&M link together distinctive features which are maintained orthogonal to each other in most phonological theories. Hence, in R&M, long vowels and voiced consonants are linked together in opposition to short vowels and unvoiced consonants. This link is prima facie a TRIC, which facilitates learning the regular past tense morphology. But, taken as a claim of universal phonological theory, it is prima facie incorrect: it would propose to explain a non-fact, the relative frequency, or ease of learning, processes which apply simultaneously to long vowels and voiced consonants or to short vowels and unvoiced consonants.

Staging the input data, and imposing a sigmoid learning function are not, strictly speaking, components of phonological theory—both devices play a role in guaranteeing overgeneralization of the regular past. Such overgeneralizations are common in mastery of other morpho-phonological phenomena, for example, the present tense in English ('Harry do-es' (rhymes with 'news')) or plural ('fishes', 'childrens'). The carefully controlled sigmoid learning function and the staging of input data necessary to yield overgeneralization phenomena, have the properties of dei ex machina—with no independent evidence of any kind.

In brief, the net effect of the TRICS is to refocus the reliable information within the central phone of Wickelphone triples. This does reconstitute the segmental property of many phonological processes, obscured by the Wickel-phonological representations. However, since those representations are not adequate in general, such reconstitution is of limited value. Most important, the specific TRICS involved in this reconstitution make wrong universal claims in some cases, and make obscure and unmotivated claims in the other cases. We conclude that even if the TRICS were fine-tuned to arrive at satisfactory empirical adequacy, they would still be arbitrarily chosen to facilitate the learning of English past tense rules, with no empirical support as the basis for phonological learning in general.

We noted above that there are theories of phonology in which more than one segment contributes to a constraint simultaneously, e.g., 'auto-segmental phonology' (Goldsmith, 1976). It might seem that such a variant of phonological theory would be consistent with Wickelphones—and the connectionist learning paradigms in general. Such claims would be incorrect. First, autosegmental phonology does not deny that many processes involve individual segments; rather, it asserts that there are simultaneous suprasegmental structures as well. Second, Wickelphones are no better suited than simple phones for the kinds of larger phonological unit to which multi-segmental constraints apply, very often the syllable. Finally, the constraints in autosegmental phonology are structural and just as rule-like as those in segmental phonology. It might also seem that the issue between traditional and autosegmental phonological theory concerns the reality of intermediate stages of derivation as resulting from the ordered application of rules like (1a–g)—another way to put this is in terms of whether rules are simple-but-ordered as in traditional phonology, or complex-but-unordered. There may be phonological theories which differ on these dimensions. But, however this issue is resolved, there will be no particular comfort for connectionist learning models of the type in R&M. The underlying object to which the rules apply will still be an abstract formula, and the output will still differentiate categorically between grammatical and ungrammatical sequences in the particular language.

5.4. Empirical evidence for rules

Up to now, we have relied on the reader's intuitive understanding of what a 'rule' is—a computation which maps one representation onto another. We have argued further that the R&M model achieves categorical rule-like behavior in the context of an analogue connectionist machine by way of special representational and processing devices. One might reply that the 'rules' we have been discussing actually compute the structure of linguistic 'competence', while the TRIC-ridden model is a 'performance' mechanism which is the real basis for the rule-like behavior. This line of reply would be consistent with the current distinction between three types of description: the computational, the algorithmic and the implementational (Marr, 1982). It is a line already taken in several defenses of connectionism (Rumelhart & McClelland, 1986a; Smolensky, in press).

The distinction between these different types of description might seem to allow for a synthesis of the connectionist and rule-based theories. On this view, rule-based theories describe the structure of language, while connectionist models explain how it 'actually' works. This would-be synthesis is not available, however, since grammatical rules are necessary for the explanation of behavior.

5.4.1. The diachronic maintenance of language systems

Consider first the operation of the processes we have used as examples: they characteristically fall into categories, often even at a physical level of description. For example, if a stop sound is 'unvoiced', it exhibits certain invariants which contrast it from its 'voiced' mode. The indicated processes occur in environments which are categorically described—e.g., /t,d/ becomes a tongue flap between two vowels (actually between two 'non-consonants' in distinctive feature terms), not between two sounds that are like vowels to a high degree. Variations in language behavior show similar discontinuities; for example, children invent phonological rules which involve rule-governed shifts rather than just groups of changed words. Similarly, dialects differ by entire rule processes, not isolated cases; finally, stable historical changes occur in precise but broad ranging shifts—the great vowel shift involved in the irregular past verbs included a complete rotation of vowel heights, not isolated changes. We are not suggesting that developmentally, synchronically and historically, there are no intermediate stages of performance; rather, we emphasize that the stable phenomena and periods are those caused by mental representations that are structural in nature.

It is possible to show that mental representations of a rule-based account of language are necessary to describe the properties of language change. The categorical nature of language change is explained in a rule-based account by the fact that rules themselves are categorical, not incremental: hence, linguistic change is resisted except at those times when it occurs in major shifts. Such facts are clearly consistent with rules, but it must be shown that they are consistent with models like that in R&M. A way to do this is to consider whether successive generations of such models could maintain an approximation of rule-governed behavior, without containing rules. The models we have considered achieve 90–95 percent correct output on their training set and considerably less on generalization trials (Pinker & Prince, 1988, calculate 66 percent correct on generalizations). This level is, of course, far below a 5-year-old child's ability, but one might argue that improved models will do better. However, if these models are to be taken as anything like correct models of the child, they must exhibit stable as well as accurate behavior, in the face of imperfect input. We can operationalize this by asking a simple question (or performing the actual experiment): what will an untrained model learn, if it is given as input, the less-than-perfect output of a trained model?

This question is divisible into two parts: how fast will the 'child' model arrive at its asymptotic performance compared with the 'parent', and what will the asymptotic level be? It is likely that for a given number of trials before asymptote is reached, the child-model will perform worse than the parent-model. This follows from the fact that the data the child-model is given are less reliably related to the actual structure of the language, and therefore must require more trials to arrive at a stable output.

It is less clear what the final asymptotic level will be. If the parent-model errors were truly random in nature, then the final asymptotic level of performance should be the same in the child model. But, in fact, the parental errors are *not* random—they tend to occur on just those forms which are hard for the model to learn. R&M offer a case in point: after 80,000 trials, the model still makes a variety of strange errors on the past tense (e.g., 'squawked' for 'squat'; 'membled' for 'mail'; see Pinker & Prince, 1988, especially for an analysis of the 'blending' mechanism which produces cases like the second). It is intuitively clear, that some of these errors occur because of phonological coincidences, others because of the overwhelming frequency of the regular past ending. In both kinds of cases, the errors have a systematic basis, and are not random—indeed, they are by operational definition, just the cases which frequency-based computations in both models discriminate with difficulty: so, we can expect the child-model to perform even worse on these cases, once given seductively misleading analyses by the parent model. Eventually, with some number of generations (itself determined by the learning curve parameters, and other TRICS), the final descendant-model will stabilize at *always* getting the critical cases wrong.

There are many indeterminacies in these considerations, and the best way to see what happens will be to train successive generations of models. We think that this is an important empirical test for any model of learning. One must not only show that a particular model can approximate rule-like behavior, given perfect input and perfect feedback information, but that successive generations of exactly the same kind of model continue to re-generate the same rule-like regularities, given the imperfect input of their immediate ancestor-models. R&M considered in this light, predicts that in successive generations, a language system will degenerate quickly towards the dominant rule, overgeneralizing most of the exceptional cases. But, this does not occur in actual linguistic evolution. Rather, it is characteristic that every systematic process has some sub-systematic exceptions. As Sapir put it, 'grammars always leak'. One can speculate as to why this is so (Bever, 1986; Sadock, 1974). The fact that it is so poses particular problems for a model based on imperfect frequency approximations by successive generations.

We do not doubt that a set of diachronic TRICS can be tacked onto the model, which would tend to maintain the rule-like regularities in the face of systematically imperfect input information. We expect by induction on the properties of the current TRICS, that two things will be true about any new TRICS: (1) insofar as they have any systematic motivation, it will not be from the connectionist framework, but from the rule-based explanation; (2) insofar as they work, it will be because of their relation to the rule-based account.

5.4.2. Linguistic intuitions

It is also striking that children seem to have explicit differentiation of the way they talk from the way they should talk. Children are both aware that they overgeneralize, and that they should not do it. Bever (1975) reports a dialogue demonstrating that his child (age 3;6) had this dual pattern.

Tom: Where's mommy?
Frederick: Mommy goed to the store.
Tom: Mommy goed to the store?
Frederick: NO! (annoyed) Daddy, *I* say it that way, not you.
Tom: Mommy *wented* to the store?
Frederick: No!
Tom: Mommy went to the store.
Frederick: That's right, mommy wennn ... mommy goed to the store.

Slobin (1978) reported extended interviews with his child demonstrating a similar sensitivity: 'she rarely uses some of the [strong] verbs correctly in her own speech; yet she is clearly aware of the correct forms.' He reports the following dialogue at 4;7.

Dan: ... Did Barbara read you that whole story ...
Haida: Yeah ... and ... mama this morning after breakfast, read ('red') the whole book ... I don't know when she readed ('reeded') ...
Dan: You don't know when she what?
Haida: ... she readed the book ...
Dan: M-hm
Haida: That's the book she read. She read the whole, the whole book.

Dan: That's the book she readed, huh?
Haida: Yeah ... *read!* (annoyed)
Dan: Barbara readed you Babar?
Haida: Babar, yeah. You know cause you readed some of it too ... she readed all the rest.
Dan: She read the whole thing to you, huh?
Haida: Yeah, ... nu-uh, you read some.
Dan: Oh, that's right; yeah, I readed the beginning of it.
Haida: Readed? (annoyed surprise) Read!
Dan: Oh, yeah — read.
Haida: Will you stop that Papa?
Dan: Sure

What are we to make of Frederick's and Haida's competence? On the one hand, they clearly made overgeneralization errors; on the other hand, they clearly knew what they should and should not say. This would seem to be evidence that the overgeneralizations are strictly a performance function of the talking algorithm, quite distinct from their linguistic knowledge. The fact that the children know they are making a mistake emphasizes the distinction between the structures that they know and the sequences that they utter. (But see Kuczaj, 1978, who showed that children do not differentiate between experimentally presented correct and incorrect past tense forms. We think that he underestimates the children's competence because of methodological factors. For example, he assumes that children think that everything they say is grammatical, which the above reports show is not true. Finally, in all his studies, the child in general prefers the correct past forms for the irregular verbs.)

In brief, we see that even children are aware that they are following (or should follow) structural systems. Adults also exhibit knowledge of the contrast between what they say and what is grammatical. For example the sentence below is recognized as usable but ungrammatical, while the second is recognized as grammatical but unusable (see discussion in Section 7 below).

Either I or you are crazy.

Oysters oysters oysters split split split

Children and adults who know the contrast between their speech and the correct form have a representation of the structural system. Hence, it is of little interest to claim that a connectionist model can 'learn' the behavior without the structural system. Real people learn both; most interestingly, they sometimes learn the structure before they master its use.

5.4.3. Language behaviors

There is also considerable experimental evidence for the independent role of grammatical structures in the behavior of adults. We discuss this under the rubric of evidence for a 'psychogrammar' (Bever, 1975), an internalized representation of the language, that is not necessarily a model of such behaviors as speech perception or production, but a representation of the structure used in those and other language behaviors. Presumably, the psychogrammar is strongly equivalent to some correct linguistic grammar with a universally definable mental and physiological representation. We set up the concept for this discussion to avoid claiming "psychological" or "physiological reality" for any *particular* linguistic grammar or mode of implementation. Rather, we wish to outline some simple evidence that a psychogrammar exists: this demonstration is sufficient to invalidate the psychological relevance of those connectionist learning models which do not learn grammars.

The fundamental mental activity in using speech is to relate inchoate ideas with explicit utterances, as in perception and production. There is observational and experimental evidence that multiple levels of linguistic representation are computed during these processes (Bever, 1970; Dell, 1986; Fodor, Bever, & Garrett, 1974; Garrett, 1975; Tanenhaus, Carlson, & Seidenberg, 1985). The data suggest that the processes underlying these two behaviors are not simple inversions, so they may make different use of the grammatical structures, suggesting separate representations of the grammar. Hence, the psychogrammar may be distinct from such systems of speech behavior; in any case, it explains certain phenomena in its own right. In standard linguistic investigations, it allows the isolation of linguistic universals due to psychogrammatical constraints from those due to the other systems of speech behavior. We think that the achievements of this approach to linguistic research have been prodigious and justify the distinction in themselves. A further argument for the separate existence of a psychogrammar is the empirical evidence that it is an independent source of acceptability intuitions. The crucial data are sequences which are intuitively well-formed but unusable, and sequences which are usable but intuitively ill-formed, as discussed above. Such cases illustrate that behavioral usability and intuitive well-formedness do not overlap completely, suggesting that each is accounted for by (at least partially) independent mental representations.

5.4.4. Conclusion: The explanatory role of rules

The evidence we have reviewed in the previous three sections demonstrates that even if one were to differentiate structural rules from algorithmic rules, it remains the case that the structural rules are directly implicated in the explanation of linguistic phenomena. That is, the rules are not merely abstract descriptions of the regularities underlying language behaviors, but are vital to their explanation because they characterize certain mental representations or processes. It is because of those mental entities that the rules compactly describe facts of language acquisition, variation, and history; they provide explanations of linguistic knowledge directly available to children and adults; they help explain those mental representations involved in the comprehension and production of behaviorally usable sentences; they are part of the explanation of historical facts about languages.

6. Learning to assign thematic roles

We now turn to a second model in which linguistic behavior is apparently learned—the assignment of thematic roles to nounphrases in different serial positions (McClelland & Kawamoto, 1986, M&K). The system which learns to assign thematic roles to nouns in specific sentences has similar properties to the model which learns past tenses. The input representational nodes are triples, consisting of a syntactic position, and two semantic features for a noun or verb—the output nodes represent a semantic feature for a noun, one for a verb, and a thematic noun-verb relation. There is a probabilistic blurring mechanism, which turns on feature/role nodes only 85 percent of the time when they should be on, and 15 percent of the time when they should not.

The semantic TRIC

Ideally (that is, in one's idealization of how this model must work to be a significant psychological theory of learning to attach thematic roles to words), one would start with an independently defined set of semantic features (human, animate, ...) taken from some semantic theory (e.g., a theory intended to account for naming behavior, or within a semantic theory, to account for synonymy and entailment). Then, the role of statistical blurring might be interpreted as allowing for some interaction between these formal features and the continuous variability which can occur when fitting nouns into thematic roles. But, for all the statistical blurring, it remains the case that the 'semantic role features', do not flow from some independent theory: rather, they are just descriptors of roles themselves. Here, the semantic features are chosen for each noun to reflect the probability that it is an agent/object/instrument/modifier. The corresponding features for verbs are chosen to capture the likelihood that the verb is an action, involves modifiers and so on (see Figure 4). Hence, any 'learning' that occurs is trivial. The 'learning' does not involve isolating independently defined semantic features which are

Figure 4. *Feature dimensions and values*

	Nouns
HUMAN	human nonhuman
SOFTNESS	soft hard
GENDER	male female neuter
VOLUME	small medium large
FORM	compact 1-D 2-D 3-D
POINTINESS	pointed rounded
BREAKABILITY	fragile unbreakable
OBJ-TYPE	food toy tool utensil furniture animate nat-inan

	Verbs
DOER	yes no
CAUSE	yes no-cause no-change
TOUCH	agent inst both none AisP
NAT_CHNG	pieces shreds chemical none unused
AGT_MVMT	trans part none NA
PT_MVMT	trans part none NA
INTENSITY	low high

Note: nat-inan = natural inanimate, AisP = Agent is Patient, NA = not applicable.

relevant to roles, but rather an accumulation of activation strengths from having the role-features available, and being given correct instances of words (feature matrices) placed in particular role positions.

One of the achievements of this model according to M&K is that it 'over-generalizes' thematic role assignments. For example, 'doll' is not marked as 'animate' and therefore is ineligible to be an agent. However, 'doll' is nonetheless assigned significant strength as agent in such sentences as 'the doll moved'. This result seems to be due to the fact that everything is assigned the gender neuter except animate objects and the word 'doll' which is assigned 'female'. Thus, 'neuter' becomes a perfect predictor of inanimacy, except for 'doll'. It is not surprising that 'doll' is treated as though it were animate.

7. The power of units unseen

It might seem that the models we have discussed are dependent on TRICS because of some inherent limitation on their computational power. We now consider connectionist learning models with more computational power, and examine some specific instances for TRICS.

Connectionist learning machines are composed of perceptrons. One of the staple theorems about perceptrons is that they cannot perform certain Boolean functions if they have only an input and an output set of nodes (Minsky & Papert, 1969). Exclusive disjunctive conditions are among those functions that cannot be represented in a two-layer perceptron system. Yet, even simple phonetic phenomena involved in the past tense involve disjunctive descriptions, if one were limited to two-level descriptions. For example, the variants of 'mounded' discussed above involve disjunction of the presence of n, lengthened vowel and the tongue flap. That is, the tongue-flap pronunciation of 't' or 'd' can occur only if the 'n' has been deleted, and the previous vowel has been lengthened. Furthermore, the distinction between /t/ and /d/ in 'mounted' and 'mounded', in some pronunciations has been displaced to the length of the preceding vowel. The solution for modelling such disjunctive phenomena within the connectionist framework is the invocation of units that are neither input nor output nodes, but which comprise an intermediate set of units which are 'hidden' (Hinton & Sejnowski, 1983, 1986; Smolensky, 1986). (A formal problem in the use of hidden units is formulating how the perceptron learning rule should apply to a system with them: there are two (or more) layers of connections to be trained on each trial, but only the output layer is directly corrected. Somehow, incorrect weights and thresholds must be corrected at both the output and hidden levels. A current technique, 'back-propagation' is the instance of such a learning rule used in the examples we discuss below—it apportions 'blame' for incorrect activations to hidden units which are involved, according to a function too complex for presentation here (see Rumelhart, Hinton & Williams, 1986).)

Recent work has shown that a model with hidden units can be trained to regenerate a known acoustic sample of speech, with the result that novel speech samples can also be regenerated without further training (Elman & Zipser, 1986). The training technique does not involve explicit segmentation of the signal, nor is there a mapping onto a separate response. The model takes a speech sample in an input acoustic feature representation: the input is mapped onto a set of input nodes, in a manner similar to that of McClelland and Elman. Each input node is connected to a set of hidden nodes, which in turn are connected to a layer of output nodes corresponding to the input nodes. On each trial, the model adjusts weights between the layers of nodes following the learning rule (the 'back-propagation' variant of it) to improve the match between the input and the output. This model uses an 'auto-associative' technique, in which weights are adjusted to yield an output that is the closest fit to the original input. After many trials (up to a million), the model is impressively successful, in regenerating new speech samples from the same speaker. This is an exciting achievement, since it opens up the possibility that an analysis of the speech into a compact internal representation is possible, simply by exposure to a sample. There are several things which remain to be shown. For example, the internal analysis which the model arrives at may or may not correspond to a linguistically relevant analysis; if it does correspond to such units, it is not clear how they can be integrated with higher-order relations between them.

7.1. A hidden unit model of syntax acquisition

Hanson and Kegl (1987, H&K) use the 'auto-association' method with hidden units to re-generate sequences of syntactic categories which correspond to actual sentences. After a period of learning, the model can take in a sequence of lexical categories (e.g., something like 'determiner, noun, verb, determiner, noun, adverb'), and regenerate that sequence. What is interesting is that it can regenerate sequences which correspond to actual English sentences, but it does not regenerate sequences which do not correspond to English sequences—in this way, the model approximates the ability to render grammaticality distinctions. Hanson and Kegl disavow their model as appropriate for the language learning child, but they make an extraordinarily strong claim for what it shows about linguistic structures which govern the ungrammaticality of certain sentences:

> If [our model] does not recognize such sentences ... after nothing more than exposure to data, this would lead us to suspect that rather than being an innate property of the learner, these constraints and conditions follow directly from regularities in the data ... . Both [our model] and the child are only exposed to sentences from natural language, they both must induce general rules and larger constituents from just the regularities to which they are exposed ... .

That is, H&K take the success of their model to be an existence proof that some linguistic universals can be learned without any internal structure. This makes it imperative to examine the architecture of their model—as we shall see, it incorporates certain linguistically defined representations in crucial ways which invalidate their empiricist conclusion.

Here is how one of the models works. The model is trained on a set of 1000 actual sentences, ranging from a few to 15 words in length. Each lexical item in every input sentence is manually assigned to a syntactic category, each coded into a 9-bit sequence (input texts were taken from a corpus with grammatical categories already assigned: Francis & Kucera, 1979). These sequences are mapped onto 270 input nodes (135 for 15 word positions, each with nine bits; another distinct set for word boundary codes). The categorized sequences are then treated as input to a set of 45 hidden nodes—each input category node is connected to each hidden node, and each hidden node is connected to a corresponding set of 270 output nodes (see Figure 5). During training, the model is given input sequences of categories—the model matches the input against the self-generated output on each trial. The usual learning rule applies to adjust weights on each trial (using a variation of back-propagation), with the usual built-in variability in learning on each trial. After 180,000 trials with the training set, the model asymptoted at about 90 percent correct on both the training set and on new sentence-based category sequences which had not been presented before.

H&K highlight four qualitative results in the trained model's responses to new cases. First, the model supplements incomplete information in input sequences so that the regenerated sequences conform to possible sentence types. For example, given the input in (3a) the model's response fills in the missing word with a verb, as in (3b). (We are quoting directly from their examples. Roughly, the lexical categories correspond to distinctions used in Francis & Kucera, 1979. 'P-verb' refers to 'verb in past-tense form'.)

Second, the model corrects

3a.   article, noun, ⟨BLANK⟩, article, noun
3b.   article, noun, p-verb, article, noun

Figure 5.

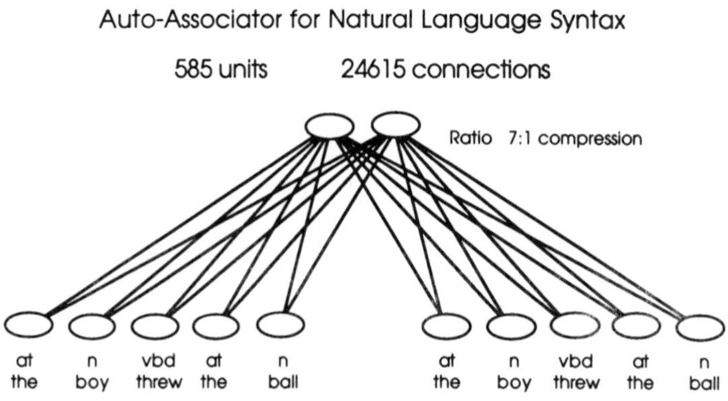

Auto-Associator for Natural Language Syntax

585 units   24615 connections

incorrect input syntactic information; for example given (4a) as input, it responds with (4b).

4a.   article, noun, p-verb, adverb, article, noun, p-verb
4b.   article, noun, p-verb, preposition, article, noun, p-verb

The interest of this case is based on the claim that (4a) does not correspond to a possible sequence (e.g., they say (4a) corresponds to *'the horse raced quickly the barn fell', while (4b) corresponds to 'the horse raced past the barn fell'. Note that (4b) is a tricky sentence: it corresponds to 'the horse *that was* raced past the barn, fell').

Third, the model regenerates one center-embedding (corresponding to 'the rat the cat chased died'): this regeneration occurs "despite the lack of even a single occurrence of a center-embedded sentence within the [1000 sentence] corpus." Furthermore, the model rejects sequences corresponding to two center-embeddings ('the rat the cat the dog bit chased died'). Given a syntactic sequence corresponding to a double embedding (5a), the model responds with (5b). H&K say that this shows that their model "can differentially generalize to sentences that can appear in natural language (center-embeddings) but cannot recognize sentences which violate natural language constraints (multiple center-embeddings)."

5a.   article, noun, article, noun, article, noun, p-verb, p-verb, p-verb
5b.   article, noun, article, noun, article, noun, p-verb, noun, verb

Finally, the model refuses to regenerate sequences in which an adverb interrupts a verb and a following 'article noun' which would have to be the verb's direct object; for example given (6a) as input (corresponding to *'John gave quickly the book'), the model responds with (6b) (corresponding to 'John quickly was the winner'). H&K say that this shows that the model has acquired one of the universal case-marking constraints as expressed in English; "a direct object must be adjacent to a verb in order to receive case from it and thereby be allowed (licensed) to occur in object position ([from] ... a Government-Binding approach (Chomsky, 1981))."

6a.   noun, verb, adverb, article, noun
6b.   noun, adverb, was, article, noun

It is enterprising of H&K to put the model to such qualitative tests, over and above the 90 percent level of correct regenerations. As in formal linguistic research, it is the descriptive claims made by a model which justify its acceptance as much as its empirical adequacy to generate correct sentences. Unfortunately, the tests which H&K cite do not provide crucial support for their model, for a variety of reasons. First, many kinds of pattern recognition models would isolate the fact that every sentence contains a verb—in their case, one of a set of pre-categorized input items, such as 'p-verb, was, do, etc ...'. It is not trivial that the model fills in a blank word as a sentence's only verb, but it is not unique either. Similarly, one would not be surprised if the model filled in a 'noun' for a blank between 'article' and 'verb', or an article or preposition for a blank between a 'verb' and a 'noun'.

The logic of the interpretation of the next two cases is contradictory. H&K cite with approval the fact that the model rejects a sequence corresponding to 'the horse raced breathtakingly the crowd roared' and corrects it to one corresponding to 'the horse raced past the barn fell'. Indeed, it is relevant that the model does not accept the input sequence, which is an obverse part of its 90 percent success in regenerating correct input sequences. In this case, the model responds by changing one lexical category so that the output corresponds to a possible English sentence—the question is, does it change the input to a correct or behaviorally salient sentence. Consider a sequence other than (4b) which would result from changing one category in (4a).

4c.   art, noun, p-verb, conj, art, noun, p-verb ('the horse raced and the crowd roared')

Yet the model apparently chose (4b). This sentence type has long been understood as an example of a sentence which is *difficult* for speakers to understand (see Bever, 1970, for discussion). Accordingly, we take the fact that the model regenerates this behaviorally difficult sequence to be an empirical failure of the model, given other options like (4c) which correspond to much easier structures. Finally, the output in (4b) does not correspond to a well-formed sentence anyway. In the Francis et al. categorization schema H&K used to categorize their input, 'past verb' is differentiated from 'past participle', so the correct category sequence corresponding to 'the horse raced past the barn fell', would be as in (4d):

4d.   article, noun, verb (past participle), article, noun, p-verb

The treatment of multiple center-embedding is conversely puzzling. Having taken the alleged success of the model at regenerating a behaviorally difficult sequence like (5a), H&K report approvingly that the model rejects doubly embedded sentences. Although they note that others have argued that such constructions are complex due to behavioral reasons, they appear to believe that in rejecting them, the model is simulating 'natural language constraints'. Others have also argued that the difficulty of center-embedded constructions shows that an adequate model of language structure should not represent them (e.g., McClelland & Kawamoto, 1986; Reich, 1969). For example, McClelland and Kawamoto write:

> The unparsability of [doubly-embedded] sentences has usually been explained by an appeal to adjunct assumptions about performance limitations (e.g., working-memory limitations), but it may be, instead, that they are unparsable because the parser, by the general nature of its design is simply incapable of processing such sentences.

There is a fundamental error here. Multiple center-embedding constructions are not ungrammatical, as shown by cases like (6c) (the unacceptability of (6d) shows that the acceptability of (6c) is not due to semantic constraints alone).

6c.   The reporter everyone I have met trusts, is predicting another Irangate.
6d.   The reporter the editor the cat scratched fired died.

In fact, the difficulty of center-embedding constructions is a function of the differentiability of the nounphrases and verbphrases: (6c) is acceptable because each of the nounphrases is of a different type, as is each of the verbphrases: conversely, (6d) is unacceptable because the three nounphrases are syntactically identical, as are the three verbphrases. This effect is predicted by any comprehension mechanism which labels nounphrases syntactically as they come in, stores them, and then assigns them to verbphrase argument positions as they appear: the more distinctly labelled each phrase is, the less likely it is to be confused in immediate memory (see Bever, 1970; Miller, 1962; for more detailed discussions). Thus, there are examples of acceptable center-embedding sentences, and a simple performance theory which predicts the difference between acceptable and unacceptable cases. Hence, H&K are simply in error to claim that it is an achievement of their model to reject center-embeddings, at least if the achievement is to be taken as reflecting universal structural constraints on possible sentences.

The other two qualitative facts suggest to H&K that their model has developed a representation of constituency. The model regenerates single embeddings without exposure to them, and rejects sequences which interrupt a verb-article-noun sequence with an adverb after the verb. Both behaviors indicate to H&K that the model has acquired a representation corresponding to a nounphrase constituent. They buttress this claim with an informal report of a statistical clustering analysis on the response patterns of the hidden units to input nounphrases and verbphrases: the clusters showed that some units responded strongly to nounphrases, while others responded strongly to verbphrases.

This seems at first to be an interesting result. But careful analysis of the internal structure of the model and the final weighting patterns are required to determine how it works. The grouping of those sequences which are nounphrases (sequences containing an article and/or some kind of noun) from those which are verbphrases (containing one of the list of verb types) might occur for many reasons. Indeed, since verbphrases often contain noun-phrases, it is puzzling that verbphrases did not excite nounphrase patterns at the same time: the very notion of constituency requires that they should. As it stands, the model appears to have encoded something like the following properties of 2–15 word sentences: they have an initial set of phrase types, and then another set of phrase types beginning with some kind of verb. This is an achievement, but not one that exceeds many item and arrangement schemata.

Hanson and Kegl's brief presentation (imposed on them by the publication format) does not allow us to examine the model completely for TRICS. We can note, however, several factors which may be important. The most serious issue involves the informativeness of the input categories, which are assigned by hand. The input is richly differentiated for the model into 467 syntactic categories. There are many distinctions made among the function words and morphemes. For example, many forms of 'be' are differentiated, personal possessive pronouns are differentiated from other pronouns, subject pro-nouns are differentiated from object pronouns, comparative adjectives are differentiated from absolutes, and so on.

Given a rich enough analysis of this kind, every English sentence falls into one kind of pattern or another. Indeed, language parsers can operate surpris-ingly successfully with differential sensitivity to 20 classes of function words and no differentiation of content words at all. The reason is straightforward: function words are the skeleton of syntax. They tend to begin English phrases, not end them: many function words offer unique information: e.g., 'the', 'a', 'my' always signal a noun somewhere to the right, 'towards' always signals a nounphrase or the end of a clause, and so on. In fact, it would be interesting to see if H&K's parser performs any worse if it is trained only on function word categorized input. As it stands, recognition of a few basic redundancies might well account for the model's 85 percent hit rate.

H&K state that their model 'begins with no assumptions about syntactic structure nor any special expectations about properties of syntactic categories other than the fact they exist.' This is a bit misleading. First, syntactic cate-gories are not independently distinguished from the syntax in which they occur. Many, if not all, syntactic categories in a language are like phonolog-ical distinctive features, in that they are motivated in part by the rule-based function they serve universally and in a particular language. For example, in English, the words, 'in, on, under ...' are all prepositions just because they act the same way in relation to linguistic constraints—i.e., they precede noun-phrases, can be used as verb-particles, can coalesce with verbs in the passive form, and so on. Giving the model the information that these privileges of occurrence coincide with a category is providing crucial information about what words can be expected to pattern together—something which a real learner would have to discover. Thus, providing the correct categories provides information which itself reflects syntactic structure.

H&K actually give the model even more information: they differentiate members of the same category when they are used in syntactically different ways. For example, the prepositions are pre-categorized differently according to whether they are used in prepositional phrases or as verb particles. In the categorized samples they provide, the prepositions below on the left are classified with the symbols on the right:

to working	'in'
on the	'in'
to the	'in'
over the	'in'
pushed *aside*	'rb'
pass it *up*	'rb'

This differentiation solves ahead of time one of the more difficult problems for automatic parsers in English, the differentiation of prepositions from particles, as reflected in the ambiguity of (7).

7.   Harry looked up the street.

H&K also differentiate the different instances of 'to', used as a preposition, above, and as a complementizer, as below:

to devote	'to'
to continue	'to'

Such syntactic pre-disambiguation of phonologically indistinguishable categories appears in other cases. For example, 'it' as subject is differentiated from 'it' as object; 'that' as conjunction is differentiated from 'that' as a relative pronoun; simple past tense verb forms ('pushed', 'sang') are differentiated from superficially identical past participle forms ('pushed', except in strong verbs, 'sung').

We have adduced the above categorization disambiguations from the four categorized sample selections which H&K present. In the categorization scheme they used (Francis & Kucera, 1979) other syntactic homophones are disambiguated in the categorization framework as well. Thus, one of the hardest problems for parsers may be solved by the categorization of the input—how to distinguish the use of a category in terms of its local syntactic function. This definitely is among the TRICS, in the sense defined above. There seems to be at least another. The categories are further differentiated according to their frequency—frequent categories were assigned to initially more active input codes. This will tend to differentiate function from content categories, which may greatly facilitate the detection of syntactic patterns.

A more complete analysis of H&K's model awaits more complete presentation of its characteristics. We tentatively conclude that insofar as it is successful, it is because of a number of TRICS, of the same general kind as those found with simpler models without hidden units. The TRICS pre-categorize the input so that relevant grammatical regularities are directly encoded or made more accessible.

The decision about how fine-grained the categories are involves a dilemma. The extremes are to give no information in the categories, and to differentiate every possible syntactic category afforded by some grammatical theory. For example, the sample sequence (8c) could be entered either as (8a) or (8b) below:

8a. word, word, word, word, word, word

8b. definite determiner modifying the following noun, singular noun in the same phrase as the preceding determiner and both grammatical subject and thematic agent of the following verb, past-tense transitive verb, definite determiner modifying the following noun, singular noun in the same phrase as the preceding determiner and both grammatical object and thematic patient of the preceding verb, adverb modifying the preceding verb.

8c. determiner, noun, verb, determiner, noun, adverb

Regenerating sequences like (8a) is of no interest: each word boundary has a different code, which is what represents serial order in the input code. Hence, regenerating the number of words in the input would be straightforward. Learning to regenerate sequences like those in (8b) would be of little interest to Hanson & Kegl for the obverse reason: all the grammatical information we can think of is encoded within the category distinctions: if the model learned to regenerate sequences of this kind, H&K could not claim that it shows that the structural universals are not innate to the learner: in this case the structural universals are embedded in the richness of the input coding scheme, which is an 'innate' part of the model.

This contrast clarifies the dilemma which H&K face: learning on a limited categorization scheme is of limited interest, learning on a complex categorization scheme would not allow them to make claims about the induction of grammatical universals from the data. What might be of interest is a model which succeeds in regenerating input at an intermediate complexity of categorization, roughly like that which may be available to a child (see Valian, 1986). For example, if the machine can learn to regenerate sequences only stated in the basic 7–8 categories as in (8c), it might provide an existence demonstration of the kind H&K seek. Even more impressive, would be a demonstration that it can learn to map inputs of the complexity in (8c) onto outputs of the complexity in (8b). That would be more like real learning, taking in lexically categorized input and learning to map it onto grammatically categorized output. In such a case, both the simple and complex categories could be viewed as innate. The empirical question would be: can the model learn the regularities of how to map simple onto complex grammatical categorizations of sentences? If such a model were empirically successful, it would offer the potential of testing some aspects of the empiricist hypothesis which H&K may have in mind.

Aside from TRICS, it is clear that auto association works both at the phonological and syntactic level because there are redundancies in the input: the hidden units give the system the computational power to differentiate disjunctive categories, which allows for isolation of disjunctive redundancies. We think that the models involve techniques which may be of great importance for certain applications. But, as always with artificially 'intelligent' systems, the importance of these proofs for psychological models of learning, will depend on their rate of success and the internal analysis both of the prior architecture of the model and of categories implied by the final weight patterns. Ninety percent correct after 180,000 trials is not impressive when compared to a human child, especially when one notes that the child must discover the input categories as well. In fact, it is characteristic of widely divergent linguistic theories that they usually overlap on 95 percent of the data—it is the last 5 percent which brings out deep differences. Many models can achieve 90 percent correct analysis: this is why small differences in how close to 100 percent correct a model is can be an important factor. But, most important is the analysis which the machine gives to each sentence. At the moment, it is hard for us to see how 45 associative units will render the subtlety we know to be true of syntactic structures.

8. Conclusions

We have interpreted R&M, M&K, and H&K as concluding from the success of their models that artificial intelligence systems that learn are possible without rules. At the same time we have shown that both the learning and adult-behavior models contain devices that emphasize the information which carries the rule-based representations that explain the behavior. That is, the models' limited measure of success ultimately depends on structural rules. We leave it to connectionists' productionist brethren in artificial intelligence and cognitive modelling to determine the implications of this for the algorithmic use of rules in artificial intelligence. Our conclusion here is simply that one cannot proclaim these learning models as replacements for the acquisition of linguistic rules and constraints on rules.

9. Some general considerations

9.1. The problem of segmenting the world for stimulus/response models of learning

In the following section we set aside the issue of the acquisition of structure, and consider the status of models like R&M's as performance models of learning. That is, we now stipulate that representations of the kind we have highlighted are built into the models; we then ask, are these learning models with built-in representations plausible candidates as performance models of language acquisition? We find that they suffer from the same deficiencies as all learning models which depend on incrementally building up structures out of isolated trials.

The learning models in McClelland & Rumelhart (1986) are a complex variant on traditional—or at least Hullean—s–r connections formed in time (with secondary and tertiary connections-between-connections corresponding to between node, and hidden-node connections). The connectionist model operates 'in parallel', thereby allowing for the simultaneous establishment of complex patterns of activation and inhibition. We can view these models as composed of an extremely large number of s–r pairs, for example, the verb-learning model would have roughly 211,600 such pairs, one for each input/output Wickelfeature pair. In fact, we can imagine a set of rats each of whose tails are attached to one of the 460 Wickelfeature inputs and each of whose nose-whiskers are all attached to one of the 460 Wickelfeature outputs: on each trial, each rat is either stimulated at his tail node or not. He then may lunge at his nose node. His feedback tells him either that he was supposed to lunge or not, and he adjusts the likelihood of lunging on the next trial using formulae of the kind explored by Hull and his students, Rescorla & Wagner (1972), and others.

We will call this arrangement of rats a Massively Parallel Rodent (MPR). Clearly, the MPR as a whole can adjust its behavior. That is, if a connection between two nodes is fixed and if the relevant input and output information is unambiguously specified and reinforced, and if there is a rule for changing the strength of the connection based on the input/output/reinforcement configuration, then the model's connection strengths will change on each trial. In his review of Skinner's *Verbal Behavior* (1957), Chomsky (1959) accepted this tautology about changes in s–r connection strengths as a function of reinforcing episodes. But he pointed out that the theory does not offer a way of segmenting which experiences count as stimuli, which as responses, and to which pairs of these a change in drive level (reinforcer) is relevant. Stimulus, response and reinforcement are all interdefined, which makes discovering the 'laws' of learning impossible in the stimulus/response framework.

We solved the corresponding practical problem for our MPR by giving it the relevant information externally—we segment which aspects of its experience are relevant to each other in stimulus/response/reinforcement triples. Accordingly, the MPR works because each rat does not have to determine what input Wickelfeature activation (or lack of it) is relevant to what output Wickelfeature, and whether positive or negative: he is hard-tailed and -nosed into a given input/output pair. Each learning trial externally specifies the effect of reinforcement on the connection between that pair. In this way, the MPR can gradually be trained to build up the behavior as composed out of differential associative strengths between different units.

Suppose we put the MPR into the field, (the verbal one), and wait for it to learn anything at all. Without constant information about when to relate reinforcement information to changes in the threshold and response weights, nothing systematic can occur. The result would appear to be as limited and circular as the apparently simpler model proposed by Skinner. It might seem that giving the MPR an input set of categories would clear this up. It does not, unless one also informs it which categories are relevant when. The hope that enough learning trials will gradually allow the MPR to weed out the irrelevancies, begs the question; which is, *how does the organism know that a given experience counts as a trial?* The much larger number of component organisms does not change the power of the single-unit machine, if nobody tells them what is important in the world and what is important to do about it. There's no solution, even in very, very large numbers of rats.

Auto-association in systems with hidden units might seem to offer a solution to the problem of segmenting the world into stimuli, responses and reinforcement relations: these models operate without separate instruction on each matching trial. Indeed, Elman & Zipser's model apparently arrives at a compact representation of input speech without being selectively reinforced. But, as we said, it will take a thorough study of the final response patterns of the hidden units to show that the model arrives at a *correct* compact representation. The same point is true of models in the style of Hanson and Kegl. And, in any case, analysis of the potential stimuli is only part of the learning problem—such models still would require identification of which analyzed units serve as stimuli in particular reinforcement relations to which responses.

So, even if we grant them a considerable amount of pre-wired architectures, and hand-tailored input, models like the MPR, and their foreseeable elaborations, are not interesting candidates as performance models for actual learning; rather, they serve, at best, as models of how constraints can be modified by experience, with all the interesting formal and behavioral work of setting the constraints done outside the model. The reply might be that every model of learning has such problems—somehow the child must learn what stimuli in the world are relevant for his language behavior responses. Clearly, the child has to have a segmentation of the world into units, which we can grant to every model including the MPR. But if we are accounting for the acquisition of knowledge and not the pairing of input/output behaviors, then there is no restriction on what counts as a relevant pair. The problem of what counts as a reinforcement for an input/output pair only exists for those systems which postulate that learning consists of increasing the probability of particular input/output pairs (and proper subsets of such pairs). The hypothesis-testing child is at liberty to think entirely in terms of confirming systems of knowledge against idiosyncratic experiences.

An example may help here. Consider two ways of learning about the game of tag: a stimulus/response model, and an hypothesis testing model. Both models can have innate characteristics which lead to the game as a possible representation. But, in a connectionist instantiation of the s/r model, the acquired representation of the game is in terms of pairs of input and output representations. These representations specify the vectors of motion for each player, and whether there is physical contact between them. We have no doubt that a properly configured connectionist model would acquire behavior similar to that observed in a group of children, in which the players successively disperse away from the player who was last in contact with the player who has a chain of dispersal that goes back to the first player of that kind. As above, the machine would be given training in possible successive vector configurations and informed about each so that it could change its activation weights in the usual connectionist way. Without that information, the model will have no way of modulating its input activation configuration to conform to the actual behavior.

Contrast this with the hypothesis testing model, also with innate structure: in this case, what is innate is a set of possible games, of which tag is one, stated in terms of rules. Consider what kind of data such a model must have: it must be given a display of tag actively in progress, in some representational language, perhaps in terms of movement vectors and locations, just like that for the connectionist model. But what it does not need is step-by-step feedback after each projection of where the players will be next. It needs instances of predictions made by the game of tag that are fulfilled: e.g., that after contact, players' vectors tend to reverse. How many such instances it needs is a matter of the criteria for confirmation that the hypothesis tester requires. Thus, both the stimulus/response pattern association model and the hypothesis testing model require some instances of categorizable input. But only the s/r model requires massive numbers of instances *in order to construct a representation of the behavior.*

9.2. The human use for connectionist models

The only relation in connectionist models is strength of association between nodes. This makes them potential models in which to represent the formation of associations, which are (almost by definition) frequent—and, in that sense, important—phenomena of everyday life. Given a structural description of a domain and a performance mechanism, a connectionist model may provide a revealing description of the emergence of certain regularities in performance, which are not easily described by the structural description or performance mechanism alone. In this section, we explore some ways to think about the usefulness of connectionist models in integrating mental representations of structures and associations between structures.

9.2.1. Behavioral sources of overgeneralization

We turn first to the 'developmental' achievement of Rumelhart and McClelland's model of past tense learning, the overgeneralization of the 'ed' ending after having achieved better-than-chance performance on some irregular verbs. This parallels stages that children go through, although clearly not for the same reasons. R&M coerce the model into overgeneralization and regression in performance by abruptly flooding the model with regular-verb input. Given the relative univocality of the regular past tense ending, such coercion may turn out to be unnecessary—even equal numbers of regular and irregular verbs may lead to a period of overgeneralization (depending on the learning curve function) because the regular ending processes are simpler. In any case, the model is important in that it attempts to address what is a common developmental phenomenon in the mastery of rule-governed structures—at first, there is apparent mastery of a structurally defined concept and then a subsequent decrease in performance, based on a generalization from the available data. It is true that some scholars have used these periods of regression as evidence that the child is actively mastering structural rules, e.g.,

9.   add 'ed' to form the past tense

Clearly, the child is making a *mistake*. But it is not necessarily a mistaken application of an actual rule of the language (note that the formula above is not exactly a rule of the language). Rather, it can be interpreted as a performance mistake, the result of an overactive speech production algorithm which captures the behavioral generalization that almost all verbs form the past tense by adding /ed/ (see Macken, 1987, for a much more formal discussion of this type). This interpretation is further supported by the fact that children, like adults, can express awareness of the distinction between what they say, and what they know they should say (section 5.4).

There are many other examples of overgeneralization in cognitive development, in which rule-based explanations are less compelling than explanations based on performance mechanisms (Bever, 1982; Strauss, 1983). Consider, for example, the emergence of the ability to conserve numerosity judgments between small arrays of objects. Suppose we present the array on the left below to children, and ask which row has more in it (Bever, Mehler, & Epstein, 1968; Mehler & Bever, 1967). Most children believe that it is the row on the bottom. Now suppose we change the array on the left below to the one on the right, and ask children to report which row now has more: 2-year-old children characteristically get the answer correct, and always perform better than 3-year-old children.

```
    *  *  *  *         *   *   *   *
   *  *  *  *  *  *       ******
```

The 3-year-olds characteristically choose the longer row—this kind of pattern occurs in many domains involving quantities of different kinds. In each case, the younger child performs on the specific task better than the older child. But the tasks are chosen so that they bring a structural principle into conflict with a perceptual algorithm. The principle is 'conservation', that if nothing is changed in the quantity of two unequal arrays, the one with more remains the one with more. The perceptual algorithm is that if an array looks larger than another, it has more in it. Such strategies are well-supported in experience, and probably remain in the adult repertoire, though better integrated than in the 3-year-old. Our present concerns make it important that the overgeneralized strategy that causes the decrease in performance is not a structural rule in any sense; it is a behavioral algorithm.

A similar contrast between linguistic structure and perceptual generalization occurs in the development of language comprehension (Bever, 1970). Consider (10a) and (10b).

10a. The horse kicked the cow
10b. The cow got kicked by the horse

At all ages between 2 and 6, children can make puppets act out the first kind of sentence. But the basis on which they do this appears to change from age

2 to age 4: at the older age, the children perform markedly worse than at the younger age on passive sentences like (10b). This, and other facts suggest that the 4-year-old child depends on a perceptual heuristic,

11. "assign an available NVN—sequence, the thematic relations, agent, predicate, patient."

This heuristic is consistent with active sentence order, but specifically contradicts passive order. The heuristic may reflect the generalization that in English sentences, agents do usually precede patients. The order strategy appears in other languages only in those cases in which there is a dominant word order. In fact, in heavily inflected languages, children seem to learn very early to depend just on the inflectional endings and to ignore word order (Slobin & Bever, 1980). The important point here is that the heuristics that emerge around 4 years of age are not reflections of the structural rules. In fact, the strategies can interfere with linguistic success of the younger child and result in a decrease in performance.

Certain heuristics draw on general knowledge, for example the heuristic that sentences should make worldly sense. 4-year-old children correctly act out sequences which are highly probable (12a), but systematically fail to act out corresponding improbable sequences like (12b).

12a. The horse ate the cookie
12b. The cookie ate the horse

The linguistic competence of the young child before such heuristics emerge is quite impressive. They perform both sentences correctly—they often acknowledge that the second is amusing, but act it out as linguistically indicated. This suggests early reliance on structural properties of the language, which is later replaced by reliance on statistically valid generalizations in the child's experience.

These examples demonstrate that regressions in cognitive performance seem to be the rule, not the exception. But the acquisition of *rules* is not what underlies the regressions. Rather, they occur as generalizations which reflect statistical properties of experience. Such systems of heuristics stand in contrast to the systematic knowledge of the structural properties of behavior and experience which children rely on before they have sufficient experience to extract the heuristics. In brief, we are arguing that R&M may be correct in the characterization of the period of overgeneralization as the result of the detection of a statistically reliable pattern (Bever, 1970). The emergence of the overgeneralization is not unambiguous evidence for the acquisition of a rule. Rather, it may reflect the emergence of a statistically supported pattern of behavior. We turn in the next section to the usefulness of connectionist models in accounting for the formation and role of such habits.

9.2.2. The nodularity of mime

Up to now, we have argued that insofar as connectionist models seem to acquire structural rules, it is because they contain representational devices which approximate aspects of relevant linguistic properties. Such probabilistic models are simply not well-suited to account for the acquisition of categorical structures. But there is another aspect of behavior to which they are more naturally suited—those behaviors which are essentially associative in nature.

Associations can make repeated behaviors more efficient, but are the source of error in novel behaviors. Accordingly, we find it significant that the most empirically impressive connectionist models have been devoted to the description of erroneous or arbitrary behavior. For example, Dell's model of speech production predicts a wide range of different kinds of slips of the tongue and the contexts in which they occur. The TRACE model of speech perception predicts interference effects between levels of word and phoneme representations. By the same token, we are willing to stipulate that an improved model of past tense learning might do a better job of modelling the mistakes which children make along the way.

All of these phenomena have something in common—they result, not from the structural constraints on the domain, but from the way in which an associative architecture responds to environmental regularities. Using a connectionist architecture may allow for a relatively simple explanation of phenomena such as habits, that seem to be parasitic on regularities in behavioral patterns. This interpretation is consistent with a view of the mind as utilizing two sorts of processes, computational and associative. The computational component represents the structure of behavior, the associative component represents the direct activation of behaviors which accumulates with practice.

Clearly, humans have knowledge of the structural form of language, levels of representation and relations between them. Yet, much of the time in both speaking and comprehension, we draw on a small number of phrase- and sentence-types. Our capacity for brute associative memory shows that we can form complex associations between symbols: it is reasonable that such associations will arise between common phrase types and the meaning relations between their constituent lexical categories. The associative network cannot explain the existence or form of phrase structures, but it can associate them efficiently, once they are defined.

This commonsense idea about everyday behavior had no explicit formal mechanism which could account for it in traditional stimulus-response theories of how associations are formed. Such models had in their arsenal single chains of associated units. The notion of multiple levels of representation and matrices was not developed. The richest attempt in this direction for language was the later work of Osgood (1968); but he was insistent that the models should not only describe associations that govern acquired behavior, they should also account for learning structurally distinct levels of representation—which traditional s/r theories cannot consistently represent or learn (see Bever, 1968; Fodor, 1965).

There are some serious consequences of our proposal for research on language behavior. For example, associations between phrase types and semantic configurations may totally obscure the operation of more structurally sensitive processes. This concept underlay the proposal that sentence comprehension proceeds by way of 'perceptual strategies' like (12), mapping rules which express the relation between a phrase type and the semantic roles assigned to its constituents (Bever, 1970). Such strategies are non-deterministic and are not specified as a particular function of grammatical structure. The existence of such strategies is supported by the developmental regressions in comprehension reviewed above, as well as their ability to explain a variety of facts about adult sentence perception (including the difficulty of sentences like (5a) which run afoul of the NVN strategy (12)). But the formulation of a complete strategies-based parser met with great difficulty. Strategies are not 'rules', and there was no clear formalism available in which to state them so that they can apply simultaneously. These problems were part of the motivation for rejecting a strategies-based parser (Frazier, 1979), in favor of either deterministic processes (production systems of a kind; Wanner & Maratsos, 1978) and current attempts to construct parsers as direct functions of a grammar (Crain & J.D. Fodor, 1985; Ford, Bresnan, & Kaplan, 1981; Frazier, Carson, & Rayner, work in progress).

On our interpretation, connectionist methods offer a richer representational system for perceptual 'strategies' than previously available. Indeed, some investigators have suggested connectionist-like models of *all* aspects of syntactic knowledge and processing (Bates & MacWhinney, 1987; MacWhinney, 1987). We have no quarrel with their attempts to construct models which instantiate strategies of the type we have discussed (if that is what they are in fact doing); however, it seems that they go further, and argue that the strategies comprise an entire grammatical and performance theory at the same time. We must be clear to the point of tedium: a connectionist model of parsing, like the original strategies model, does not explain away mental grammatical structures—in fact, it depends on their independent existence elsewhere in the user's mental repertoire. Furthermore, frequency based behavioral heuristics do not necessarily comprise a complete theory of performance, since they represent only the associatively based components.

Smolensky (in press) has come to a view superficially similar to ours about the relation between connectionist models and rule-governed systems. He applies the analysis to the distinction between controlled and automatic processing (Schneider, Dumais, & Schiffrin, 1984). A typical secular example is accessing the powers of the number 2. The obvious way to access a large power of two, is to multiply 2 times itself that large number of times. Most of us are condemned to this multiplication route, but computer scientists often have memorized large powers of two, because two is the basic currency of computers. Thus, many computer scientists have two ways of arriving at the 20th power of two, calculating it out, or remembering it. Smolensky suggests that this distinction reflects two kinds of knowledge, both of which can be implemented in connectionist architecture—'conscious' and 'intuitive'. 'Conscious' knowledge consists of memorized rules similar to productions. Frequent application of a conscious rule develops connection strengths between the input and the output of the rule until its effect can be arrived at without the operation of the production-style system. Thus the production-style system 'trains' the connectionist network to asymptotic performance.

The conscious production-style systems are algorithms, not structural representations. For example, the steps involved in successive multiplications by two depend on available memory, particular procedures, knowledge of the relation between different powers of the same number, and so on. Thus, this proposal is that the slow-but-sure kind of algorithms can be used to train the fast-but-probabilistic algorithms. Neither of them necessarily represents the structure. Smolensky, however, suggests further that a connectionist model's structural 'competence' can be represented in the form of what the model would do, given an infinite amount of memory/time. That is, 'ideal performance' can be taken to represent competence (note that 'harmony theory' referred to below is a variant of a connectionist system).

> It is a corollary of the way this network embodies the problem domain constraints, and the general theorems of harmony theory, that the system, when given a well-posed problem, and infinite relaxation time, will always give the correct answer. So, under that idealization, the competence of the system is described by hard constraints: Ohm's law, Kirchoff's law. It is as if it had those laws written down inside of it.

Thus, the system conforms completely to structural rules in an ideal situation. But the ability to conform to structure in an infinite time is not the same as the representation of the structure. The structure has an existence outside of the idealized performance of a model. The structure corresponds to the 'problem domain constraints'.

Smolensky directly relates the production-style algorithms to explicit potentially conscious knowledge, such as knowing how to multiply. This makes the proposal inappropriate for the representation of linguistic rules, since they are generally not conscious, and most of them operate on abstract objects. Consider for example, the seven rules involved in the description of the pronunciation of the regular past tense. Many of them operate over abstract phones, which are by definition unpronounceable (similarly, in autosegmental terms, the structures are abstract schemata). It is not meaningful to think of explicit learning or teaching of such operations. But, this has been the problem all along: language has a rich and abstract structure, whatever the algorithms are that humans use when they speak and understand it.

9.3. The end—habits and rules

We have attempted to put the connectionist debate about rules in perspective. The debate was initially among those interested in cognitive modelling, contrasting propositionally-based algorithms such as those used in many production systems with constraint satisfaction algorithms. That form of debate has been extended to include the question of whether connectionist models can learn to exhibit rule-governed behavior without acquiring rules. With differing shades of emphasis, there have been three answers to the specific challenge to rule-based theories of language acquisition posed by R&M's and H&K's models.

- Some mental processes require rules anyway (Fodor & Pylyshyn)
- R&M's model, in particular, does not work, empirically or theoretically (Pinker & Prince)
- Our emphasis in this paper has been on the fact that the connectionist models we have considered arrive at rule-like regularities in language behavior only insofar as the models already contain architectures and devices explained in humans by mental representations of categorical rules.

This is not surprising since there is no natural way for an associative device to represent categorical rules: hence, as adult models, such artificially intelligent systems require a built-in sensitivity to the rules or their equivalents. As acquisition devices, the connectionist machines share the limitation of all models which change their behavior as the accumulated result of pairing stimuli and responses: namely, they can never discover structural rules. The positive feature of connectionist models is that they provide a rich associative framework for the description of the formation of complex habits.

In sum, we have reminded the reader that the structure of human behaviors such as language cannot be explained by associative networks. But it is equally obvious that *some* behaviors are habits—the result of associations between structurally defined representations. We think that connectionist models are worth exploring as potential explanations of those behaviors: at the very least, such investigations will give a clearer definition of those aspects of knowledge and performance which cannot be accounted for by testable and computationally powerful associationistic mechanisms.

References

Anderson, J.A. (1983). *The architecture of cognition.* Cambridge, MA: Harvard University Press.
Bates, E., & MacWhinney, B. (1987). Competition variation and language learning. In B. MacWhinney (Ed.), *Mechanisms of language acquisition* (pp. 157–197). Hillsdale, NJ: Lawrence Erlbaum Associates.
Bever, T. (1968). A formal limitation of associationism. In T. Dixon & D. Horton (Eds.), *Verbal behavior and general behavior theory.* Englewood Cliffs, NJ: Prentice-Hall, Inc.
Bever, T. (1970). The cognitive basis for linguistic universals. In J.R. Hayes (Ed.), *Cognition and the development of language* (pp. 277–360). New York, NY: Wiley & Sons, Inc.
Bever, T. (1975). Psychologically real grammar emerges because of its role in language acquisition. In D. Dato (Ed.), *Developmental psycholinguistics: Theory and applications* (pp. 63–75). Georgetown University Round Table on Languages and Linguistics.
Bever, T. (1982). Regression in the service of development. In T. Bever (Ed.), *Regression in mental development* (pp. 153–188). Hillsdale, NJ: Lawrence Erlbaum Associates.
Bever, T., & Langendoen, D. (1963). (a) The formal justification and descriptive role of variables in phonology. (b) The description of the Indo-European E/O ablaut. (c) The E/O ablaut in Old English. *Quarterly Progress Report RLE.* MIT, Summer.
Bever, T., Carroll, J., & Miller L.A. (1984). Introduction. In T. Bever, J. Carroll & L.A. Miller (Eds.), *Talking minds: The study of language in the cognitive sciences.* Cambridge, MA: MIT Press.
Bever, T., Mehler, J., & Epstein, J. (1968). What children do in spite of what they know. *Science, 162,* 921–924.
Brown, R. (1973). *A first language: The early stages.* Cambridge, MA: Harvard University Press.
Bybee, J., & Slobin, D. (1982). Rules and schemes in the development and use of the English past tense. *Language, 58,* 265–289.
Chomsky, N. (1959). Review of Skinner's Verbal Behavior. *Language, 35,* 26–58.
Chomsky, N. (1964). The logical basis of linguistic theory. In Proceedings of the 9th International Conference on Linguistics.
Chomsky, N. (1981). *Lectures on government and binding.* Dordrecht: Foris.
Chomsky, N., & Halle, M. (1968). *The sound pattern of English.* New York, NY: Harper and Row.
Crain, S., & Fodor, J.D. (1985). How can grammars help parsers? In D.R. Dowty, L. Kartunen, & A. Zwicky (Eds.), *Natural language parsing: Psychological, computational and theoretical perspectives.* Cambridge: Cambridge University Press.
Dell, G. (1986). A spreading-activation theory of retrieval in sentence production. *Psychological Review, 93,* 3, 283–321.
Elman, J.L., & McClelland, J.L. (1986). Exploiting the lawful variability in the speech wave. In J.S. Perkell & D.H. Klatt (Eds.), *Invariance and variability of speech processes.* Hillsdale, NJ: Lawrence Erlbaum Associates.
Elman, J.L., & Zipser, D. (1987). Learning the hidden structure of speech. USCD Institute for Cognitive Science Report 8701.
Feldman, J. (1986). Neural representation of conceptual knowledge. University of Rochester Cognitive Science Technical Report URCS-33.

Feldman, J., & Ballard, D. (1982). Connectionist models and their properties. *Cognitive Science, 6,* 205–254.

Feldman, J., Ballard, D., Brown, C., & Dell, G. (1985). Rochester Connectionist Papers: 1979–1985. University of Rochester Computer Science Technical Report TR-172.

Fodor, J.A. (1965). Could meaning be an r_m? *Journal of Verbal Learning and Verbal Behavior, 4,* 73–81.

Fodor, J.A., Bever, T.G., & Garrett, M. (1974). *Psychology of language.* New York: McGraw Hill.

Fodor, J.A., & Pylyshyn, Z.W. (1988). Connectionism and cognitive architecture: A critical analysis. *Cognition, 28,* 3–71, this issue.

Ford, M., Bresnan, J., & Kaplan, R. (1981). A competence-based theory of syntactic closure. In J. Bresnan (Ed.), *The mental representation of grammatical relations.* Cambridge, MA: MIT Press.

Francis, W.N., & Kucera, H. (1979). *Manual of information to accompany a standard sample of present-day edited American English, for use with digital computers.* Providence, RI, Department of Linguistics, Brown University.

Frazier, L. (1979). On comprehending sentences: Syntactic parsing strategies. Doctoral Thesis, University of Massachusetts.

Frazier, L., Carson, M., & Rayner, K. (1985). Parameterizing the language processing system: Branching patterns within and across languages. Unpublished.

Garrett, M. (1975). The analysis of sentence production. In G. Bower (Ed.), *The psychology of learning and motivation.* New York: Academic Press (pp. 133–177).

Goldsmith, J. (1976). An overview of autosegmental phonology. *Linguistic Analysis, 2,* No. 1.

Grice, H.P. (1975). Logic and conversation. In P. Cole and J.L. Morgan (Eds.), *Syntax and semantics 3: Speech acts.* New York, NY: Seminar Press.

Grossberg, S. (1987). Competitive learning from interactive activation to adaptive resonance. *Cognitive Science, 11,* 23–63.

Halle, M. (1962). Phonology in generative grammar. *Word, 18,* 54–72.

Hanson, S.J., & Kegl, J. (1987). PARSNIP: A connectionist network that learns natural language grammar from exposure to natural language sentences. *Proceedings of the Ninth Annual Cognitive Science Society Meeting.* Hillsdale, NJ: Lawrence Erlbaum Associates.

Hinton, G., & Anderson, S. (Eds.) (1981). *Parallel models of associative memory.* Hillsdale, NJ: Lawrence Erlbaum Associates.

Hinton, G., & Sejnowski, R. (1983). Optimal perceptual inference. *Proceedings of the IEEE Conference on Computer Vision and Pattern Recognition,* Washington, D.C.

Hinton, G., & Sejnowski, T. (1986). Learning and relearning in Boltzmann machines. In D. Rumelhart & J. McClelland (Eds.), *Parallel distributed processing: Explorations in the microstructure of cognition: Vol. 1. Foundations.* Cambridge, MA: MIT Press.

Hopfield, J. (1982). Neural networks and physical systems with emergent collective computational abilities. *Proceedings of the National Academy of Science USA: Vol. 79. Biophysics* (pp. 2551–2558).

Kuczaj, S. (1978). Children's judgments of grammatical and ungrammatical irregular past-tense verbs. *Child Development, 49,* 319–326.

Kuroda, S.Y. (1987). Where is Chomsky's bottleneck? Reports of the Center for Research in Language, San Diego, Vol. 1, No. 5.

Langackre, R. (1987). The cognitive perspective. In Reports of the Center for Research in Language, San Diego, Vol. 1, No. 3.

Macken, M. (1987). Representation rules and overgeneralizations in phonology. In B. MacWhinney (Ed.), *Mechanisms of language acquisition* (pp. 367–397). Hillsdale, NJ: Lawrence Erlbaum Associates.

MacWhinney, B. (1987). The competition model of the acquisition of syntax. In B. MacWhinney (Ed.), *Mechanisms of language acquisition* (pp. 249–308). Hillsdale, NJ: Lawrence Erlbaum Associates.

Marr, D. (1982). *Vision.* San Francisco, CA: Freeman.

McClelland, J., & Elman, J. (1986). Interactive processes in speech perception: The TRACE model. In J. McClelland & D. Rumelhart (Eds.), *Parallel distributed processing: Explorations in the microstructure* of cognition: Vol. 2. Psychological and biological models. Cambridge, MA: MIT Press.

McClelland, J. & Kawamoto, A. (1986). Mechanisms of sentence processing: Assigning roles to constituents. In J. McClelland & D. Rumelhart (Eds.), Parallel distributed processing: Explorations in the microstructure of cognition: Vol. 2. Psychological and biological models. Cambridge, MA: MIT Press.

McClelland, J., & Rumelhart, D. (1981). An interactive activation model of context effects in letter perception: Part 1: An account of basic findings. Psychological Review, 88, 5, 60–94.

McClelland, J. & Rumelhart, D. (Eds.) (1986). Parallel distributed processing: Explorations in the microstructure of cognition: Vol. 2. Psychological and biological models. Cambridge, MA: MIT Press.

Mehler, J., & Bever, T. (1967). A cognitive capacity of young children. Science, Oct. 6, 141.

Miller, G.A. (1962). Some psychological studies of grammar. American Psychologists, 17, 748–762.

Minsky, M., & Papert, S. (1969). Perceptrons. Cambridge, MA: MIT Press.

Neches, R., Langley, P., & Klahr, D. (1987). Learning, development and production systems. In D. Klahr, P. Langley & R. Neches (Eds.), Production system models of learning and development. Cambridge, MA: MIT Press.

Osgood, C.E. (1968). Toward a wedding of insufficiencies. In T. Dickson & D. Horton, Verbal behavior and general behavior theory, Englewood Cliffs, NJ: Prentice-Hall, Inc.

Pinker, S., & Prince, A. (1988). On language and connectionism: Analysis of a parallel distributed processing model of language acquisition. Cognition, 28, 73–193, this issue.

Reich, P.A. (1969). The finiteness of natural language. Language, 45, 831–843.

Rescorla, R.A., & Wagner, A.R. (1972). A theory of Pavlovian conditioning: Variations in the effectiveness of reinforcement and non-reinforcement. In A.H. Black & W.F. Prokosy (Eds.), Classical conditioning. New York: Appleton-Century-Crofts, pp. 64–99.

Rosenblatt, F. (1962). Principles of neurodynamics. New York, NY: Spartan.

Rumelhart, D., Hinton, G.E., & Williams, R. (1986). Learning internal representations by error propagation. In D. Rumelhart, J. McClelland & the PDP Research Group, Parallel distributed processing: Explorations in the microstructure of cognition: Vol. 1. Formulations. Cambridge, MA: MIT Press/Bradford Books.

Rumelhart, D., & McClelland, J. (1982). An interactive activation model of context effects in letter perception: Part 2: The contextual enhancement effect and some tests of the model. Psychological Review, 89, 1, 60–94.

Rumelhart, D., & McClelland, J. (Eds.) (1986a). Parallel distributed processing: Explorations in the microstructure of cognition: Vol. 1. Foundations. Cambridge, MA: MIT Press.

Rumelhart, D., & McClelland, J. (1986b). On learning the past tenses of English verbs. In J. McClelland & D. Rumelhart (Eds.), Parallel distributed processing: Explorations in the microstructure of cognition: Vol. 2. Psychological and biological models. Cambridge, MA: MIT Press.

Sadock, J. (1974). Toward a linguistic theory of speech acts. New York: Academic Press.

Sampson, G. (1987). A turning point in linguistics: Review of D. Rumelhart, J. McClelland and the PDP Research Group (Eds.), Parallel distributed processing: Explorations in the microstructure of cognition. Times Literary Supplement, June 12, 1987, p. 643.

Sapir, E. (1921–49). Language. New York: Harcourt, Brace and World.

Savin, H., & Bever, T. (1970). The nonperceptual reality of the phoneme. Journal of Verbal Learning and Verbal Behavior, 9, 295–302.

Schneider, W., Dumais, S., & Shriffrin, R. (1984). Automatic and control processing and attention. In R. Parasaraman & D. Davies (Eds.), Varieties of attention. New York: Academic Press, Inc.

Skinner, B. (1957). Verbal behavior. New York, NY: Appleton-Century-Crofts.

Slobin, D. (1978). A case study of early language awareness. In A. Sinclair, R. Jarvella, & W. Levelt (Eds.), The child's conception of language. New York, NY: Springer-Verlag.

Slobin, D., & Bever, T.G. (1982). Children use canonical sentence schemas: A crosslinguistic study of word order. Cognition, 12, 219–277.

Smolensky, P. (1986). Information processing in dynamical systems: Foundations of harmony theory. In D. Rumelhart & J. McClelland (Eds.), *Parallel distributed processing: Explorations in the microstructure of cognition: Vol. 1. Foundations.* Cambridge, MA: MIT Press.

Smolensky, P. (in press). The proper treatment of connectionism. *Behavioral and Brain Sciences.*

Strauss, S., & Stavy, R. (1981). U-shaped behavioral growth: Implications for theories of development. In W.W. Hartup (Ed.), *Review of child development research* (Volume 6), Chicago: University of Chicago Press.

Tanenhaus, M.K., Carlson, G., & Seidenberg, M. (1985). Do listeners compute linguistic representations? In D. Dowty, L. Kartunnen, & A. Zwicky (Eds.), *Natural language parsing: Psychological, computational, and theoretical perspectives* (pp. 459–408). Cambridge: Cambridge University Press.

Wanner, E., & Maratsos, M. (1978). An ATN approach to comprehension. In M. Halle, J. Bresnan and G. Miller (Eds.), *Linguistic theory and psychological reality.* Cambridge, MA: MIT Press.

Wickelgren, W. (1969). Context-sensitive coding, associative memory, and serial order in (speech) behavior. *Psychological Review, 76,* 1–15.

Name Index

Subject Index

Acoustic features, 199
Acquisition, stages of, 201
Activation level, 1, 5, 12, 15, 63, 73, 75, 76, 196, 223
Actors, 15
Algorithm, 65, 80
vs. implementation, 74
Algorithmic use of rules in AI, 233, 234
All-or-none character of conventional rule systems, 53
Animal thought, 41, 44, 45
Architecture, associative, 240
classical, 7, 14, 55, 60
connectionist, 5, 28, 54, 78
von Neumann, 52n, 63
Associationism, 27, 31, 49n, 63
Associative learning, 208
Associative strengths between units, 235
Atomic predicates, 22
Atomic representations, 12
Augmented transition networks, 35
Auto-association, 225, 233, 235
Autosegmental phonology, 216
Auxiliary, *does,* 103
Auxiliary, *has,* 103

Back propagation, 6, 181, 183, 224, 225
Back-formation, 111
Bandwidth of communication channels, limits on, in serial machines, 75
Bistability of the Necker tube, 7
Blended responses, in the RM model, 155, 156, 157, 159, 161, 162, 165, 167
Blurring, of wickelfeature representation, 99, 101, 210
Boltzman machine, 30, 181
Boolean algebra, 196
Brain-style modeling, 62

Categorial operations, 201
rules, discrete, 180
symbols, 201
Categorization disambiguations, 231
Center-embedded sentences, 35, 227–229
Central processing unit, 52n, 59
Central-informativeness TRICS, in the R&M model, 214, 215
Classical machines vs. connectionist machines, 16, 17
Cognitive architecture, 9, 10, 35

Cognitive level, 8, 9, 66
Cognitive processes, 76, 77, 85
Combinatorial structure, of mental representations, 13, 14, 15, 37
Competence versus performance, 34, 35, 80, 128, 242
Complex symbols, 22
Compositionality of cognitive representations, 33, 41, 43, 44, 48
Computation, syntax-based notion of, 50
Computational vs. algorithmic vs. implementational description, 217
Concatenative structure, 174
Concept-level theories, 20
Conceptual level, 9, 19
Conscious vs. intuitive knowledge, 242
Conservation, 238
Conservatism versus overregularization, 139, 140, 142, 143
Consistency relations, 77
Consonant shifts, 153
Consonant-cluster voicing, 104 (see also Voicing assimilation)
Constituency relations, 12, 17, 19, 21, 23, 24, 175
Constrained nature of linguistic entities, 181
Constraint satisfaction, 1, 2, 53, 196, 243
Content-addressable memory, 172
Continuous variation, in degree of applicability of principles, 53, 57
Conventional machines, 5 (*see also* Von Neumann machines)
Correlation extraction, unconstrained, 180

Damage-resistance of connectionist over classical machines, 52, 56
Data-structures, 61
Decoding/Binding network, 92
Default structure, in the regular forms, 121
Degemination, 148
Derivational morphology, 178
Developmental psycholinguistics, 80
Diachronic maintenance, of language systems, 217
Diachronic vs. synchronic behavior of a network, 31
Distance between representations, 20n
Distinctive features, 201, 202, 204, 215
Distributed representations, 1, 2, 5, 19, 172, 173, 174, 175, 176, 177